Dilemmas of Lone Motherhood

Women have entered the workplace in greater numbers worldwide. They are increasingly expected to earn wages but are still primarily responsible for raising children. While all parents confront the tensions of this double burden, the situation is especially complex and acute for the lone mother, simply because she has no other adult who shares responsibilities and no access to a male wage. Without strong family networks, decent part-time employment opportunities, extensive and high quality care for children of all ages, or government income support, lone mothers are much more likely to live in poverty and cannot compete with married parents for the resources they need to raise children.

The essays in this volume address these dilemmas and at the same time distinguish important differences among lone mothers. How can governments help lone mothers without undermining their ability to enter the workforce? Should the state indefinitely support lone mothers? How should we measure the success of a policy? What roles do ethnicity, race, religion, class, and sexual orientation play? The authors in this volume speak from many perspectives and study a variety of places, including Sri Lanka, the US, Germany, England, and Norway, allowing the reader to draw powerful conclusions by comparing across different policies and contexts.

This book was previously published as a special issue of *Feminist Economics*.

Randy Albelda, **Susan Himmelweit**, and **Jane Humphries** are associate editors of the journal *Feminist Economics* and each has served on the board of the International Association for Feminist Economics. Albelda is Professor of Economics at University of Massachusetts Boston, Himmelweit is Professor of Economics at the Open University, and Humphries is Reader in Economic History at Oxford University and Fellow of All Souls College.

Dilemmas of Lone Motherhood

Edited by

Randy Albelda,
Susan Himmelweit, and
Jane Humphries

Routledge
Taylor & Francis Group

LONDON AND NEW YORK

First published 2005
by Routledge, an imprint of Taylor & Francis
2 Park Square, Milton Park, Abingdon, Oxon OX14 4RN

Simultaneously published in the USA and Canada
by Routledge
270 Madison Ave, New York, NY 10016

Routledge is an imprint of the Taylor & Francis Group

© 2005 IAFFE

Typeset in NewBaskerville by Elite Typesetting Techniques Ltd,
Eastleigh, Hampshire, UK
Printed and bound in Great Britain by Antony Rowe Ltd,
Chippenham, Wiltshire

British Library Cataloguing in Publication Data
A catalogue record for this book is available from the British Library

Library of Congress Cataloging in Publication Data
A catalog record for this book has been requested

ISBN 0-415-36017-X (hbk)
ISBN 0-415-36018-8 (pbk)

CONTENTS

This book was previously published as a special issue of the journal, *Feminist Economics*, the official journal of the International Association for Feminist Economics (IAFFE). All contributions have been subjected to the journal's rigorous peer review process and comply with the journal's editorial policies, as overseen by the editor, Diana Strassmann, and the journal's editoral team, including the associate editors, the editorial board, numerous volunteer reviewers, and the journal's in-house editorial staff and freelance style editors. The special issue and book have been made possible by the generous financial support of Rice University and the Ford Foundation.

THE DILEMMAS OF LONE MOTHERHOOD: KEY ISSUES FOR FEMINIST ECONOMICS

Randy Albelda, Susan Himmelweit, and Jane Humphries

Feminist economists have been at the forefront of research on the institutions and social norms that perpetuate gender inequality. They have contributed to growing literatures on family structure, the division of responsibility for caring work, welfare policies, pay discrimination, and gender-segregation in labor markets, all of which act together to perpetuate women's economic dependence. This exploration of lone motherhood encompasses each and all of these areas and highlights one of the key questions of our era, how to raise children while earning a living.

The diversity of terms used in this issue to refer to lone mothers – "single mothers," "sole parents," and "female-headed households," to name a few – reflects a real diversity of meanings and experiences. Even the term "lone mothers" for women who raise children with little or no support from men is not entirely satisfactory. Most obviously, lone mothers are not alone in one important sense – they have children, who can in themselves be sources of support. Further, many lone mothers have support from wider family and from friends. However, a lone mother is almost always both the primary breadwinner and the primary caregiver for her family.

Lone motherhood is not new, nor are policy measures designed to cope with its causes and consequences. However, the growth in the numbers of lone mothers worldwide and in the proportion of children raised in families headed by women has given a new urgency to the tasks of investigating lone motherhood and formulating policy that will improve their position. While all parents confront the tensions that arise from the need to care for their children while also earning a living, these tensions are much more acute for lone mothers, simply because they have no other adults to share them with and no access to male wages. Not only do their households lack a second earner, but also the primary earner is female and so likely to be poorly paid.

A lone mother also has less time than a couple. As a result, lone mothers are caught on the horns of a dilemma: if they work the long hours necessary to provide an acceptable standard of living from a poorly paid job, they condemn their children (and themselves) to insufficient time together as a family. Further, when they must pay for childcare the dilemma becomes even more acute, since paying for high-quality childcare will require even longer hours at work. And for many lone mothers even that dilemma is out of their reach; those who cannot find jobs and/or childcare have to rely on the state to provide, if it will. In other words, lone mothers are at the sharpest of sharp ends of the key dilemma of our time: how to reconcile work and family life.

The economic well-being of lone mothers and their children depends on a host of relationships and a network of support structures. For economic survival, lone mothers must interact with and depend on men (including the fathers of their children); other family members; friends and neighbors; communities; the state; and the labor market. This means that lone mothers can rarely be economically independent.

The deck has long been stacked against lone mothers. Market-based societies have evolved a sexual division of labor that is built into the institutions of marriage and family. Historically, mothers have been discouraged from participating in paid labor, and women's wages were, and in many cases remain, low. In recent years, women's earnings in many countries have made an increasingly important contribution to their households' standard of living, but wages that make a significant contribution to a dual-earner household often remain inadequate to support an entire family. Social insurance programs were constructed on the same basis, designed to reinforce and shore up families comprising heterosexual, married couples with a primary male breadwinner, and their children. Social policy is only slowly adapting to the changed reality in which dual-income households are increasingly prevalent and in which family breakdown, lone motherhood, and living in reconstituted households are normal stages of life for many people.

2

Political and economic discourse has yet to catch up with these changing realities. Lone mothers are still seen as deviant, even though the likelihood that any mother will at some time in her life become a lone mother is high and growing; and the odds that any child will live in a lone-parent household at some point during childhood are close to even in many parts of the world. Raising children and at the same time earning enough to support them alone is an unfair burden on lone mothers and disadvantages their children. Without strong family networks, decent part-time employment opportunities, extensive and high-quality care for children of all ages, and/or government income support, lone mothers cannot possibly "compete" with married parents for the resources they need to raise children. Indeed, as women's labor force participation increases and their economic contribution to households becomes larger, the income disparities between single-adult and two-adult households – with or without children – are growing. Lone mothers occupy the bottom rungs of the income distribution, contributing heavily to the feminization of poverty. Their children grow up materially disadvantaged in comparison with children who live in households with two adults, however those two adults divide their time.

Market forces will not remedy the unevenness of the economic playing field that lone mothers face. Nor will special treatment that relies on the goodwill of employers or neighbors. Without legal compulsion, firms or individual employers are unlikely to change workplace practices and culture so as to level the field for parents with primary caregiving responsibilities. Similarly, while it would be ideal if families and communities fully supported all of their members, some do, some cannot, and some will not. Such patchy support leaves too many families disadvantaged. To begin closing the gap between lone-parent families and others, government policies must take up the task of easing the tension between raising children and earning an income. The policies that are designed to help lone parents should also be open to others in need, since policies that are perceived as privileging one kind of family could prove divisive. Family-friendly employment practices, high-quality affordable childcare, and financial support for poor families with children would not only help lone mothers, but would also benefit other workers, parents, and children.

While lone mothers clearly face hardships that other mothers escape, they are by no means all alike. The road to "loneness" varies and may not always be "lonely." Family structure is remarkably fluid, easily and frequently reconfigured by death, desertion, marriage, remarriage, divorce, births, migration, wars, disease, and despair. Many lone mothers suffer moral admonitions while raising children outside marriage; widows on the whole do not, though they may share in other hardships that lone mothers face. However, attitudes are neither monolithic nor immutable, but shaped by the economic, political, cultural, and national contexts. In becoming

3

lone mothers, many women change their self-perceptions – reconfiguring their life strategies, reassessing their opportunities, and, far more often than not, successfully managing to raise their children. All the differences, visible and invisible, that exist among women generally, including unequal access to economic opportunities, surface among lone mothers as well.

These differences are articulated in the articles collected here. This special issue of *Feminist Economics* was not intended to provide comprehensive coverage of the debate about lone motherhood. Rather, it provides a sampler of feminist economic thinking on the strategies of lone mothers in different circumstances, and on the policy debates that have surrounded them.

Margaret Nelson explores how lone mothers in the rural United States replace the work that men once did in their households in an article that addresses a gap in feminist research: its neglect of the work that men do around the houses, yards, and vehicles of families. Nelson uncovers an additional disadvantage faced by lone mothers as they struggle to substitute not only for lost male earnings but also for the unpaid labor that men typically contribute, and the skills and physical strength they use to do it.

In different national settings and using different methodologies, Judith Record McKinney and Randi Kjeldstad and Marit Rønsen examine the impacts of economic policies through the lens of lone motherhood. Judith Record McKinney traces the ways in which economic supports for lone mothers changed over various Soviet and Russian regimes in the twentieth century. Assuming that centrally planned economies would do a better job at socializing the costs of raising children, McKinney finds that lone mothers always had a difficult time, intensified by wars, purges, and housing and consumer shortages. She argues that in the transition to a market-based economy, lone-mother families are faring even worse, but not because of the loss of commitment to mothers raising children. Rather, it is the state's commitment to improving the position of women in the labor market that is at fault.

Randi Kjeldstad and Marit Rønsen use longitudinal data interpreted through a hazard model to analyze individual labor market transitions in Norway. The analysis reveals large differences in the labor market behavior of single and nonsingle mothers and fathers, even when controlling for differences in human capital and care responsibilities. Changes in the demand for labor and welfare reforms that sharpen the incentive to perform paid work have both affected the employment dynamics of lone parents. But the most striking finding is that favorable economic conditions and tight labor markets appear to have played a larger role than welfare policies in increasing the economic activity of lone parents. Counter-cyclical macroeconomic policy to maintain demand for labor emerges as more significant in enabling the labor market participation of lone parents than

4

providing specific subsidies or assistance that are unavailable to other working parents. Of benefit to all working people, such policy avoids the divisions and resentments that targeted subsidies tend to create.

Anne Skevik compares two countries, Norway and the UK, that have both traditionally been seen as strong male-breadwinner regimes. By looking at the special case of widows, she questions why the transition to the dual-earner regimes that characterize both countries today took such different forms and happened at such different rates. Lisa Giddings, Irene Dingeldey, and Susan Ulbricht chime in on the welfare-state debates by focusing on the recent changes in US and German policies toward lone mothers. They argue that policies that enable lone mothers to enter employment, as found in Germany, proved just as effective in encouraging paid employment as coercive US workfare policies.

Karen Christopher provides a feminist critique of the seemingly endless stream of US welfare-reform research that highlights caseload reduction over economic well-being. Christopher focuses on how researchers have approached the task of examining and interpreting the effects of recent US welfare policies directed toward poor unmarried or divorced lone mothers. In the 1990s in the US, radical changes in policies toward poor-mother families emphasized employment and marriage as a substitute for government cash assistance. These changes, in turn, have inspired a spate of research that has largely focused on the "success" of the new measures as defined by framers of the policy. Christopher argues that neither the policy goals nor much of the prominent research has been influenced by feminist understandings of family, labor markets, or the role of the state. She concludes by defining a feminist research agenda for welfare reform.

The next two articles in the issue focus on differences among lone mothers. In their exploration of lone mothers in eastern Sri Lanka, Kanchana Ruwanpura and Jane Humphries examine survival strategies of Muslim, Tamil, and Sinhala women. They find that female headship is not solely the result of two decades of intense conflict, and therefore should not be seen as a temporary phenomenon. Based on interviews with both *de facto* (women with absent husbands) and *de jure* (legally single) lone mothers, Ruwanpura and Humphries find that the paths to loneness and income-generating avenues differ substantially by ethnicity. Further, while women may not have chosen their lone motherhood, amidst the hardship, some find it empowering.

Like Kjeldstad and Rønsen, Shireen Kanji mobilizes longitudinal data, in her case from Russia, to investigate the situation of lone mothers there. She shows that within Russia there is enormous diversity in the circumstances and sources of income of lone-mother households, and therefore in the levels of material disadvantage children in such households suffer. Like several contributors to this issue, Kanji associates these differences with the circumstances that led to individual women becoming lone mothers.

5

Divorce, widowhood, and bearing and raising children while never married: each different situation conditions the opportunities for earning a living and influences the support forthcoming from wider kin and community. Important as these differences are, Kanji's careful decomposition of inequality among two-adult households with children and lone-mother households shows that inequality between types of lone-mother households contributes only modestly to overall inequality. The latter remains dominated by inequality within the different types. Thus, the heterogeneity in household well-being that derives from the specific status of the lone mother is but the tip of the iceberg of unseen differences among lone-mother households, even those that appear to be the same type. As do other authors, Kanji counsels against lumping together all lone mothers and applying a one-size-fits-all policy prescription, especially if that policy selectively benefits lone mothers, leaving other working parents aggrieved and resentful.

In the Explorations, June Lapidus stirs the "lone-mother" pot by launching a discussion based on her experiences as a lesbian lone mother. Besides calling attention to the different ways in which women become "lone," Lapidus's piece raises a set of provocative questions for feminists: can, do, or should lesbians "pass" as straight women when they are lone mothers? What is the relationship of lesbian mothers in two-parent households to lone mothers (lesbian or straight)? What political and analytical motives explain why the conservative movement in the US wishes to push poor women into marriage, while vehemently denying gays and lesbians the right to marry?

Finally, this special issue includes a dialogue section, in which four authors discuss distinct approaches to policies for lone parents. Authors were given freedom to write about the policies they would like to see governments adopt. The articles are not exhaustive; they do not address all the same issues and they certainly do not all agree. In particular, the pieces reflect current debates within feminist economics about the relative values for women of having employment and of having time for caring. The range of ideas shows how attempts to develop policy for lone mothers cut to the heart of feminist economics about care and family responsibilities. Is care similar to other goods or do caring responsibilities imply particular obligations and rights? Are these individual or social responsibilities? What is the role of individual choice in allocating such responsibilities? How should care be treated as an economic good? In the implicit cost–benefit analysis involved in social decision-making, is care valued too low and employment too highly? Does feminist economics need to develop better ways of valuing care and measuring the effects of care (and lack of care)? Should we be aiming for financial independence for women or recognition of mutual dependence? Who should be responsible for the welfare of children? These debates capture real dilemmas that lone mothers face in their daily lives, dilemmas that policy-makers around the world should begin to address.

The guest co-editors would like extend thanks to all the reviewers for this issue. We owe particular gratitude to Cheryl Doss, Lynn Duggan, Michael Ellman, Barbara Hopkins, Mary King, Charlotte Koren, Elaine McCrate, Meike Meurs, Ellen Mutari, Ingrid Robeyns, and especially to Deb Figart and Anita Nyberg, for their sterling work in reviewing several manuscripts. We thank all the contributors to this special issue; all the authors for their patience and good humor in dealing with successive rounds of revisions and also the office staff of *Feminist Economics*. This includes Cheryl Morehead and Amy Rowland, for their exceptional organizational skills and gentle handling of guest editors; Rebecca Jensen and Polly Morrice for their careful and skillful copyediting of the articles; and Diana Strassmann for her unsparing support and encouragement of this special issue. Finally, we would like to acknowledge the generous financial support of the Ford Foundation and Rice University.

HOW MEN MATTER: HOUSEWORK AND SELF-PROVISIONING AMONG RURAL SINGLE-MOTHER AND MARRIED-COUPLE FAMILIES IN VERMONT, US

Margaret K. Nelson

INTRODUCTION

Since the publication of Ann Oakley's (1974) and Joan Vanek's (1974) classic studies of housework in Great Britain and the US, women's and gender studies have highlighted the importance of women's unpaid work in the home. Through numerous – and quite marvelous – studies, we have come to understand that if the activities of cooking, cleaning, and caring for children and other family members are expressions of love and attachment, they are also daily, unremitting, and exhausting labor that make significant economic contributions to the well-being of the household (and, indeed, to society as a whole) (Janet Finch and Dulcie Groves 1983; Emily Abel and Margaret Nelson 1990; Susan Himmelweit 2000; Nancy Folbre 2001).

We also know that in the "developed" world these central responsibilities – cooking, cleaning, and caring for children – are unevenly divided between men and women. Quite simply, a substantial body of literature suggests that no matter what the household configuration is regarding the labor force involvement of its adult members and whether those adults are married, cohabiting, or remarried, when heterosexual couples live together, not only do men and women focus their energies on different tasks, but women do more housework and childcare than do their male partners.[1] To be sure, this literature tells us that men do make significant contributions to the survival of the households to which they are attached, and that this contribution is growing in the US both because of women's increased labor force participation (Harriet Presser 1988) and because women therefore have increased bargaining power within the home (Elaine McCrate 1992). However, much of the literature from both the US and Britain continues to emphasize the fact that men do considerably less than women, even when their wives are employed full-time.[2]

Nothing in this paper challenges any of these well-documented findings. But I do want to suggest that the scholarship emphasizing comparisons between men and women with respect to their contributions to the household often treats the contributions that men do make to household survival quite dismissively (see, for example, Scott South and Glenna Spitze 1994; Suzanna Bianchi *et al.* 2000; Maximilliane Szinovacz 2000). As a result, we fail to understand what happens when a man is not available to make those contributions, as is the case in single-mother households.

The motivations for research on housework might explain some of the "blind spots" of feminist scholarship. This scholarship aimed to make visible what had long been invisible. It also aimed to make the economic significance of that work more visible, as well as how capitalism and patriarchy – both separately and together – built on that invisible labor (Heidi Hartmann 1976; Michele Barrett and Mary McIntosh 1980; Nona Glazer 1990; Himmelweit 2000). But it told a story that was biased towards understanding household economics as a simple matter of earned income and unpaid housework.

For well over a decade now, Hochschild's *The Second Shift* (1989) has been a major touchstone for understanding housework in the households of married couples in the US (but for a critique, see Rosalind Barnett and Caryl Rivers 1996). In this analysis, men and women are shown through their participation in two sets of activities: they work outside the home for wages/salaries and they do the required unpaid work of maintaining the home and caring for the children. Some significant activities, however, are utterly ignored. Are we to assume that no one in these couples (many of whom are economically pressed) ever does significant home repair, mows the lawn, rotates the tires on the car, builds a bookshelf, grows vegetables in the backyard, or makes gifts to cut down on holiday expenses? That is, there is a tendency to focus on family survival as being a simple (or not so simple) matter of employment and women's "traditional" housework.

Yet, the substantial success of businesses like Home Depot (*New York Times* 2002) in the US; B&Q Warehouse, Focus Do It All, Wickes, BuildStore, Homebase, and Great Mills in the United Kingdom (Brian Gorman 2001); Hornbach Holding in Germany; and Castorama in France might lead one to wonder whether only hired contractors and handymen buy all these hammers and cans of paint. What are generally called self-provisioning and do-it-yourself activities (Ray Pahl 1984; Ray Pahl and Claire Wallace 1985; Enzo Mingione 1991; Margaret Nelson and Joan Smith 1999) make no appearance at all in the homes of the couples with whom Hochschild had her intimate conversations about diapers and vacuum cleaners, even though to forget about these self-provisioning activities is to miss an important part of the true household economy (Colin Williams and Jan Windebank 2001). It might also lead to misunderstandings about what happens when men leave – or are kicked out.

Along with motivations, part of the explanation for this oversight might be a middle-class and urban bias in the research on housework.[3] Because middle-class couples can purchase the services of a handyman (or handy woman!) (Patricia Cohen 1998) and urban couples find it difficult to engage in many traditional self-provisioning activities (*Daily Star* 2002), many scholars forget its existence. But ignoring self-provisioning not only overlooks a crucial element of the survival strategy of many rural (and quite possibly some urban) households (and how that survival is shaped by class location), but it might well conceal the true poverty of the lives of single mothers who might not be able to include these activities in their survival strategy.

This paper takes on these challenges.

METHODS

Sample

This paper draws on interviews conducted with a nonrandom sample of thirty single mothers in a rural county in Vermont called by the pseudonym of Coolidge County. Initially, I located respondents through a variety of techniques, such as placing notices about the research on the bulletin boards of organizations that serve single parents specifically (e.g., a Parent-Child Center that provides resources for teenage mothers and their children), organizations that serve the poor (e.g., a welfare office), and organizations that serve children (e.g., a daycare center). Then I asked those women who responded to the notices and agreed to be interviewed to provide the names of other single mothers.

To the greatest extent possible, the thirty single-mother households were similar to the married-couple households Joan Smith and I studied in the same county six years ago (Nelson and Smith 1999). For that study, we drew on two datasets: a random telephone survey of 158 married-couple households and face-to-face interviews conducted with a nonrandom, snowball sample of eighty-one married-couple households in the same county. The married-couple households were all white (as is the vast majority of Vermont's population), two-parent, heterosexual couples and any children living with them; in each couple at least one person currently had as his or her principal source of income employment in the formal waged labor force and the second worker was eligible for employment as well (Nelson and Smith 1999: 3–4). None of these households were welfare (AFDC) reliant, although some relied on other means-tested programs.

The single mothers were living on their own, without another adult in the household; they were also white, self-defined as heterosexual, and not currently relying on welfare grants (although, as is the case in the married-couple sample, members of the single-parent sample might have been receiving other means-tested assistance and many of the women had been welfare-reliant in the past). The two samples differ in that the single-mother sample included several women whose primary source of income was self-employment (rather than exclusively waged employment).

Because the single-mother sample is not random, no inferences can be made about single mothers as a whole in Coolidge County from these data. For the purposes of this paper, however, we can compare the two samples. (See Table 1.) One major difference between single-mother and married-couple households is that the single mothers all had children, whereas the earlier sample included married-couple households whether or not they had children. In comparison with their married neighbors, the single mothers in this study are less varied in age (with about 60 percent of households having an adult under forty), and in spite of their higher levels

Table 1 Comparison of married-couple household sample and single-mother sample, Coolidge County, Vermont

	Married-couple households*			Single-mother households (N=30)
Household characteristic	Married-couple households (N=156)	Without children (N=67)	With children (N=89)	
At least one adult under age 40	59%	48%	66%	58%
Total income under $35,000	39%	37%	41%	67%
Own home	76%	70%	81%	40%
Have children	57%	0%	100%	100%
Have preschool-aged children	20%	0%	35%	57%
At least one adult with more than a high school education	53%	51%	54%	87%

*Recalculated from Nelson and Smith (1999)

of education, the single mothers are considerably poorer and less likely to own their homes. While the random sample of married-couple households are quite representative for the area (see Nelson and Smith 1999), the single mothers are quite privileged in comparison with other single mothers in the same region (Joy Livingston and Elaine McCrate 1993: 6) in part because of the restriction to those who were not welfare reliant. Among the group of single mothers included in this study, the median household income is $23,000 (the range is from $12,000 to $45,000); in Vermont as a whole, in 1995 the median income for single mothers with children was a paltry $16,000 ($44,000 was the median income for all Vermont families) (Institute for Women's Policy Research 1998). In short, this is a relatively privileged group of single mothers by virtue of their race, education, and income. The difficulties they face would certainly be compounded in a less advantaged population. I address the issue of the extent to which these findings can be generalized to other populations in the conclusion.

Definitions

In what follows, I look at two sets of activities that are essential to household survival: housework and self-provisioning.

Housework
In the random survey of households in Coolidge County, Joan Smith and I took a simple route to measuring household labor: in each telephone interview we asked whether the men and the women in the household "routinely" participated in the activities of housework, childcare, lawn work, and car repair. The first two fit under what are generally thought of as being "feminine tasks" even though many studies of housework explicitly exclude childcare from the analysis (for a discussion of this point see South and Spitze 1994: 334, fn. 2); the latter two are generally coded as "masculine tasks."

In the interviews with single mothers, I did not specifically ask about participation in the tasks of caring for children and housework because I assumed that all women did at least some of this work on a routine basis. I did ask whether they did their own yard work and car maintenance. I also asked if they ever received assistance with any of these four activities.

Self-provisioning
In *Working Hard and Making Do*, Joan Smith and I define self-provisioning as "the efforts that household members make to provide, through their own labor (and for themselves), goods and services they would otherwise have to purchase in the (formal or informal) market" (Nelson and Smith 1999: 10). We further subdivide self-provisioning into two sets of activities.

13

Routine self-provisioning is defined to include those activities which "help to guarantee the daily life of the household" (Nelson and Smith 1999: 10) and it was measured in the random survey by asking whether anyone in the household had raised an animal for food, grown vegetables in a garden, changed the oil in the car, cut and gathered their own firewood for heating purposes, or plowed the driveway during the past year.[4] A similar question was asked of the single mothers (with the exception of plowing which so clearly applied only to those who owned their own homes). This measure of routine self-provisioning focuses on goods and services for which extensive markets have already existed for a long time and thus does not include a broad range of activities (like parental childcare) which families traditionally provided for themselves, even if purchased substitutes may now be available.[5] It also excludes a range of activities (e.g., sewing, knitting, raising chickens) traditionally done by women because in the rural area in which the research was conducted – where women's labor force participation has been high for some time – women's involvement in many of such activities (for home consumption, exchange, or money) had all but disappeared.[6]

Substantial self-provisioning is defined as those activities that "help to improve the family's living conditions" (Nelson and Smith 1999: 10), and it was measured by asking respondents whether they engaged in home construction and major home renovation projects; it thus focused on the production of durable goods, which – as is the case of routine self-provisioning – is often a male activity.

HOUSEWORK AND SELF-PROVISIONING IN COOLIDGE COUNTY

Housework

Given the research reported above, it should come as no surprise that Joan Smith and I (1999) found that housework was a common activity among married women and more common among wives than among husbands in the rural married couples we interviewed whether or not they had children. It should also come as no surprise that we found that, among those married couples with children, childcare was more commonly a responsibility of married women than of married men. (See Table 2.) The data also demonstrate that in almost half of the households, men do routinely participate in housework and two-thirds of the men do routinely participate in childcare within those families with children. In married-couple households in Coolidge County, Vermont, then, women's work of caring for their children and of maintaining the home are ongoing responsibilities, but they may not be unremitting. Even the most chauvinist husband

14

Table 2 Housework in Coolidge County: percent of men and women in married-couple households who say they routinely participate in each activity*

	All married-couple households (N = 156)	Married-couple households without children (N = 67)	Married-couple households with children (N = 89)
Housework			
Men	48%	47%	49%
Women	94%	94%	94%
Childcare			
Men	Does not apply	Does not apply	69%
Women	Does not apply	Does not apply	97%
Lawn work			
Men	90%	90%	89%
Women	64%	59%	65%
Car repair			
Men	68%	63%	71%
Women	10%	12%	8%

*Recalculated from Nelson and Smith (1999: 144)

might watch the baby while a woman runs to the supermarket for the day's needs; even those who believe housework is beneath them might take out the trash.

Polly Fassinger's (1993: 208) comparison of single mothers and single fathers in the US suggests that because married women do most of the housework and feel responsible for it, some women find that it is easier to manage housework when they are living without a male partner (see also Catherine Riessman 1990 and Melissa Ludtke 1999). Some of the single women interviewed for this study reported similarly that housework was more straightforward after they had separated because they did not have to deal with their anger at a partner who did not do his share of the work and they did not have to pick up after him. As one woman, the mother of two, said: "[After we were separated] it seemed like a great relief not to have three children."

But these comments competed with those reflecting the simple fact that, as single mothers, they had no ready-made relief from the ongoing responsibility for these tasks. Diana Spenser,[7] for example, described how hard it was to clean house with a toddler running around and said that it was for this reason she believed that families might do well to have two parents: "It's just really impossible to get anything done. Like because you do the dishes, and she's just destroying another room. That's why there's two parents, I'm sure. It's just very hard [alone]." Later in the interview, when asked what kind of social policy would make her life easier, she returned to this struggle:

You know [I would like to see] some day care that could come to your house, or that could come or, I mean, somehow, some way, taking the place of what the other parent would do in terms of work, or help, just every once in a while. I mean, it would be really nice to have someone watch [my daughter] for a few moments sometimes, a few hours while I make dinner, or do get my house cleaned.

If wives in Coolidge County have daily responsibility for housework and childcare (albeit assisted by men), they participate less in the male tasks of yard work and car maintenance (whether or not they have children) both in comparison with the men in their households and in comparison with the efforts men put into housework and childcare (see Table 2.) That is, these data show that men are more likely to engage in the traditional women's work than women are to engage in traditional men's work. This difference is especially noteworthy around car repair.

Single women also have to find ways to accomplish this work. In fact, many commented on how bewildered they were when they first found themselves responsible for the chores their husbands had previously handled:

When we first split up ... I didn't know how to do anything in the house. I just didn't take care of the house. ... I never lived alone in my entire life – 39 years old and I'd never lived alone.... I didn't deal with the wood stove [and] I didn't take care of any of the stuff in the basement.

When I moved in here ... I didn't know how to clean up my wood stove so I had to have help with that.

If some women – like Diana Spenser quoted above – fantasize about having someone come to help them with the daily routines normally considered women's work, others fantasize about having enough money to pay for the full range of household activities, responsibility for which weighs heavily on their daily lives. When asked by the interviewer how much money she would need in order to live comfortably, Tiffany Morrow said:

[I would need] five thousand a month.... And in there, I'm thinking about lawn mowing, I'm thinking about house cleaning, I'm thinking about childcare, I'm thinking about repairs to the house, I'm thinking about snow plowing, I'm thinking about entertainment for the three of us, [and] I'm thinking about what it would take to help us live comfortably, not extravagantly, but comfortably, less of a strain. ... I mean, it's not like I'm asking anybody to come and put an in-ground pool in my backyard! I'm just asking for stuff to be done and so I can come home and not look at the laundry, or the carpet that needs vacuuming, or the dishes that need doing, or the floor that needs sweeping. And all that stuff is what I face every night. And it's like, oh my God, I don't want to go home!

Routine and substantial self-provisioning

Routine self-provisioning

Joan Smith and I found high rates of engagement in most of these self-provisioning activities among married-couple households: 72 percent grew some vegetables; 83 percent changed the oil in their vehicles by themselves; 46 percent of all families gathered some wood for heating by themselves; 62 percent took care of their own snow plowing; and 22 percent grew their own meat (see Table 3). Moreover, having children appeared to increase (slightly) the rate at which families engaged in these activities. Indeed, these activities were so frequent that in analyzing the determinants of participation in routine self-provisioning, Joan Smith and I divided the sample into high and low self-provisioners, with the dividing line at four or more of these activities (and a third of the families – 30 percent of those without children; 38 percent of those with children – crossed that line).[8]

Among single-mother households, however, these ways of saving money were far less common even though single-mother households faced serious economic pressures of the sort that frequently drove married-couple households to self-provision.[9] The only activity found with any frequency among this group was growing vegetables (slightly more than a third of the women said that they had a garden); no woman told an interviewer that she changed the oil in her car by herself (although every woman interviewed

Table 3 Routine self-provisioning in Coolidge County

| Percent engaging in each self-provisioning activity | Married-couple households* | | | Single-mother households (N = 30) |
	All married-couple households (N = 156)	Married-couple households without children (N = 67)	Married-couple households with children (N = 89)	
Change oil	83%	81%	83%	0%
Cut own wood	46%	42%	50%	3%
Grow meat	22%	16%	26%	3%
Garden	72%	68%	75%	37%
Plow	62%	53%	68%	[Not asked]
Percent with high rates of self-provisioning (four or more activities)	34%	30%	38%	0%

* Recalculated from Nelson and Smith (1999)

did own a car); only one said she actually gathered her own wood (although several said that they used wood to heat their homes); and only one woman had a household member (her son) who raised an animal to supply meat. Moreover, the number of different women who participated in these activities is smaller yet since the woman who cut her own firewood was the same woman whose son raised a pig; she also grew a garden.

Although the data here are too limited for extensive quantitative analysis, it is interesting to note that in contrast to the finding in *Working Hard and Making Do* (Nelson and Smith 1999: 56) that married-couple households are more likely to engage in these activities when incomes are lower, the exact opposite appears to be the case among single mothers.[10] (See Table 4.) Moreover, a closer look at the data on single mothers suggests two other significant factors: home ownership and job flexibility. Having access to one's own home and its adjacent land is a crucial variable that, even more strongly than income, determines whether or not a single mother engages in the specific self-provisioning activity of growing a garden (17 percent of those who rent compared to 67 percent of home owners). Having a flexible job appears to be even more important (15 percent of those in regular year-round full-time jobs in contrast with 80 percent of those whose jobs have built-in flexibility). Put differently, among the eleven women who gardened, five had jobs which left them essentially free during the summer (as teachers or as childcare workers in a day care center that closes during the summer), two were self-employed and therefore had some control over their hours, and one was not working but was living on an inheritance in a house owned by her parents. The importance of this flexibility can be heard when Liz Miles (the childcare worker) talks about how she schedules her extensive yard work:

> In the summer it takes me six hours to mow the lawn because I have a cheap little lawnmower. And that's probably done weekly. And then you add the garden, it's a lot more [time] in the summer because

Table 4 Determinants of self-provisioning among single mothers in Coolidge County

	Percent of single mothers who self-provision
Income	
Low income (< $25,000)	20% (15)
High income (> $25,000)	60% (10)
Home ownership	
Own home	67% (12)
Rent home	17% (18)
Job flexibility	
No job flexibility	15% (20)
Job flexibility	80% (10)

you add the garden work. . . . I would say, because I'm off in the summer, I would bet that I put in at least twenty hours a week, because I tend to do most of [the outside work] in the summer.

Those who can engage in these activities reap enormous savings. Hope Fleming had never calculated these savings for the simple reason that she never bought vegetables. However, in a household where vegetables constitute a main source of nutrients, those savings might well be significant: "I guess I do [save money] because I'm a vegetarian. I guess I suppose I do. . . . I don't save anything because I've never bought them. I have a big freezer downstairs and it's always full by the end of the summer." Joanna Darling was somewhat more certain that her garden saved her money on her food: "My garden is coming along pretty well. I probably save, when it's really blooming, I probably save fifty bucks a week, maybe, for food." Megan Paige acknowledged that the produce from the garden enriched her in other ways. She enjoys the activity itself and she uses the garden's output in her barter and gift economy:

> I do have a garden and I'm not really sure it saves money. It's a hobby and it gives me some surplus to barter with. I don't do any of what I call real specific barter, I give them this and they give me this back, I just like to give away everything that I can, food from my garden or cooking for people or watching their kids – anything that I can do I do – and I feel like eventually that will come back to me.

Substantial self-provisioning
Among married-couple households, substantial self-provisioning in Coolidge County followed a very different pattern from that of routine self-provisioning. Rather than income alone, the quality of employment mattered: whereas almost half of the households in which one adult had year-round, full-time, regular employment in a job with benefits (what Joan Smith and I define as a "good job" (Nelson and Smith 1999: 9–10)) had built their own homes or had recently engaged in a major home improvement; no household without a recent history of a good job had done either of these (Nelson and Smith 1999: 97).

But good job or not, as was the case for routine self-provisioning, substantial self-provisioning was much less common among single-mother households. Only four women said that they (alone, or in conjunction with friends and relatives) had engaged in this kind of project. Doris Davis essentially built her own home following a fire; although she does not calculate the savings, they might well be considerable. Hope Fleming (the vegetarian quoted above) did large construction projects such as rebuilding the beautiful porch that rings the front of her home; Joanna Darling also built a porch for her home; and Janet Linden not only built a porch and laid the hardwood floor in her home (before her child was born), but she also put together a swing set for her daughter, ensuring considerable savings in the process.

Like routine self-provisioning, substantial self-provisioning makes the most sense when combined with home ownership, and therefore 60 percent of the single mothers are essentially precluded from enriching their lives in this way. But, as these data indicate, home ownership does not ensure the capacity to engage in these kinds of activities. Many of the women suggested that they were limited in overall skills. Liz Miles, who saved money from mowing, said that in spite of the range of tasks she had learned how to do, she still could not handle even the most basic repairs:

> I do the mowing myself, I do the plowing myself, I take the garbage [to the dump] instead of having it collected. Basically I do all, all of it, anything I can do myself, I do ... Well [not] home maintenance because I don't know how to do it. ... I mean I do do stuff like painting and things like that ... but I don't know how to do repairs. If I did, I would do them.

HOUSEWORK AND SELF-PROVISIONING STRATEGIES

The comparison above has shown that not only are the single-mother households considerably poorer than are their married-couple counterparts in the same region of the US, but that single-mother households are disadvantaged when it comes to the capacity to manage routine and non-routine household activities. How, then, do they accomplish these tasks to ensure their own and their children's survival? In what follows, I look at four sets of strategies that are not mutually exclusive.

Lowered standards and avoidance

Fassinger (1993) reported that single mothers put less effort into housework when they became single. The single mothers Fassinger interviewed gave four reasons for this shift: following separation their values changed and they no longer cared as much; they had more demands on their time and thus less time available to devote to housework; they felt fewer social pressures; and they no longer had to meet a spouse's needs and standards. In fact, Fassinger (1993: 212) insists that the single mothers she interviewed weakened the connection between housework and their self-esteem.

The single mothers in this study reported similarly that they had allowed their standards to drop well below levels they believed that they themselves had formerly found acceptable and below levels they assumed others (including, sometimes, the interviewer) still held. Phoebe Stark said cooking had been a catch-as-catch-can affair in her house for many years: "We're not into, like the three-meals-a-day kind of thing. If [the boys are] around, they eat lunch if they're hungry. ... Nobody likes to cook. ... We eat a lot of [take-out] pizza." Diana Spenser reported that not only did she let her standards drop, but also she assumed that her habits resembled those of all single mothers: "Have you ever seen the houses where single women live? You should come to my house. It would totally scare you, it's the worst thing in the world. That's probably my one, you know, total worst point is cleaning my house. It's just ... like this [mess] everywhere." Other women indicated that they ignored maintenance and repairs: "Oh maybe like 5 percent of things you don't [have to do], they're not essential. Leaky faucets, I let slide"; "The house is in perpetual need. We get done what we can and the rest just has to go."

Avoidance carries its own obvious (and not so obvious) dangers. If Diana Spenser is confident that her house is no messier than that of other single women, she may not so easily as Fassinger (1993) suggests shed the notion that she should be doing a better job in this domain; she refers to her housecleaning as her "total worst point." And Megan Paige lives with leaky faucets and risks having her well run dry. Moreover, Megan Paige, like other single mothers, cannot enjoy the benefits of improving the value of the house she does own. When men and women in married couples devote their time and energy to fixing up their houses, they not only garner the immediate benefits of better living conditions, but they can anticipate getting returns on their investments at some future time.

An alternative to ignoring these tasks is to find ways to avoid having them arise at all. Women can choose to live in rental housing and avoid the hassles of home ownership altogether. In some cases, renting is not a choice so much as it is a necessity: many single mothers do not have sufficient savings to make a down-payment on a home.[11] But, several of the women, who might easily have afforded to own their own homes, or might have opted to keep the house they previously shared with a partner, made the decision not to do so because they did not want the additional burden of upkeep. When Carol Poirier was asked about how she managed home repairs, she adamantly asserted that there were not any, on purpose. Another woman spelled out even more clearly her reasons for renting rather than owning:

> I must say I'm really glad to rent. ... I came in one night from work ... [and it was] freezing cold in the house. ... I called the landlady, left a message on her machine, took [the children] to their dad's, [and I] went over to [a friend's] house overnight. ... It wasn't my problem. It's expensive to rent ... but God, the weight off my soul! ... Sooner or later the lawn will get mowed. And there are things that I wish weren't this way. I wish we had a different heating system, obviously. But

on the whole, the weight of not renting, because of the things like who's going to help me fix this, that, and the other thing are just great.

As Samantha Stuart implies, however, renting has its own costs, including settling for conditions which are less than perfect and dealing with unreliable landlords. Individuals who rent also do not have an important asset that, under current economic conditions, might well increase substantially in value. And, as shown above, renting rather than owning generally precludes the possibility of relying on one's own self-provisioning efforts.

Purchasing necessary goods and services

To be sure, it is possible to hire someone to do many housework tasks as well as to provide the goods and services of routine and substantial self-provisioning. However, as Michael Bittman's (1999) analysis of Australian households has shown, food preparation is the only "housework" activity that is currently "outsourced" on a regular basis. Moreover, the cost of purchasing necessary goods and services can play havoc with the precarious budgets of single mothers (Cohen 1998; Glenna Spitze 1999).[12] Liz Miles, explained that her decision to do her own yard work was motivated by financial considerations: "Well, you know, every time you have to have the lawn mowed [by somebody else], it's probably ten or fifteen dollars." Other women made reference specifically to car repair as having cast into disarray their new efforts of trying to survive in straitened circumstances: "My car got fixed last week and that was $145"; "Well, just a couple of months ago I had an $850 bill for new brakes and brake pads and stuff so that really took a chunk out [of my budget]"; "I would like to have food stamps but I can do without them, but ... you know, my car insurance is due, oh my God ... I got a flat tire, I need a new tire, what am I going to do?" Moreover, as anyone who has tried to find a plumber on a weekend or even a babysitter for a last-minute engagement knows, money is not the only obstacle to getting needed help.

Skill acquisition

One way of avoiding the expense and hassle of purchasing services is, of course, to acquire the necessary skills to do these jobs by one's self. Although learning requires both a teacher ("Once I had a flat tire and I didn't know how to change a flat tire ... so I had [my boyfriend] on the phone") and time ("Not only do you have to do it, you have to learn how to do it first; it's like a double time investment and time is scarce"), this tactic carries rewards. The two women who commented on their bewilderment when they separated, both learned how to do more of these tasks and expressed pride in their new-found skills: "I've learned a lot, I'm much more independent." "I stack all my own firewood. As time goes on, I'm getting more and more self-sufficient." And there is evidence from the US as well as other high-income countries that in general women are getting more involved in these activities (*Marketing to Women* 2001; *News of the World* 2001; *Times-Picayune* 2001).

Some tasks remain out of most women's reach. For example, Samantha Stuart said that she had extensive abilities but that she needed help when a job required heavy lifting: "[I'm] Yankee capable ... on my mother's heels ... but I have had to ask for major help [to move] a pair of bunk beds." And Doris Davis, who built her own house, said that she too needed this kind of help: "I had to get a new bed upstairs – up that spiral staircase. So, I had to get someone to remove the stairwell and put the bed up there. [I always need help] moving things."

Even if women have learned how to do many of the things they formerly relied on their partners to do, they still need to fit those activities into days already stretched thin by the demands of paid employment, childcare, and routine housework. As one woman said, in response to the question about self-provisioning activities, "[Those things] you mentioned – they're all great ideas, but I don't have the time or the energy."

Reliance on others

An alternative to managing on one's own, of course, is to rely on the kindness of friends and family (Rosanna Hertz and Faith Ferguson 1997: 204). This tactic solves some problems; it can also create new ones. I look briefly at the issues involved in relying on children, men, members of one's family of origin, and female friends and neighbors.

Children
In her US study, Fassinger (1993) noted single fathers often enlisted children in the business of housework. Like the children of single fathers, the children of single mothers might be taught independence at an early age. Phoebe Stark, for example, said that her sons had "always made their own breakfast since they were 2 or 3", and that now that they were older, "they take initiative; they wash all their own clothes, they make their own beds [and] that kind of stuff." Women with older children can rely on them to care for their younger siblings. But Liz Miles, who needed her daughter to babysit for her much younger brother, found this strategy had serious drawbacks: she worried about whether her son was being adequately cared for by his sister and she worried about the integrity of her own relationship with her daughter:

I'll have made plans for her to babysit and then she's just really being obnoxious to him, ... to the point where I feel it's not safe, that she's going to really be abusive to him. ... I resent that I'm in that position where I have to ask her. I resent that she has the power to babysit. I feel like if I could say to her, "You cannot babysit unless you can be right with him," then she would treat him better. But she sort of knows a little bit that I'm stuck.

Men: Ex-husbands, current boyfriends, and male friends

Because many of the skills relevant to the issues under consideration here have traditionally been considered "male" skills, it should come as no surprise to find that women rely on the men in their lives.

A number of women said that they relied on their former partners for assistance in maintenance of their households. This strategy has the obvious advantage of convenience and of getting someone with "insider" knowledge. Yet this strategy also carries its own risks. Joanna Darling found that to rely on her ex-husband was to awaken troublesome feelings on her side: "There was one time all my pipes froze and burst. And he's who I called. ... He helps me make decisions about the house. He built the fire escape. ... There were times when it was really difficult for me to try to rely on him, because I was so hurt [when he left]." Jessica Walsh, who had recently left her husband, worried that by letting him help she was sending the wrong message: "He still wants to help me like fix my car and stuff like that but I'm trying not to let him, ... 'cause he still has that hope that we're going to get back together."

Ex-husbands are not the only men who might expect something in return or might take being asked to do chores as a sign of intimacy. Doris Davis talked about the expectations that arose when a single male friend of hers had helped with home construction: "Even with this man who helped us with the house – [I thought] nothing's free, you're going to want something from me. ... And eventually he did. It was something sexual." Other women also indicated that they were aware that in asking for help from men who were "just friends" or with whom they were beginning a relationship, they were risking an intimacy, and creating expectations, they might not yet be ready to handle (Kathryn Edin and Laura Lein 1997).

Kin

Although a substantial body of literature in the US suggests that single mothers get more instrumental support than do those who are married, another body of literature suggests just the reverse (Naomi Gerstel 1988; Spitze 1999). My data cannot resolve this question, but they do reveal that single mothers in Coolidge County do often rely on the members of their families for assistance, that they do so in highly gendered ways, and that

24

here too they have to find ways to handle the obligations of reciprocity (Stacey Oliker 2000b).

When asked about assistance with childcare and home and car repairs, many of those interviewed mentioned members of their family first. This help was patterned. The single mothers say that it is their mothers, aunts, and sisters who assist them with childcare. Even if they do not rely on this assistance for the regular care of children during work hours (Harriet Presser 1986; Karen Kuhlthau and Karen Mason 1996; Holly Hunts and Rosemary Avery 1999; Peter Brandon 2000), they do find it invaluable to cover unexpected gaps in normal arrangements: "I've had to change my schedule [at work] and then I've had to ask people to babysit. Like, it's usually my mom or my sister I will ask to babysit." Others take advantage of free babysitting (on the assumption that their parents are eager to spend time with their grandchildren) to take leisure time for themselves: "I pretty much don't even have to ask any more, my parents just automatically take [my daughter] every weekend. If they don't get to see her, they get very upset."

The women also report that their fathers and brothers assist with the heavy work of home maintenance and renovation (Spitze 1999): "Eventually my dad did come, and helped me build a porch"; "And my brother. When he's up, once in a while, he makes a good handy-person"; "Once in a while my dad will help me with something. ... Once in a very great while, I mean it's not so much heavy chores, it's, you know, my toilet needed some work and so he came up and did that."

Interestingly, in contrast to the strategy to be described next, of relying on female friends and neighbors, many women deny that relying on family carries with it extensive obligations of tit-for-tat reciprocity (Karen Seccombe 1999; Margaret Nelson 2000). If what goes round comes round (Carol Stack 1974), it may take a very different form as it moves among family members. But this is not to say that there are no reciprocal obligations or costs. In the US, at least, reliance on kin is often associated with psychological distress (Gerstel 1988). And although the women sometimes deny that they have any immediate obligations at all, as Oliker (2000a: 462) writes, "In the long run ... studies of social networks suggest that stark asymmetries undermine even the more trusting and committed ties of generalized exchange. Those who give a lot but do not receive begin to feel exploited or just 'burn out.'"

Friends and neighbors
The same general body of US scholarship that addresses the patterns of giving and receiving support between single mothers and their families also often looks at relationships with friends (Ann Roschelle 1997). Once again, these qualitative data cannot resolve the issue of frequency, but they do reveal some interesting patterns. The women in this study say that they rely

on friends for emotional support, assistance with childcare and transportation, and that occasionally they shared the burdens of cooking by trading dinner invitations or getting together to cook with their children. But, ongoing assistance with housework, car repair, and routine maintenance are not common occurrences. One woman at first suggested that she and another single mother (Diana Spenser) shared support regularly. When questioned more fully, she acknowledged that this had happened but once:

> *Melanie Jones:* Well, when Diana moved into that apartment, we did a little bit of cleaning and painting, kind of stuff. But we did a trade. ... And if I go over to her house – she has laundry facilities, I don't – I might bring my diapers, do a load of diapers, and then clean her kitchen for her. You know, we just sort of balance it out. And then, in the meantime, that gives us both the chance to get what we need done, and still hang out with each other. So you feel like you've both gained from it.

> *Interviewer:* Has it always been this kind of relationship?

> *Melanie Jones:* Well, that's only happened once, but I guess it sort of works out that way somehow.

Reliance on friends also, as Melanie Jones implies, requires a more balanced reciprocity than does reliance on the family (Edwina Uehara 1990; Oliker 2000b). As Megan Paige mentioned above, her garden gave her goods to exchange for assistance from friends. Sheila Davis said she was careful to maintain balance in her relationships with neighbors: "And then my neighbors, my elderly neighbors, I do their tax return and do dinner for them and they mow my lawn." Given these expectations, women may be especially reluctant to call for this kind of assistance, knowing that they will have to take time out from their own lives to return the favor.

DISCUSSION AND CONCLUSION

This research suggests that (at least in rural areas of the US) the feminization of poverty is even deeper and more profound than can be measured by income levels alone because it extends to an inability to participate in a range of activities which can relieve the pressure on the wage. To be sure, the single mothers included in this study were relatively privileged by virtue of income, race, and residence in a state with generous means-tested programs (Jason Zengerle 1997; Jon Margolis 2000; Administration for Children & Families 2002).[13] Yet even these women found it difficult to manage (and got little support for) the traditional female tasks of cooking, cleaning, and caring for children. If their married counterparts did not have spouses who shared equally in these activities, they at least had spouses who made significant contributions towards them. Even more importantly, most single mothers had to make special arrangements to manage the traditional male tasks of yard work and car repair. And a much smaller percentage of these women – in comparison with the members of married-couple households – had the time, skills, or resources to engage in self-provisioning activities. Searching for ways to manage on their own, single mothers in the study engage in a variety of strategies for managing daily life. They lower their standards for housework or avoid necessary tasks altogether; they purchase what they can; they acquire new skills; and they rely on the assistance of those in their social networks. Each of these strategies has associated drawbacks. The avoidance of some tasks has a way of coming round to bite you in the back; buying necessary services cuts into the income available for other expenses; the acquisition of skill adds time to already overburdened daily schedules; and reliance on network support embeds the women in complex relationships and requires reciprocity of some sort or another.

Because this study was conducted in a rural US county with a relatively privileged group of single mothers, the question of the degree to which the findings reported here can be generalized elsewhere might well arise. To the extent that in many high-income countries men (in heterosexual couples) do make contributions to housework (even if their contributions are both different from, and lesser than, those of their female partners), the finding that single mothers are disadvantaged when it comes to completing these tasks should have broad applicability. And this relative disadvantage might be especially substantial for those single mothers who are poorer than the women in this study because they will be even less able than their more advantaged peers (whether living as part of a single-parent or married-couple household) to afford to "outsource" that work (Bittman 1999).

The degree to which the findings about self-provisioning can be generalized to a broader population is somewhat different because we have less information altogether about the extent to which families elsewhere in the world engage in this kind of activity. (I address this paucity of information below.) However, since my argument about self-provisioning rests, as it did for housework, on the issue of disadvantage *in comparison* to two-adult families, I would argue that in any place where these activities play an important role in the household economy, single mothers will be less able than their married counterparts to make ends meet by substituting their own labor for purchased goods and services.

To be sure, single mothers in the US are altogether disadvantaged relative to single mothers in countries (like Finland, as in Bittman 1999) that have more generous state provisions for supporting the full range of kinds of families. The US context frames much of the discussion of the implications of my findings.

I fear that the reader has concluded from this analysis that, as conservatives in the US now recommend, single mothers would do well to find themselves husbands (Hedieh Rahmanou and Amy LeMar 2002; Robin Toner and Robert Pear 2002). Alternatively, and from a more feminist orientation, it might be suggested that the women acquire the skills necessary to do without men.

Neither of these seems to be the solution – or at least the whole solution. Husbands can and do help with the activities of car repair, lawn mowing, and self-provisioning; they also can do so in ways that are very costly (Alan Acock and David Demo 1994). Marriage or co-residence for convenience is, at best, dissatisfying and, at worst, dangerous for women and for children (Andrew Cherlin and Paula Fomby 2002; Ellen Scott, Andrew London, and Nancy Myers 2002; Robin Toner 2002). And even when women do learn how to repair the leaky faucet, costs do not entirely disappear; they still need to purchase the necessary tools and squeeze the time from already overburdened days.

However, having more information about the depth of the relative disadvantage of single mothers could provide the basis for more appropriate social policy solutions. For example, although the academic scholarship on single mothers has, for many years, stressed the feminization of poverty (Diana Pearce 1978), to understand fully the poverty of these lives, we need to know more about how these women handle the routine tasks associated with daily living and we need to know more about the direct and indirect costs of various strategies they employ to make do.

We also need more studies that compare single-parent households to both married-couple households and households with gay partners, with respect to the *full* range of activities that enable a household to get by (for an example in the US see Rosanna Hertz 1999). The practices of studying single mothers separately from other kinds of domestic units and of drawing comparisons within a sample of single mothers (for examples in the US, see Edin and Lein 1997 and Ludtke 1999) highlight some problems but conceal others. Studies that compare single mothers and single fathers might also be attentive to issues of home maintenance and self-provisioning as well as housework and contributions from friends and relatives (Leslie Hall, Alexis Walker, and Alan Acock 1995; D. Terri Heath and Dennis Orthner 1999).

We could then apply evidence about the real costs of daily survival in different family structures to social welfare programs that rely on income and family size as the eligibility criteria, as is often the case in the US. New programs might be developed as well (Jane Millar 2001 on Britain). For example, in areas that lack public transportation, funds might be made available for emergency car repair grants or loans of working vehicles that, like emergency fuel assistance, would respond to the urgent needs of those who live in poverty (Jessica Wasilewski 2002 in a study of Vermont, US).

Throughout the developed world, employers, schools, and the broader community could also play a role. Many of the proposals put forth to make employers more family friendly in Britain (*Economist* 2000) and the US (Joan Williams 2000) – such as flexible schedules – may be of more use to those who can easily make the infrastructural arrangements to support that flexibility. But this is not to say that employers don't have other roles in creating other useful benefits, particularly in countries like the US where the state provides so little support for employment. On-site childcare is an obvious one, so too are parental leaves, vacations, and time off to care for sick children. Employers who offer their employees a choice among benefits (through what are sometimes called "cafeteria" plans) might consider including in those plans car insurance, insurance to cover losses to property for those who rent their living accommodation, and support for the cost of transportation to and from work.[14]

Schools could be more sensitive to distinctive needs and consider carefully the possibility of homework completion by children in different family structures (Stephanie Coontz 1997; Katherine Newman and Margaret Chin 2003). In addition, the single mothers in this study often talk bitterly about the fact that attendance is required (or encouraged) at school events, but that no childcare is provided to enable a single parent with more than one child to participate in meaningful ways (for a similar problem in Britain, see Kay Standing 1999). This too could be easily solved. Other community agencies might also provide childcare at their events (such as Vermont's famous town meetings). Community agencies might also encourage meaningful fund-raising efforts: instead of having a bake sale, why not sell the services of a "handy-person" at a low hourly rate so that single parents could purchase some needed home repair rather than yet another plate of brownies? Indeed, by contributing their time on a team of "handy-people," single mothers might acquire some of the skills they lack.

The social policy solutions suggested above range from the academic to the practical. If the former seem too abstract, they actually constitute the real thrust of this research because they address the point on which the concrete recommendations rest. To be sure, much research seeks to measure the value of women's unpaid and unreported work. For example, a recent United Nations study suggests that women work twice the unpaid time as do men (around the globe) and that "the value of women's unpaid housework and community work is estimated at between 10–35 percent of GDP worldwide, amounting to $11 trillion in 1993" (United Nations 1996). However, in emphasizing women's contributions, this study slights both the fact that men's unpaid work was worth approximately $5.5 trillion in the same year and that these trillions were far more likely to go to women (and their children) who lived with men than they were to women living on their own.

In short, now that feminist scholarship has taught us that housework and childcare are real work, we need to be more attentive to the contributions of men's domestic labor (whether it be changing the baby's diapers or changing the car's oil) and we need to examine more closely the way households – especially, but not exclusively, those in rural areas – extend their wages and thereby relieve the pressure on the income with which they make do.[15] Only then will the full cost of single parenting be understood in a way that can lead to meaningful social change.

ACKNOWLEDGMENTS

I thank the Middlebury College Faculty Development Fund for supporting this research. I appreciated the insightful comments offered by Naomi Gerstel, Karen Hansen, and the two anonymous reviewers for, and the editors of, *Feminist Economics*. Finally, I am grateful to Jessica Lindert, Bethany Johnson, and Carol McMurrich for their help in interviewing and transcribing.

NOTES

[1] Studies on the gender division of labor include those by Sarah Berk (1985); Arlie Hochschild (1989); Myra Ferree (1991); and Julia Heath and W. David Bourne (1995) in the US; Oriel Sullivan (2000) for Britain; and Michael Bittman (1999) for a comparison of Australia and Finland. Bittman (1999: 27) notes that "[t]hroughout the 'developed' world, unpaid domestic labor remains stubbornly divided by gender." For additional studies that focus on the different tasks done by men and women see Sanjiv Gupta (1999) (on the effects of marital transitions in the US); Joan Twiggs, Julia McQuillan, and Myra Ferree (1999) (on couples in Connecticut, US); and Suzanne Bianchi, Melissa Milkie, Liana Sayer, and John Robinson (2000) (on trends in the US); see also Scott South and Glenna Spitze (1994) for a comparison of marital and nonmarital households in the US. In his 1999 article, Bittman notes, as well, that in all "OECD countries on which there is information," the ratio of men's to women's average time spent in housework is unequal (1999: 30). For some studies of the distribution of time spent on housework by men and women in Britain, see Jane Wheelock (1990); Lydia Morris (1993); and Oriel Sullivan (1997). For some studies of the US see Ferree (1991); Maximilliane Szinovacz (2000); and Hochschild (1989). For a study unique in its focus on cohabiting couples in Australia, see Jo Lindsay (1999).

[2] For studies on this issue in the US, see Ferree (1991); Rosalind Barnett and Yu-Chu Shen (1997); Yoshinori Kamo (1988); and Bianchi, Milkie, Sayer, and Robinson (2000). For a study of Britain, see Sullivan (2000).

[3] There is also a contemporary bias to much of this research. Indeed, historical research is much more aware of women's self-provisioning efforts and efforts to bring in additional, casual income through such activities as keeping chickens or taking in boarders. (See, for example, Joan Jensen 1980 and Christine Bose 1987.)

[4] The potential economic significance of these activities varies widely. Gathering wood

lessens heating costs that, global warming notwithstanding, loom large in Vermont's cold climate. The most common alternative – relying on fuel oil – costs approximately $12 per BTU of heat produced (in comparison with less than $10 per BTU for wood heat) (Andy Netzel 2003). Average heating costs for a single-family home with fewer than three bedrooms run at about $850 a year (in comparison with approximately $420 for heating with wood that has been purchased) (Department of Social Welfare 1996). Individuals can save approximately $15 each time they change the oil themselves and approximately $20 each time it snows by plowing their own driveways. To be sure, there are direct and indirect costs of all of these activities. Those who cut their own wood need to purchase chain saws and axes, a wood stove itself, and, perhaps, a vehicle adequate for transporting logs. Those who change their own oil might need appropriate tools as well. Presumably, however, in the long run these activities are cost-efficient. And if households that engage in these activities have less available free time or leisure, they also live somewhat better than income levels alone would suggest, especially in comparison with those at the same level of income who have to purchase all of these goods and services. Individuals who participate in these activities might even gain pleasure from ensuring their own survival in these very direct ways.

[5] I appreciate the comments of an anonymous reviewer for clarification of this point.

[6] This appeared to be the case both because "the ready availability of market goods has a clear advantage over spending the time to make things oneself" and because "some of these goods might even be more economical to purchase than to make" (Nelson and Smith 1999: 49–50). Joan Smith and I also found that when women did engage in these activities – knitting, sewing, preserving – they did so as part of a gift economy rather than for household use; they thus saved the family money in a different way. But, "whether from choice or circumstance … the same is not true of many activities of routine self-provisioning that customarily have been under the direction of men" (Nelson and Smith 1999: 49–50). The exception to this general rule is gardening: although individual households may have deviated from the more general pattern, both men and women work in gardens. Thus, the difference in the proportion of married-couple and single-parent households that have gardens (72 percent versus 37 percent) is probably a good representation of the actual differences in the proportion of married versus single women who engage in this activity.

Other money-raising activities that were common among women in the past – such as raising chickens for "egg money" – also have largely disappeared from this rural landscape. Although doubling-up on housing was a frequent response to economic stress, the married-couple households Joan Smith and I interviewed did not often take in "strangers" as boarders in their homes. Taking in boarders was also uncommon among the single mothers interviewed for this study, few of whom had sufficient room to house another adult. Several women did say that they had others living with them from time to time (e.g., a friend or relative undergoing her own marital disruption) and that on some of those occasions they did collect rent from their "boarders."

[7] All names are pseudonyms.

[8] Similarly, Pahl (1984), in the study of the Isle of Sheppey, divides self-provisioners into those who do between two and four activities (in each of six different clusters) and those who do more than five. Over half of the married-couple households surveyed ranked high on this scale.

[9] Pahl (1984: 235) finds a similar difference by family structure with only 10 percent of households headed by women engaging in self-provisioning at a high rate.

[10] By way of contrast, Pahl and Wallace (1985: 215) find that self-provisioning rises with

social class rather than, as might be expected, substituting for the resources associated with a more advantaged position in society. For a full discussion of this issue, see also Pahl (1984); Leif Jensen, Gretchen Cornwell, and Jill Findeis (1995); Colin Williams and Jan Windebank (1995); and Nelson and Smith (1999).

[11] In Great Britain, 35 percent of single mothers own their own homes in comparison with 77 percent of other families (Alison Walker, Joanne Maher, Melissa Coulthard, Eileen Goodard, and Margaret Thomas 2002). The *American Housing Survey* (1993) cited in Maya Federman, Thesia Garner, Kathleen Short, W. Bowman Cutter, John Kiely, David Levine, Duane McGough, and Marilyn McMillan (1996) reports that among nonpoor families, 77.6 percent owned their own homes in contrast with 24.3 percent of single-parent poor families and 40.8 percent of married-couple poor families.

[12] In the US, a service wryly called Rent-a-Husband, Inc., costs anywhere from thirty-nine dollars an hour in Maine to sixty-five dollars an hour in Massachusetts (Gary Dymski 2001).

[13] In an interesting study of the real effects of poverty on material living conditions, see Federman *et al.* (1996), which shows, as just one example, that only two-fifths of single-parent poor families have a clothes dryer in comparison with almost 90 percent of nonpoor families (whether married or not).

[14] It should be noted that these arrangements may well carry the risk of having individuals sacrifice long-term needs (e.g., for pensions) for more immediate needs (e.g., for healthcare).

[15] Increasingly, in US scholarship attention *is* being focused on what it is men do contribute to the household. See, for example, Annette Lareau (2000); Karen Hansen (2001); and Nicholas Townsend (2002).

REFERENCES

Abel, Emily K. and Margaret K. Nelson. 1990. *Circles of Care: Work and Identity in Women's Lives*. Albany, NY: State University of New York Press.

Acock, Alan C. and David H. Demo. 1994. *Family Diversity and Well-Being*. Thousand Oaks, CA: Sage.

Administration for Children & Families, Office of Planning, Research and Evaluation. US Department of Health & Human Services. 2002. Table 13:18: Benefit Levels for Family of 3 (1 adult, 2 children) with No Income. In *Temporary Assistance for Needy Families: Annual Report to Congress*, Fourth Annual Report to Congress (May, 2002). Washington, DC: Government Printing Office. Available www.acf.dhhs.gov/programs/opre/ar2001/1318t.htm

Barnett, Rosalind C. and Caryl Rivers. 1996. *She Works/He Works: How Two-Income Families Are Happier, Healthier, and Better-Off*. San Francisco: Harper San Francisco.

Barnett, Rosalind C. and Yu-Chu Shen. 1997. "Gender, High- and Low-Schedule-Control Housework Tasks, and Psychological Distress: A Study of Dual-Earner Couples." *Journal of Family Issues* 18(4): 403–28.

Barrett, Michele and Mary McIntosh. 1980. *The Anti-Social Family*. London: Verso.

Berk, Sarah F. 1985. *The Gender Factory: The Apportionment of Work in American Households*. New York: Plenum.

Bianchi, Suzanne M., Melissa A. Milkie, Liana C. Sayer, and John P. Robinson. 2000. "Is Anyone Doing the Housework? Trends in the Gender Division of Household Labor." *Social Forces* 29(1): 191–228.

Bittman, Michael. 1999. "Parenthood Without Penalty: Time Use and Public Policy in Australia and Finland," *Feminist Economics* 5(3): 27–42.

Bose, Christine E. 1987. "Devaluing Women's Work: The Undercount of Women's Employment in 1900 and 1980," in Christine Bose, Roslyn Feldberg, and Natalie Sokoloff (eds.) *Hidden Aspects of Women's Work*, pp. 95–116. New York: Praeger.

Brandon, Peter D. 2000. "An Analysis of Kin-Provided Child Care in the Context of Intrafamily Exchanges: Linking the Components of Family Support for Parents Raising Young Children." *American Journal of Economics and Sociology* 29(21): 191–216.

Cherlin, Andrew J. and Paula Fomby. 2002. "A Closer Look at Changes in Children's Living Arrangements in Low-Income Families." Welfare, Children and Families: A Three-City Study, Working Paper 02-01, Johns Hopkins University.

Cohen, Patricia. 1998. "Daddy Dearest: Do You Really Matter?" *New York Times*, July 11, late edition, Arts and Ideas/Cultural Desk.

Coontz, Stephanie. 1997. *The Way We Really Are: Coming to Terms with America's Changing Families*. New York: Basic Books.

Daily Star. 2002. "Britons Give Up Holidays for DIY." February 14.

Department of Social Welfare, Vermont. 1996. "Primary Heating Fuel Costs for the 1996-97 Heating Season." In *Bulletin No. 96-57*. Available http://www.dsw.state.vt.us/policy/part9/2906!4S.htm

Dymski, Gary. 2001. "Home Work." *Newsday*, August 30. Nassau and Suffolk Edition.

Economist (US). 2000. "Family Policy – Leave It to Me (Family-Friendly Employment Practices Gain Ground in Britain)." April 29.

Edin, Kathryn and Laura Lein. 1997. *Making Ends Meet*. New York: Russell Sage Foundation.

Fassinger, Polly A. 1993. "Meanings of Housework for Single Fathers and Mothers: Insights into Gender Inequality," in *Men, Work and Family*, pp. 195–216. Newbury Park, CA: Sage.

Federman, Maya, Thesia I. Garner, Kathleen Short, W. Bowman Cutter, John Kiely, David Levine, Duane McGough, and Marilyn McMillan. 1996. "What Does It Mean to Be Poor in America?" *Monthly Labor Review* 119(5): 3–17.

Ferree, Myra Marx. 1991. "The Gender Division of Labor in Two-Earner Marriages." *Journal of Family Issues* 12: 158–60.

Finch, Janet and Dulcie Groves. 1983. *A Labour of Love: Women, Work and Caring*. London: Routledge & Kegan Paul.

Folbre, Nancy. 2001. *The Invisible Heart Economics and Family Values*. New York: New Press.

Gerstel, Naomi 1988. "Divorce and Kin Ties: The Importance of Gender." *Journal of Marriage and the Family* 50: 109–219.

Glazer, Nona. 1990. "Servants to Capital: Unpaid Domestic Labor and Paid Work," in *Work Without Wages*, pp. 142–67. Albany, NY: SUNY Press.

Gorman, Brian. 2001. "Expansion of B&Q is Key to Kingfisher's Growth." *The Scotsman*, September 13.

Gupta, Sanjiv. 1999. "The Effects of Transitions in Marital Status on Men's Performance of Housework." *Journal of Marriage and the Family* 61: 700–11.

Hall, Leslie D., Alexis J. Walker, and Alan C. Acock. 1995. "Gender and Family Work in One-Parent Households." *Journal of Marriage and the Family* 57: 685–92.

Hansen, Karen V. 2001. "Men in Networks of Care For Children." Paper presented at the Carework, Inequality and Advocacy Conference at the University of California, Irvine. Department of Sociology, Brandeis University.

Hartmann, Heidi. 1976. "Capitalism, Patriarchy, and Job Segregation by Sex." *Signs* 1(3): 137–67.

Heath, Julia A. and W. David Bourne. 1995. "Husbands and Housework: Parity or Parody?" *Social Science Quarterly* 76(1): 195–202.

Heath, D. Terri and Dennis K. Orthner. 1999. "Stress and Adaptation among Male and Female Single Parents." *Journal of Family Issues* 20(4): 557–87.

Hertz, Rosanna. 1999. "Working to Place Family at the Center of Life: Dual-Earner and Single-Parent Strategies." *Annals of the American Academy of Political and Social Science,* March: 16–31.

—— and Faith I. T. Ferguson. 1997. "Kinship Strategies and Self-Sufficiency Among Single Mothers by Choice: Post Modern Family Ties." *Qualitative Sociology* 20(2): 187–209.

Himmelweit, Susan (ed.). 2000. *Inside the Household: From Labour to Care.* London: Macmillan Palgrave.

Hochschild, Arlie. 1989. *The Second Shift.* New York: Avon Books.

Hunts, Holly J. and Rosemary J. Avery. 1999. "Relatives as Child Care Providers." *Journal of Family and Economic Issues* 19(4): 315–41.

Institute for Women's Policy Research. 1998. *State of the States: Vermont.* Washington, DC: IWPR.

Jensen, Joan M. 1980. "Cloth, Butter and Boarders: Women's Household Production for the Market." *Review of Radical Political Economics* 12(2): 14–23.

Jensen, Leif, Gretchen T. Cornwell, and Jill L. Findeis. 1995. "Informal Work in Nonmetropolitan Pennsylvania." *Rural Sociology* 60(1): 91–107.

Kamo, Yoshinori. 1988. "Determinants of Household Division of Labor: Resources, Power, and Ideology." *Journal of Family Issues* 9: 177–200.

Kuhlthau, Karen and Karen Oppenheim Mason. 1996. "Market Child Care Versus Care by Relatives: Choices Made by Employed and Nonemployed Mothers." *Journal of Family Issues* 17(4): 561–78.

Lareau, Annette. 2000. "My Wife Can Tell Me Who I Know: Methodological and Conceptual Problems in Studying Fathers." *Qualitative Sociology* 23: 407–33.

Lindsay, Jo. 1999. "Diversity but Not Equality: Domestic Labour in Cohabiting Relationships." *Australian Journal of Social Issues* 34(3): 267–75.

Livingston, Joy and Elaine McCrate. 1993. *Women and Economic Development in Vermont: A Study for the Governor's Commission on Women.* Montpelier, VT: Governor's Commission on the Status of Women.

Ludtke, Melissa. 1999. *On Our Own: Unmarried Motherhood in America.* Berkeley, CA: University of California Press.

Margolis, Jon. 2000. "Vermont: The Greening of Welfare." *The American Prospect* 11: 34.

Marketing to Women. 2001. "Women Take on Major Home Improvement." October 10, p. 9.

McCrate, Elaine. 1992. "Accounting for the Slowdown of the Divorce Rate in the 1980s." *Review of Social Economy,* Winter: 404–19.

Millar, Jane. 2001. "Establishing Family Policy in Britain?" *Family Matters,* Autumn: 28–33.

Mingione, Enzo. 1991. *Fragmented Societies: A Sociology of Economic Life Beyond the Market Paradigm.* Oxford: Blackwell.

Morris, Lydia. 1993. "Domestic Labour and Employment Status among Married Couples: A Case Study in Hartlepool." *Capital and Class* 49: 37–49.

Nelson, Margaret K. 2000. "Single Mothers and Social Support: The Commitment to and Retreat from Reciprocity." *Qualitative Sociology* 23(3): 291–319.

—— and Joan Smith. 1999. *Working Hard and Making Do: Surviving in Small Town America.* Berkeley, CA: University of California Press.

Netzel, Andy. 2003. "The Price of Winter." *Burlington Free Press,* September 23, p. A1.

Newman, Katherine D. and Margaret M. Chin. 2003. "High Stakes: Time Poverty, Testing, and the Children of the Working Poor." *Qualitative Sociology* 26(1): 3–34.

New York Times. 2002. "Home Depot's Earnings Soar More Than 50%." February 27.

News of the World. 2001. "Girls Get DIY Bug." November 25.

Oakley, Ann. 1974. *The Sociology of Housework.* New York: Pantheon.

Oliker, Stacey. 2000a. "Challenges for Studying Care After AFDC." *Qualitative Sociology* 23(4): 453–65.

——. 2000b. "Family Care After Welfare Ends." *National Forum* 80(3): 29–33.

Pahl, Ray E. 1984. *Divisions of Labour.* Oxford: Blackwell.

—— and Claire Wallace. 1985. "Household Work Strategies in Economic Recession," in *Beyond Employment: Household, Gender and Subsistence*, pp. 189–228. London: Blackwell.

Pearce, Diana. 1978. "The Feminization of Poverty: Women, Work and Welfare." *Urban and Social Change Review*, February: 28–36.

Presser, Harriet. 1986. "Shift Work Among American Women and Child Care." *Journal of Marriage and the Family* 48(3): 551–64.

Rahmanou, Hedieh and Amy LeMar. 2002. *Marriage and Poverty: An Annotated Bibliography.* Institute for Women's Policy Research. IWPR Publication No. B239, Washington, DC.

Riessman, Catherine Kohler. 1990. *Divorce Talk: Women and Men Make Sense of Personal Relationships.* New Brunswick, NJ: Rutgers University Press.

Roschelle, Anne R. 1997. *No More Kin: Exploring Race, Class, and Gender in Family Networks.* Thousand Oaks, CA: Sage.

Scott, Ellen K., Andrew S. London, and Nancy A. Myers. 2002. "Dangerous Dependencies: The Intersection of Welfare Reform and Domestic Violence." *Gender and Society* 16(6): 878.

Seccombe, Karen. 1999. *"So You Think I Drive a Cadillac?": Welfare Recipients' Perspectives on the System and Its Reform.* Needham Heights, MA: Allyn & Bacon.

South, Scott J. and Glenna Spitze. 1994. "Housework in Marital and Nonmarital Households." *American Sociological Review* 59: 327–47.

Spitze, Glenna. 1999. "Getting Help with Housework." *Journal of Family Issues* 20(6): 724–45.

Stack, Carol. 1974. *All Our Kin: Strategies for Survival in a Black Community.* New York: Harper & Row.

Standing, Kay. 1999. "Lone Mothers and 'Parental' Involvement: A Contradiction in Policy?" *Journal of Social Policy* 28(3): 479ff.

Sullivan, Oriel. 1997. "The Division of Housework Among 'Remarried' Couples." *Journal of Family Issues* 18(2): 205–23.

——. 2000. "The Division of Domestic Labour: Twenty Years of Change?" *Sociology* 34(3): 437–56.

Szinovacz, Maximilliane. 2000. "Changes in Housework After Retirement: A Panel Analysis." *Journal of Marriage and the Family* 62: 78–92.

Times-Picayune. 2001. "More Women Tackling Home Improvements: Renovations, Repairs Not Just for Men." August 4, Real Estate.

Toner, Robin. 2002. "2 Parents Not Always Best For Children, Study Finds." *New York Times*, February 20, p. A21.

—— and Robert Pear. 2002. "Bush Urges Work and Marriage Programs in Welfare Plan." *New York Times*, February 27.

Townsend, Nicholas W. 2002. *The Package Deal: Marriage, Work, and Fatherhood in Men's Lives.* Philadelphia: Temple University Press.

Twiggs, Joan E., Julia McQuillan, and Myra Marx Ferree. 1999. "Meaning and Measurement: Reconceptualizing Measures of the Division of Household Labor." *Journal of Marriage and the Family* 61(3): 712–24.

Uehara, Edwina. 1990. "Dual Exchange Theory, Social Networks, and Informal Social Support." *American Journal of Sociology* 96: 521–7.

United Nations. 1996. "Women at a Glance." Women and Labour. Available http://www.un.org/ecosocdev/geninfo/women/women96.htm

Vanek, Joan. 1974. "Time Spent in Housework." *Scientific American* 231: 116–20.

Walker, Alison, Joanne Maher, Melissa Coulthard, Eileen Goodard, and Margaret Thomas. 2002. "Table 4.7: Housing Profile by Family Type: Lone-Parent Families Compared with Other Families," in *Living in Britain: General Household Survey 2000/01*. London: Crown copyright. Available www.statistics.gov.uk/lib2001/viewerChart4743.html

Wasilewski, Jessica. 2002. "Low-Income Credit Rationing and Social Return on Investment: Welfare-to-Work Car Loans in the State of Vermont." Senior thesis, Department of Economics, Middlebury College, Middlebury, VT.

Wheelock, Jane. 1990. "Capital Restructuring and the Domestic Economy: Family Self Respect and the Irrelevance of 'Rational Economic Man'." *Capital and Class*, Summer: 103–41.

Williams, Colin C. and Jan Windebank. 1995. "Social Polarization of Households in Contemporary Britain: A 'Whole Economy' Perspective." *Regional Studies* 29(8): 723–8.

—— and Jan Windebank. 2001. "Note: Paid Informal Work in Deprived Urban Neighborhoods: Exploitative Employment or Cooperative Self-Help?" *Growth and Change* 32(4): 548–57.

Williams, Joan. 2000. *Unbending Gender: Why Family and Work Conflict and What to Do About It*. New York: Oxford University Press.

Zengerle, Jason Gray. 1997. "Welfare as Vermont Knows It." *The American Prospect* 30 (January–February): 54–5.

Lone Mothers in Russia: Soviet and Post-Soviet Policy

Judith Record McKinney

INTRODUCTION

After more than a decade of attempted transition, it is clear that the Russian "revolution" of 1991, like that of 1917, has failed to deliver quickly on its promise to bring about dramatic improvement in the lives of ordinary Russians. Rather than bringing prosperity and empowerment, this attempt to make fundamental changes in the economic, political, and social system of the country has imposed enormous hardship on much of the population, especially on women and their children, and most particularly on women raising their children alone.

Because centrally planned socialist systems are designed to socialize the costs and benefits of many activities, including childrearing, one might expect them to be particularly supportive of lone mothers. It would therefore make sense that the transition to a market economy in Russia would have hurt lone mothers and their children more than other groups. Many of the difficulties lone mothers in Russia face today are not new at all, however. The Soviet system clearly failed to solve the "woman question"[1] and the legacy from that period – particularly the structure of the existing stock of both physical and human capital and the appalling state of the environment – continues to impose costs on Russian women. What has made life harder for lone mothers in the post-Soviet period, beyond the sharp drop in GDP and the state's difficulty collecting taxes, is not retreat from the commitment to women as mothers but retreat from the commitment to women as workers.

The demographic situation in post-Soviet Russia, characterized by low birth rates, high mortality rates, and negative population growth, is widely viewed as a crisis and has sparked considerable discussion about how best to encourage Russian women to bear more children. While a striking variety of solutions to the demographic problems has been proposed, most rest on the assumption that the government still has an important role to play. Indeed, the basic assumptions of both the Russian legislature and the general population about the role of the government in ensuring the welfare of the population have changed little from the Soviet period (Linda Cook 2002). At the same time, concerns about unemployment, social ills, and excessive government spending have created a political environment in which there is much less support than in the past for the idea that the government should make it easy for women to work outside the home.

SOCIALISM: THEORY VS. SOVIET PRACTICE

As Wendy Goldman argues in her book *Women, the State and Revolution: Soviet Family Policy and Social Life, 1917–1936*,[2] Bolshevik theorists "believed that capitalism had created a new contradiction, felt most painfully by women, between the demands of work and the needs of family" (1993: 2). With industrialization, mass production in factories substantially replaced household production by women. At the same time, women were forced to enter the paid labor force, since their husbands did not receive a wage high enough to support their families. Since women still had full responsibility for the household and children, they bore a heavy double burden that made it impossible for them to play a role in public life equal to that of men as well as to take adequate care of their children.

The Bolsheviks believed that socialism would resolve this dilemma and ease women's burden by creating arrangements for the public provisioning of the population. Eventually, the family – like the state – would wither away, but until that time children would be reared by some combination of the state and the parents. According to Goldman, the policy implications of this were clear: "If the state was serious about women's liberation, it had to implement policies to abolish wage differentiation, to raise wages, to establish broad social services, and to socialize household labor" (1993: 48).

While the liberation of women was never in fact a central concern to Soviet leaders, ensuring a supply of workers and soldiers large enough to "build socialism in one country" and protect it from the hostile capitalist world clearly was. The catastrophic demographic consequences of World War I, the Civil War, World War II, and the brutal Stalinist campaigns of forced collectivization of agriculture and the Great Terror made this need all the more urgent. Because young adult males were most likely to have been killed during both the wars and the Stalinist excesses, the state had a strong interest in making it possible for women to be simultaneously engaged in both productive and reproductive labor, whether or not they were married.

The Soviet centrally planned socialist system should have been able to devote substantially more resources to the creation of human capital via investment in childcare, healthcare, and education. Because the system was designed to socialize both costs and benefits, it should also have been able to structure wages, prices, and social benefits to spread the burden of raising children more broadly.

The actual record of the Soviet state in resolving the tension between women as workers and women as mothers was mixed. While it achieved extremely high rates of labor force participation by women, including those with young children, it failed to prevent birth and fertility rates from falling, just as it failed to reduce women's double burden significantly. Soviet investment policy focused on other goals, and the promise offered by a progressive family policy was undercut by inadequate funding.

Soviet mothers were hurt both by the high level of forced saving, which resulted in scant provision of household appliances and other goods and services designed to make it easier to maintain a household, and by the choices leaders made in allocating the resulting investment funds.[3] Most investment resources were directed toward creation of physical capital, especially in heavy industry. Investment in light industry, housing, and services was extremely low. Investment in human capital was spotty. It was much better in education than in healthcare, and most impressive in the early years, when the new leaders felt compelled to turn a predominantly rural and largely illiterate population into a modern industrial labor force.

The Soviets did devote significant investment resources to childcare, where the link with women's participation in the industrial labor force was inescapable. The first big investment in childcare facilities came with the huge labor requirements of the First Five-Year Plan: the number of nurseries for infants was over 5 million in 1932, twenty times greater than in 1928, while the number of pre-school facilities, which was only 2,155 in 1927, had reached 25,700 in 1934–35 (Gail Lapidus 1978: 130; Goldman 1993: 313–34). Investment in childcare facilities continued throughout the Soviet period, with another major campaign taking place under Brezhnev. In 1990, 66.4 percent of all children of pre-school age attended such facilities, a slight decrease from 68.3 percent in 1985 (Gosudarstvennyi komitet rossiskoi federatsii po statistike 1992: 231).

Brezhnev's government also directed resources to the development of after-school care and summer camps for older children. In 1970, about 10 percent of Soviet children aged 5 to 14 received after-school care; ten years

39

later, more than twice as many children were in after-school care even though the total number in this age group had fallen by about 15 percent. About 18 percent of children aged 5 to 14 attended summer camp in 1970 and almost 29 percent did in 1980 before attendance fell slightly to 27 percent in 1990 (Gosudarstvennyi komitet SSSR po statistike 1991: 74, 219; Judith Harwin 1996: 39).

If Soviet investment in childcare facilities was exceptionally high by international standards, investment in housing was extremely low. This sector was almost completely neglected until after Stalin's death, and despite the greater attention it received under subsequent leaders, especially Khrushchev, at the end of 1986 there was a total of only about 4 billion square meters of useful living space for a population of just under 280 million (Gosudarstvennyi komitet SSSR po statistike 1987: 373, 517). This lack of housing space created significant stress in the lives of urban families, who often lived either in communal apartments, with shared bath and kitchen, or in crowded worker dormitories.

There was also little investment in light industry. Although far greater attention was paid to private consumption under Khrushchev and Brezhnev than under Stalin, both the stock of household appliances and their quality remained low, and consumer services were still woefully inadequate in the mid-1980s. While the provision of childcare services sharply reduced the amount of time women spent caring for their children, there was no corresponding effort by the state to reduce the time it took to maintain a household. Women's burden was further increased by the paucity of retail establishments[4] and by Soviet distribution policy, which kept prices of necessities – in particular, housing, basic foodstuffs, and children's clothing – artificially low and relied on mechanisms other than prices to allocate many goods and services.

Time-budget studies carried out in the 1960s in the Soviet Union found that while men and women spent roughly the same number of hours a week working and meeting physiological needs (slightly less in both cases for women), women spent over twice as much time as men performing housework (Lapidus 1978: 270–1). In a survey conducted in March of 1980, Soviet women who worked for state enterprises (that is, all employed women except those on collective farms) were found, on average, to spend over six hours a week on acquiring goods and services, and 29.5 hours a week on housework (Tsentral'noe statisticheskoe upravlenie SSSR 1985: 89).

Soviet investment and distribution policy thus imposed heavy costs on all Soviet mothers, and did relatively little to address the particular challenges facing lone mothers. While the provision of childcare facilities might be expected to have made the greatest difference to lone mothers, who could not rely on the income of a spouse, Soviet wages were kept so low that even married mothers felt a financial compulsion to work outside the home and therefore relied heavily on these facilities. While the decision to keep the prices of necessities low might be expected to have provided greatest help to low-income families – a category to which most families headed by lone mothers belonged – allocation on the basis of "first-come, first-served" required the expenditure of significant amounts of time, which for lone mothers may have been even more scarce than money. Although this might also be expected to mean that the lack of labor-saving household appliances placed a heavier burden on lone mothers, time-budget studies indicate that the reverse was true. In a study published in 1965, G. S. Petrosian found that the number of hours of housework performed by a working mother with one child dropped by between three and eight hours a week in the absence of a husband (Lapidus 1978: 272–3).

The very low levels of investment in housing had the effect of changing the configurations of lone motherhood. It essentially created lone mothers out of young married women forced to live with their children in female dormitories while their husbands lived in male dormitories, but also meant that not all women raising their children without partners were truly lone mothers. In some cases, lone mothers were likely to be living with other adults. If never married, a lone mother would almost certainly have continued to live at home (unless she was one of the large numbers of young girls who moved away from their home towns to a larger city, in which case she almost certainly lived in a dormitory with other workers); if divorced, she might very well continue to live with the father of her children for lack of alternative housing. While the latter situation was clearly undesirable, an unmarried mother living with her mother or grandmother might in fact be better off in many ways (though not financially) than her married counterpart, since the older woman would have been more likely to provide assistance with childcare and housework than the average Soviet father. (Of course, for a married woman there were *two* possible *babushki* to turn to.)

If Soviet investment policy generally neglected the needs of mothers, family policy was designed with these needs clearly in mind. While the specific provisions changed over the decades in response to changes in the availability of resources, in the strength of the perceived need for female participation in the labor force, in the degree of concern over declining birth rates, and in attitudes about the role of the family in creating – and redressing – social problems, the underlying perception of children as public goods remained constant. Soviet family codes were generally remarkably progressive in their treatment of marriage, divorce, and out-of-wedlock births relative to those in other countries (Goldman 1993: 57).[5] Insofar as policy explicitly distinguished between lone mothers and those with husbands, it generally attempted to provide additional support for the former.

In the early years of Bolshevik rule, ideology supported the use of large public institutions for rearing children. These were to be part of a broader drive to socialize household responsibilities through the development of public dining facilities, public laundries, and the like, thereby freeing women from dependence on men and enabling them to raise children outside of marriage. Bolshevik practice, however, fell far short of ideology, as the drains of the Civil War and reconstruction made it impossible to provide adequately even for those millions of children left without families as a result of the wars and famine.

The New Economic Policy of the 1920s, which temporarily allowed private enterprise and the operation of market forces in parts of the economy, may have been successful in boosting agricultural and industrial output back to pre-war levels, but it took a tremendous toll on Soviet women. Fired from their jobs to make room for returning soldiers, abandoned by husbands quick to take advantage of the so-called "post-card divorce," and faced with the challenge of providing both financial and physical care for their children, many women were forced to turn to prostitution (Goldman 1993: 101–43).

By the mid-1930s, Stalin made virtue of necessity and asserted that the family was indeed the best setting for raising children. Divorce became both more difficult and more expensive, while the penalties for failure to pay alimony increased (Goldman 1993: 331). Despite the renewed official commitment to traditional families, however, the Soviet state continued to play a far more active role in providing for its children than was the norm in capitalist countries. Monthly allowances for large families – those with at least eight children – were introduced in 1936; in 1944, with the population losses of World War II a serious concern and with urbanization reducing average family size, families with as few as four children became eligible for these allowances (Mary Buckley 1989: 133–4; Goldman 1993: 331–2; Harwin 1996: 19–20).

The Family Code of 1944 is strikingly pro-natalist. In general, neither marital status nor income level played a role in determining state benefits (or taxes). All that mattered was the number of children and whether any of them were born after 1944 (David Ransel 2000: 77).[6] Single and married women were treated identically, receiving a one-time grant upon the birth of a third child and a monthly subsidy for subsequent children until they turned 5. Anyone, married or not, with two or fewer children was subject to a special tax (Buckley 1989: 133–4; Harwin 1996: 19–20, 24).

Other features of the 1944 law were shaped by concern over the dearth of young males, and were designed to make life easier both for lone mothers and for the men who fathered their children.[7] Children born to unmarried women no longer had any claims on their fathers and could not even have the father's name appear on their birth certificates, presumably freeing men to sire more children than they could personally afford to support. Instead, the state was to provide the necessary financial support for children up to the age of 12. Should the mothers choose, the state would also rear the children in institutions, either temporarily or permanently (Harwin 1996: 19–20).

By the late 1960s, Soviet leaders faced many of the problems of both the 1940s (low birth rates) and the 1920s (family instability, unsupervised children, and other social ills). Their response to the first was to continue trying to reduce the private costs of raising children through both increased maternity leave and increased investment in childcare facilities (Harwin 1996: 38–40). They did not, however, increase the size of monthly allowances.

In 1980, lone mothers still received only 5 rubles per month for one child, 7.5 rubles a month for two, and 10 rubles a month for three, exactly the same amounts they were entitled to in the late 1940s and only a fraction of the official monthly poverty line of 66.6 rubles per capita (Mervyn Matthews 1986: 23, 122).[8] Although family allowances were not increased, there was an attempt to target families with especially low per capita income by introducing small monthly allowances for every child under the age of 8 in such families (Lapidus 1978: 305; Harwin 1996: 40).

To address family instability, unsupervised children, and the like, the leaders tried to increase parents' sense of personal responsibility. In 1968, for the first time since 1944, women could file paternity suits (John Dunstan 1980: 134). Although the state apparently wanted fathers to assume greater financial responsibility mothers received the bulk of attention by Soviet analysts, who attributed social problems primarily to women's failure to perform adequately as mothers. The only significant assistance mothers received, however, was the longer maternity leave, both paid and unpaid, mentioned above. The state continued to pay far more to care for children outside the home (in childcare facilities, day schools, boarding schools, and orphanages) than it paid to women directly in the form of child-related allowances (payments to pregnant women, to children up until their first birthday, to lone mothers and mothers of large families, and to children in poor families). In 1983, the former figure was 17.6 billion rubles, the latter only 4.4 (Tsentral'noe statisticheskoe upravlenie SSSR 1985: 84–5).

Popular attitudes toward lone mothers varied over time more than state policy did, but like policy they tended to reflect economic and demographic circumstances. It was in the immediate aftermath of World War II that lone mothers were portrayed most positively. Not only women who had actually lost their husbands during the war but also those who had lost *potential* husbands were viewed with great sympathy. David Ransel, in his study of three generations of rural women in Russia, quotes a woman who married in the late 1930s:

Yes, there were many widows here who had children. . . . Some of the women gave birth without fathers. Well, these were decent women and they did this consciously. They didn't want to have to go through life

43

alone, and that meant they had to have a child, or even two, or even three without fathers.... And [these] mothers are respected. No one here treated them with contempt, we didn't shun them or reproach them. After all, what was one to do? (Ransel 2000: 115)

A slightly less generous view is expressed in comments recorded by two British marriage counselors visiting the Soviet Union in the 1960s. The first is unattributed; the second is by a lawyer.

In the years just after the war ... [the mother alone] was considered to be a *very* important person. She was rendering a great service to the state, by helping to make up for our terrible war losses. She was such a privileged person that you didn't dare utter a word of criticism of her. (David Mace and Vera Mace 1964: 253)

I can remember these "mothers alone" coming into my office to demand their legal rights. Some of them behaved as if they were the privileged class in our society. (Mace and Mace 1964: 253)

The relatively sympathetic view seems to have eroded with time, as conditions changed. By the 1960s, never-married mothers began to be condemned in print for irresponsibility. Women of childbearing age were no longer in cohorts whose sex ratio was skewed by the terror and the wars, and abortion was again legal, so there were no longer extenuating circumstances for the birth of a child outside of marriage (Dunstan 1980: 134). By the late 1980s, in the first flurry of free-wheeling discussion sparked by Gorbachev's introduction of *glasnost'*, a Soviet version of the "welfare queen" started to appear in the press (Elizabeth Waters 1992: 128–30). Women, especially unmarried women, were condemned for having children in order to receive state benefits and for taking advantage of the law which allowed mothers to leave their children in state care for an indefinite period. Within a few years, however, the attitude had softened, as the economic difficulties faced by these women became more obvious (Waters 1992: 131–2).

Changes in conditions and attitudes were accompanied by changes in behavior. In the immediate aftermath of World War II, roughly one-third of all births were outside of marriage, but in 1970 this proportion had fallen to 10.6 percent. The proportion then climbed again, reaching 12.0 percent in 1985 and 14.6 percent in 1990 (Sergei Zakharov 1999: 50).

REFORM AND TRANSITION

Gorbachev's attempts to revitalize Soviet socialism had a number of consequences for state policy toward families. At the same time that *glasnost'* led to much more public discussion of a wide range of social ills, increased attention to economic efficiency threatened to create significant unemployment.[9] In the eyes of Gorbachev and other leaders at the time, these two problems could be solved simultaneously by encouraging women to return to their role as wives and mothers.[10] Since Soviet women had never actually abandoned these roles, the real idea was that they could now shed the additional role of employee. In addition to refraining from taking jobs from the men who were believed to need them more, women would be in a position to address any number of social ills by staying home and tending to the needs of both their children (thus preventing them from becoming drug abusers, prostitutes, or juvenile delinquents) and their husbands (thus preventing them from becoming alcoholics or emasculated drones). Not only would Soviet men then find it easier to meet the demands of the reformed system, but Soviet children would receive the maternal nurturing and supervision necessary to help them mature into responsible citizens and workers (the latter presumably now only in the case of sons). The belief that having women stay home would reduce social ills was not new; but the expectation that it could be done without sacrificing current production was. There also seemed to be little recognition during these discussions that the return to their "purely womanly mission" would be possible for the sizeable (and increasing) number of lone mothers only with a substantial increase in government assistance.

As it became obvious that Gorbachev's reforms would lead to considerable redistribution of economic well-being, there was more and more discussion about the need to buffer the population from the costs of these reforms. Since a key element of the reforms was the deliberate privatization of a larger share of costs and benefits, not *all* groups could be protected. There was, however, widespread agreement among government officials that "families with children" should not be harmed. At the same time, officials agreed that family assistance policies needed to be overhauled. In a roundtable discussion of the family published in the journal *Nedelya* in 1987, for example, M. Kravchenko, Vice Chair of the USSR State Committee on Labor and Social Questions, noted that the 6 billion rubles paid out annually in family assistance were paid in the form of benefits that had been "established in different years and for the solution of different problems. Some of them no longer play the role they were intended to play" (*Nedelya* 1987: 17–18). Gorbachev struck a similar note in his speech to the Congress of People's Deputies in May of 1989 when he called for an "audit" of all social benefits and privileges (Mikhail Gorbachev 1989: 1–3).

The difficulty lay in establishing appropriate criteria, but for the most part in this period the government simply increased benefits in recognition of increasing need. In late summer of 1990 the newspaper *Izvestiia* reported that the Council of Ministers had "adopted a resolution on additional measures to provide social safeguards for families with children in connection with the changeover to a regulated market economy" (*Izvestiia*

1990: 1). The monthly allowance for lone mothers was increased from a fixed rate of 20 rubles to an amount equal to half the minimum wage (that is, to half of 70 rubles) (*Izvestiia* 1990: 1; Government of the Russian Federation 1994: 41). With this change in the method of calculation, moreover, the frequent upward revisions in the minimum wage, which took place starting in 1991, automatically led to increases in the monthly allowance as well.

There was some attempt to distinguish between those who genuinely needed this assistance and those who did not. For example, the resolution "On Urgent Measures for Improving the Position of Women, Safeguarding Mother and Child and Strengthening the Family," adopted by the Supreme Soviet in the spring of 1990, called for monthly allowances for children living in families with a per capita income of no more than twice the minimum wage. On the other hand, that same resolution also called for a one-time payment on the birth of every child, without regard to family income (William Moskoff 1993: 105). Thus, Gorbachev-era policy, like that of the earlier Soviet period, combined targeted assistance to the most needy with a basic commitment by the state to recognize that society as a whole should bear some of the costs of raising children.

Even after the dissolution of the Soviet Union and Yeltsin's embrace of market capitalism, policy-makers continued to stress the importance of protecting the especially vulnerable from the costs of transition. Continuing Soviet practice, this group was defined primarily by demographic, not economic, characteristics and included the very young, single-parent families, families with many children, and the retired. Thus, in a decree on social benefits issued in the spring of 1993, Yeltsin raised the one-time payment for the birth of every child, the monthly and quarterly payments to families with children, and the monthly food allowance for all children enrolled in school (Tatyana Khudyakova 1993: 29). It was not until July of 1998 that the law "On State Benefits for Citizens with Children" was amended to restrict payment of such allowances to those families considered most needy.[11]

Despite the official commitment to provide support for raising children, economic constraints made it an increasingly empty promise. A shrinking state budget – due both to declining production and to failure to collect taxes – limited the state's ability to make payments. Old programs remained officially in existence and new ones were created, but these programs have often not received the necessary funds, even when those funds have technically been budgeted for them (Nick Manning, Ovsey Shkaratan, and Natalya Tikhonova 2000: 59, 212). Responsibility for funding benefits has been passed down to the level of the *oblast'*, and assistance at that level has been increasingly characterized by reliance on in-kind transfers, primarily because of lack of funds (Mark C. Foley and Jeni Klugman 1997: 194).

At the same time, inflation, which outstripped government measures to adjust the size of payments, quickly reduced the purchasing power of state allowances to virtually nothing. By November of 1995, the Russian newspaper *Segodnya* commented in an article describing a meeting between President Boris Yeltsin and then Minister of Social Protection of the Population Lyudmila Bezlepkina: "It is not known whether Ms. Bezlepkina told the President that the state allowance per child (38,500 rubles [a month]) is enough for exactly two long pieces of cooked sausage, but many parents wait for months for even that money, along with their wages" (Natalya Gorodetskaya 1995: 9). Despite the small size of these payments, their share in total family income rose in the early 1990s, and at the end of 1996 reached 8.9 percent for truly lone mothers (compared to 6.0 percent for all single-parent families) (Michael Lokshin, Kathleen Mullan Harris, and Barry Popkin 2000: 24). Overall, social transfers constituted 16.7 percent of total monetary income of the population in 1995, up from 14.0 percent in 1992 (Anders Aslund 1997: 139).

If the transition did little to weaken the view that the state should help bear the cost of raising children, it had a much greater impact on women's role as worker and on the provision of the childcare that made it possible. In the Soviet period, when all enterprises were state-owned, the distinction between benefits provided from the government budget and those provided by places of employment was largely artificial. With Gorbachev's self-financing reform and Yeltsin's privatization policies, this distinction became real. Despite strong recommendations from Western advisers and international organizations to do otherwise, in the mid-1990s Russian enterprises – especially those that were the only significant employer in a community – continued to provide such benefits as housing and healthcare to their employees. According to a study carried out by the Organization for Economic Co-operation and Development (OECD), however, enterprises were less likely to continue to provide childcare services (Jacques Le Cacheus 1996: 20). Since municipal governments generally lacked the funds to take over these facilities, many were closed. In 1995, there were 658 pre-school slots for every 1,000 children under the age of 7 (Gosudarstvennyi komitet statistiki 1996: 201); by 1999, the number of daycare centers had fallen by 16,000 from the number in 1994 and 1.7 million fewer children were enrolled (Itar-TASS 1999a).

Nor has significant easing of other household responsibilities offset the extra effort needed to arrange for childcare. Although the freeing of retail prices has meant that the shortages of consumer goods so characteristic of the Soviet period are less common, shopping remains a much more time-consuming and difficult task than in the United States. Outside of Moscow and St. Petersburg, large retail outlets with a wide range of products scarcely exist, and even in the biggest cities people rely heavily on small, specialized kiosks, street vendors, and outdoor markets. Self-service is rare and most stores still operate much as they did in Soviet days, with a single purchase requiring three separate stages – placing the order at a counter, paying in another part of the store, then returning with the receipt to collect the good (Olga Alexeitchik and Yelena Zheberlyaeva 2001: 4; Polina Belkina 2003: 7).

Housing, too, remains a source of frustration. Despite the decline in population, the number of households in Russia has increased, which puts more demand on the housing stock (Maria Lodahl 2001: 195). While there has nonetheless been a marked drop in the number of households on waiting lists, a third of those remaining on the lists have been waiting for over a decade (Lodahl 2001: 195). Lack of an effective credit market puts home purchase or construction far beyond the reach of many, and the essentially free privatization of state-owned apartments has been largely meaningless, since the owners are charged no more than renters of state property for maintenance and are eligible for state housing subsidies on the same grounds as renters (Lodahl 2001: 196–7; Nadezhda Kosareva, Andrei Tkachenko, and Raymond Struyk 2000: 156).

RUSSIA TODAY

While poverty afflicts a great many Russians in all types of families – for the last several years the official figure has fluctuated between about 27 and 40 percent of the population, depending on the period and the method of computation – the proportion of families in this position is unambiguously related to the number of children and is especially high for single-parent families. In the third quarter of 1999, when the poverty rate for all households was 41.9 percent, that for families with children up to the age of 16 was 57.8 percent, and that for single-parent families, which are overwhelmingly female-headed, was 62.7 percent (Cook 2002: 119).

The number of children in single-parent families is increasing. In 1998, 27 percent of births were outside of registered marriages, there were 59.1 divorces per 100 marriages, and one of every seven children under the age of 18 lived in an "incomplete family" (*Materialy ministerstva truda i sotsial'nogo razvitiia Rossiiskoi Federatsii* 1999; Itar-TASS 1999b). At the same time, the share of lone mothers actually living in households with no other adult present is falling, presumably in response to the greater economic difficulty these women face. According to data from the Russian Long-itudinal Monitoring Study, in September of 1992, 55.5 percent of single-mother families lived in households without another adult, while 32.4 percent lived with at least one of the parents of the mother; in October of 1996, these proportions were 43.8 percent and 42.0 percent (Lokshin, Harris, and Popkin 2000: 22).

The greater poverty of lone mothers and their children in Russia is due both to the smaller number of wage earners in the family and to the generally poorer earning opportunities for women. The lower wages are in large measure a result of the vertical and horizontal job segregation inherited from the Soviet period, and in particular the heavy concentration of women in sectors like education and public health that have not been privatized. This employment pattern results both in lower wages – official statistics put average earnings of women at 56 percent of the average for men in 2000, down from 70 percent for much of the Soviet period (*Nezavisimaya gazeta* 2001) – and in a much more serious problem with wage arrears.

Official figures, we know, do not provide an entirely accurate picture of the state of the Russian economy or of the lives of Russian citizens. The unofficial economy, though difficult to measure, is undeniably large. The Minister of Labor and Social Development estimates that "gray economy" – and therefore unreported – wages constitute around 60 percent of earnings (Sergei Kalashnikov 1999).[12] According to a recent article in *Moscow News*, the millions of poor in Russia, most of whom hold jobs, survive in large measure because of food received from personal plots, often belonging to parents still living in villages (Erlen Bernshtein 2002). The average value of food grown on small plots for personal consumption has been estimated at 250 rubles per family per year (*Golovachev* 2000), more than the average per capita income of families with four or more children (*Materialy ministerstva truda i sotsial'nogo razvitiia Rossiiskoi Federatsii* 1999).

These averages are sure to mask considerable variation and may not be representative of the amounts received in families with lone mothers. Lone mothers in Russia participate in the labor force more than married mothers, with labor force participation rates in late 1996 of 81 percent and 71 percent, respectively (Lokshin, Harris, and Popkin 2000: 9), and are unlikely to have time to moonlight in the unofficial economy.[13] Furthermore, they may well resist getting involved in potentially dangerous economic activities in order to protect their children, which would further reduce their income from unofficial sources.

The poverty of lone mothers in Russia today is certainly harsher than that experienced in the late Brezhnev era, but it is not a new phenomenon. In his study of poverty in the Soviet Union, Mervyn Matthews (1986: 28) used a variety of sociological studies and émigré surveys (since official data on poverty were not published, if indeed they existed) and posited "'poverty contingents' of up to two-fifths of all workers and employees' families, and rather more of the population at large." Among the groups that Matthews identified as especially likely to experience poverty were women and members of large or "incomplete" families (Matthews 1986: 37–9).

One consequence of Russian poverty is the high incidence of nutritional deficiencies and of various infectious diseases associated with low income. Recent studies have found that significant numbers of Russian women are deficient in such nutrients as folic acid, iron, calcium, and some of the B vitamins, and nearly half of pregnant women are malnourished. During the 1990s, there was a decline in the average weight, height, chest size, and muscle strength of Russian children (Alla Malakhova 1999: 1, 5; Alexandre Zouev 1999: 24; Stephen Massey 2002: 2).

To the extent that these health problems are due to inadequate diet, drug use, or sexually transmitted diseases, they can be attributed in large measure to the economic hardships and social dislocations arising from the transition period. Daily per capita caloric intake in Russia fell from 2,589 in 1990 to 2,427 in 1994 (Bertram Silverman and Murray Yanowitch 1997: 26). According to the Russian Ministry of Health, drug use rose by almost 400 percent in the 1990s (Francesca Mereu 2002). Some experts claim that a sharp rise in the mortality rate for children and young women since 1997 is due in large measure to increased prostitution (*BBC Monitoring* 2001).

Many of the negative trends began well before 1991, however. The sickness rate among Russian newborns climbed from 82.4 per 1,000 in 1981 to 173.7 per 1,000 in 1991, while the incidence of birth defects in the early 1990s was about 15 percent (*Nezavisimaya gazeta* 1992: 6; Yelena Shafran 1994). Deaths per 1,000 members of the Russian population rose from 7.4 in 1960 to 10.4 in 1986, then, much more rapidly, to 15.7 in 1994 (Gosudarstvennyi komitet SSSR po statistike 1987: 407; Boris Gorzev 1996: 35). Life expectancy at birth for males in Russia fell from 63.1 years in 1969–70 to 61.5 in 1979–80, then rose to 63.9 in 1990 (possibly because of the anti-alcohol campaigns of Andropov and Gorbachev), before falling sharply to 57.7 in 1994 (Gosudarstvennyi komitet SSSR po statistike 1987: 409; 1991: 94).

Many of the sources of today's health problems lie in the past. Soviet-era degradation of the environment was responsible for about 20 percent of illnesses in the 1980s, according to a study by the All-Union Central Research Institute for Occupational Safety (D. J. Peterson 1993: 7), and its impact will be felt for generations. Soviet vaccination practices also contributed to current problems. The isolation of Soviet medical researchers from their counterparts in the rest of the world resulted in a distinctive approach to immunology and much lower vaccination rates than deemed desirable in the West. Pediatricians were officially discouraged from giving vaccinations to children with any of a long list of contra-indications, very few of which would be considered problems in the West (Laurie Garrett 1998: 4). In 1989, for example, "one-quarter of Soviet children who should have been vaccinated against polio were not; one-fifth were not immunized against diphtheria, and one-third did not get a whooping cough vaccination" (Arthur Hartman 1992).

Inadequacies in the Russian healthcare system make dealing with health problems difficult, and these, though exacerbated by the transition, also have a long history. According to an article published in *Nezavisimaya gazeta* in 1992,

"one-fourth of all currently operating hospitals were built before 1940. A total of 46 percent of all hospitals and almost one-third of all outpatient clinics need capital repairs. As many as 42 percent of all hospitals and 30 percent of all outpatient clinics have no hot-water supply; 18 percent and 15 percent, respectively, have no sewerage systems; and 12 percent and 7 percent have no water supply at all." (*Nezavisimaya gazeta* 1992: 6)

These long-term problems with the physical capital stock have been joined by more recent shortages of personnel (due to low wages and serious wage arrears) and of medicines. Furthermore, because of a shortage of pharmacists, people without the necessary training prepare medicines, and there is a growing problem with fraudulent production (*RFE/RL Newsline* 2001a). Medicines for children are particularly hard to find. According to Aleksandr Baranov, chair of the executive committee of the Russian Pediatricians' Union, few Russian medicines are available except in adult doses, and foreign medicines, which do come in appropriate doses, are at least twice as expensive; less than 5 percent of the medicines needed for Russian children are currently available (Itar-TASS 2002).

The costs of the country's poor health fall heavily on Russian women: they suffer poor health themselves, bear the burden of caring for sickly children, and face an increased likelihood of becoming lone mothers because of the high mortality rate for young males. In addition, more very young women are giving birth outside of marriage, and the incidence of premature births is significantly higher for teenaged mothers (Lokshin, Harris, and Popkin 2000: 10).

At a time when Russians are deeply concerned about a shrinking population and when the number of births to married women has been falling, both the absolute number and the share of births to unwed women have been rising. In 1989, 1.87 million babies were born to married women and 291,700 to unmarried women; in 2000, the figures were 912,500 (a 51 percent drop) and 354,300 (a 21 percent increase), respectively (*Demoscope Weekly* 2001). For women over 40, 35 percent of births are to unmarried women, while for girls between the ages of 15 and 19 almost 20 percent are to those who are not married (*Demoscope Weekly* 2001).

The trend toward increasing numbers of very young lone mothers is worrisome. Not only are premature births, and the resulting health problems, more common for these women, but their educational achievement is below that of other women in their age group (Lokshin, Harris, and Popkin 2000: 10). With less education, they have fewer employment opportunities and lower incomes; with sicker children, they need more healthcare, and are likely to need more leave time, which makes them unattractive to potential employers.

In these conditions, many lone mothers in Russia simply cannot cope, and end up turning to state-run orphanages. By all reports, over the last decade the number of children in Russian orphanages and boarding schools has risen sharply.[14] The exact numbers are not easy to establish, however, because of ambiguity about the terms used. At the beginning of 1998, official figures indicated that about 600,000 children (or about 22.8 per 1,000 under the age of 18) were not under parental supervision, and of these about a quarter lived in children's homes or boarding schools, with the number in infant and children's homes having doubled since 1993 (Otto Latsis 1999; Malakhova 1999). This compares with 8.0 per 1,000 children in the United States living in foster care in 2000 (Office of the Assistant Secretary for Planning and Evaluation, US Department of Health and Human Services 2001), but international comparisons must be treated with considerable caution because arrangements for the care of children without supervisory parents depend so heavily on cultural norms. The overwhelming majority – some estimates say over 90 percent – of children in Russian orphanages are so-called "social orphans" with at least one living parent. In some cases these children have run away from home to escape abuse or neglect, in others the authorities have terminated parental rights. Of the children entering orphanages each year, however, about 30 percent are brought to the homes by lone mothers no longer able to take care of them (Itar-TASS 1999b).

As with poverty and ill health, however, the plight of lone Russian mothers unable to care for their children is not new. In the early period of *glasnost'* the Soviet press was full of articles about the large number of institutionalized children and the poor conditions in which they lived. Data presented at a roundtable in 1987 mentioned 284,000 children in state care for the Soviet Union as a whole (Waters 1992: 124). Remarkably, compared to the entire population, this works out to be about the same proportion as for Russia in 1998.[15]

As the number of divorces, deaths among young men, and births outside of marriage increase and concerns about the shrinking Russian population become more intense, it seems probable that lone mothers will face less and less social censure. Surveys suggest that fewer Russians than before disapprove of premarital sex (1upInfo 1996). On the other hand, there are some profoundly conservative groups, such as the leadership of the Russian Orthodox Church, who have been given greater voice in the new era. While these groups stress the desirability of traditional families, they have also been successful in deterring efforts to increase the availability of sex education and information about contraception, so are unlikely to reduce the incidence of lone mothers in Russia.

Since becoming president, Vladimir Putin has devoted his energies more to tightening control than to fundamentally changing economic or social policies. Despite considerable discussion of the importance of targeting state assistance more carefully, there has been very little change in practice. A poll conducted by VTsIOM (the All-Russian Center for the Study of Public Opinion) in late 2001 found that 49 percent of the population receives some type of government benefit, while Deputy Prime Minister for Social Affairs Valentina Matvienko put the share at two-thirds and argued that only a small percentage of these recipients are people with low incomes (*RFE/RL Newsline* 2001d; Alla Startseva 2001). It is difficult, however, to reconcile Matvienko's latter claim with the data on poverty. The legislature did pass a bill to introduce means-testing for child benefits, but it has proved hard to implement and so far has had little impact (Cook 2002: 121). In any event, most lone mothers would continue to be eligible, given their low incomes.

In the last couple of years the minimum wage has increased modestly, and therefore so have the myriad social benefits, including allowances to lone mothers, based upon this number, but these amounts remain very low. Plans called for raising the minimum wage from about 14 percent of the (unrealistically low) official subsistence minimum in 2000 to 60 percent of the subsistence level in 2002 and 100 percent in 2003, but according to the Minister of Labor such an increase is well beyond the capacity of the government to fund (Startseva 2001). Monthly child support is only 5 percent of the subsistence minimum (Muraviera 2002),[16] and continues to be subject to lengthy delays. As of January of 2002, child allowance arrears were equal to 17 billion rubles (approximately $558 million), a bit higher than the figure for 1998 although considerably lower than the 25.4 billion rubles for 1999 (World Bank Group in Russia 2002).

Wage arrears, too, continue to be a problem, despite some initial success under Putin at reducing them. According to the chair of the State Statistics Committee, wage arrears in June of 2002 were only 40 percent of those in September 1998 (*RIA Novosti* 2002). They were higher, however, than at the end of 2001, and in July 2002 equaled $101 million, of which over 40 percent were owed to workers in the healthcare sector and over 53 percent to education workers, both groups that are overwhelmingly female (Alex Rodriguez 2002; *RFE/RL Newsline* 2002b; Karpova 2002). Arrears to workers in healthcare and education affect not only the incomes of women, but also the availability of services they need for their children.

Putin has called for "transition to the principle of paying for medical care through insurance," while recognizing the need to increase government spending on healthcare (Vladimir Putin 2001: 10), but it is clear that problems in this area will not be resolved soon. The Russian Minister of Health, Yurii Shevchenko, argued in mid-2001 that a 50 percent increase in spending was needed in 2002 while the government was planning only a 10 percent increase (*RFE/RL Newsline* 2001b).

There are three areas in which Putin's policies are likely to have a significant, if not immediate, effect on the lives of lone mothers. First, his tax reform of 2001, which replaced a progressive income tax with a flat 13 percent tax; second, his reduction and gradual elimination of subsidies for housing and municipal services; third, his simplification of registration procedures for small and medium-sized businesses, which went into effect on July 1, 2002, and promises of less intrusive monitoring and regulation of these businesses.

The primary goal of the tax reform was to increase revenues from the abysmally low levels of most of the post-Soviet period. Difficulties collecting taxes have stemmed from the inherited fiscal arrangements among the various levels of government, the hidden nature of most Soviet taxation (and thus the lack of any cultural norm of tax payment) and rampant corruption (greater today but already a serious problem in the late Brezhnev era). Initial results of the reform were mildly encouraging. Speaking in October of 2001, Tax Minister Gennadii Bukaev said that collection in 2001 was 2 percent more of GDP than in 2000 (*RFE/RL Newsline* 2001c). Since the main reason for the inadequate allowances received by lone mothers and others in need in Russia has been the inability of the government budget to fund larger amounts, improved tax revenues could make a considerable difference. While the tax rates are no longer progressive, under the new law single parents receive double the regular tax deduction per child and people with relatively low incomes are entitled to larger standard deductions than are the better off (Ministry of Taxation of the Russian Federation 2003).

Although the plan to bring market reform to the area of communal services over the next decade would seem likely to hurt the poor by significantly increasing the cost of housing and utilities, one of the goals of the reform is better targeting of assistance. If the reforms are indeed accompanied by the promised increase in assistance to those with low income, the net effect for lone mothers could prove to be positive. Still, assistance is contingent upon government priorities and availability of money for these reforms. In addition, these communal service reforms are extremely unpopular, and it is unclear whether Putin will succeed in implementing them.

Reforms in the small business sector should be unambiguously beneficial to lone mothers, if indeed they are implemented as intended at the local level. Not only would these reforms increase the tax base and increase the opportunity for women to start their own small businesses, but they should also make shopping for goods and services easier, since small businesses in Russia tend to be concentrated in trade and catering.[17] At least as important as simplification of registration procedures is the idea of reducing the degree of state monitoring. According to Irina Khakamada, who was appointed as head of the State Committee for the Support and Development of Small Business in 1997 and is now deputy chair of the Duma, inspections are a particular problem for female entrepreneurs, who tend to experience about twice as many visits – around fifty each year – from government officials (or those who claim to hold such positions) as do male entrepreneurs (Nora Boustany 2002).

CONCLUSION

Life for lone mothers in Russia today is indeed hard, but many of the difficulties they face have their roots deep in the Soviet period. The shortage of housing and the health consequences arising from environmental degradation are clearly the result of Soviet-era policies, while the difficulties the federal government encounters in collecting taxes to fund assistance programs stem both from the inherited administrative structure and from attitudes instilled in the earlier period. While lone mothers are not the only segment of the population to be affected by these legacies, they are more likely to be operating at the limits of what they can manage in terms of both time and money and are therefore likely to be more seriously hurt.

The transition to a new economic and political system has of course also played an important role. What is apparent, however, is that the problems do not arise from a change in the state's official commitment to women as mothers. There has been remarkably little erosion in the belief that the state is responsible for ensuring that the basic needs of the population are met, and correspondingly little change in welfare legislation since 1991 (Cook 2002). In particular, the state has not retreated from its view of children as public goods, nor has it retreated in principle from its responsibility for providing healthcare and education to the population.

What has changed is the state's attitude toward employment. It has abandoned its commitment to over-full employment and its desire to ensure high labor force participation rates for women, and this has resulted in far fewer and less affordable childcare facilities.[18] For some married women in Russia this may have provided welcome encouragement to stay at home and escape the dual burden; for the increasing number of lone mothers it has made the burden that much heavier.

ACKNOWLEDGMENTS

I am indebted to Jo Beth Mertens, Randy Albelda, Jane Humphries, and anonymous reviewers for their suggestions. I received support while conducting the research for this article from the University of Illinois Russian, East European, and Eurasian Summer Research laboratory and the U.S. Department of State Title VIII Program.

NOTES

[1] For the most part, the Bolsheviks treated the "woman question" – the proper role for women in society and the problem of women's oppression – as secondary to the class struggle. The proletarian revolution was expected to result more or less automatically in the liberation of women. See, for example, Chapter 1 in Gail Lapidus (1978) and Nancy Folbre (1993).

[2] See Goldman's book for a thoughtful discussion of the different positions expressed by individual theorists.

[3] Although the consequences of Soviet investment and family policy might be felt by all parents, childcare and housework in the Soviet Union were almost exclusively women's responsibility. I therefore use the term "mother" throughout.

[4] The number of retail trade outlets per 10,000 people increased from 21 in 1940 to only 25 in 1986 (Gosudarstvennyi komitet SSSR po statistike 1987: 496).

[5] In both Soviet and post-Soviet legislation the term "lone mothers" generally refers only to women who have never married, despite the considerable number of divorced mothers in the country (UNICEF-MONEE 1999: 9); the categories "lone mothers" and "mothers of large families" are generally combined, while "insufficiently provisioned families" constitute a separate category, despite the high proportion of lone mothers and families with many children who are "insufficiently provisioned."

[6] An exception was the reduction in fees for childcare for low-income families (Buckley 1989: 134).

[7] These provisions, however, had the effect of recreating distinctions between children born within and outside of registered marriages (Buckley 1989: 134–5; Harwin 1996: 20).

[8] In the late 1970s the official minimum wage was 70 rubles per month, up from 27–35 in 1956, and the average gross wage was 163.3 rubles per month (Matthews 1986: 11–12, 27).

[9] Officially vanquished in the USSR by the beginning of the 1930s, unemployment was expected to re-appear as enterprises found it advantageous to shed relatively unproductive labor.

[10] Gorbachev's views are captured in this comment from his book *Perestroika: New Thinking for Our Country and the World* (1987: 116): "[we must consider] what we should do to make it possible for women to be returned to their purely womanly mission."

[11] In particular, the benefits were to be paid only to families with per capita income less than one and a half times the official minimum living standard (Svetlana Babayeva, Dmitri Dokuchayev, Stepan Pavlovsky 1998: 6–7).

[12] This figure seems to come from comparing official earnings with expenditures. Thus, in an interview in *Moscow News*, June 21–27, 2000, Deputy Prime Minister for Social Affairs Valentina Matvienko is quoted as saying, "Do you know, for example, that statistically, Russians spend three times more than what they officially earn?"

[13] Somewhat fewer women than men work informally, with official statistics for May 2002 indicating 5.21 million men and 4.96 million women involved (Alexander Protsenko 2002). Since the bulk of informal activity involves the production and sale of food, a predominantly female occupation, the share of women in nonfood-related informal businesses must be relatively small.

[14] A boarding school in the Russian context is essentially an orphanage for children of school age, not a place for an expensive private education.

[15] I have been unable to find any data to indicate the distribution of children in institutions by republic in the Soviet period.

[16] The figure is provided by Professor Natalia Rimashevskaya, director of the Socio-Economic Problems of the Population Institute at the Russian Academy of Sciences.

[17] Even if much of the effect is just to bring existing businesses out of the shadows, this will have the important effect of increasing the tax base and is likely to simplify shopping as well.

[18] In addition to the decline in year-round childcare, only 9 percent of children attended summer camp in 2002 (*RFE/RL Newsline* July 15, 2002).

REFERENCES

1upInfo. 1996. "Sexual Attitudes," in *Country Guide for Russia.* Available http://www.1upinfo.com/country-guide-study/russia/russia96.html (November 12, 2002).

Alexeitchik, Olga and Yelena Zheberlyaeva. 2001. "Retail Trade Gains Momentum in Russia." *BISNIS Bulletin*, July, pp. 1, 4. Available http://www.bisnis.doc.gov/BISNIS/BULLETIN/july01-web.pdf (September 30, 2003).

Aslund, Anders. 1997. "Social Problems and Policies in Postcommunist Russia," in Ethan B. Kapstein and Michael Mandelbaum (eds.) *Sustaining the Transition: The Social Safety Net in Postcommunist Europe*, pp. 124–46. New York: Council on Foreign Relations.

Associated Press. 2002. "Russia Suffers Shortage of Children's Medicines." July 26. Available http://www.cdi.org/russia/johnson/6348-4.cfm.

Babeyeva, Svetlana, Dmitry Dokuchayev, and Stepan Pavlovksy. 1998. "Anticrisis Program Will Lighten Everybody's Wallet by Four Percent." *Izvestiia*, July 21, pp. 1–2. Trans. *Current Digest of the Post-Soviet Press* 50(29): 6–7.

BBC Monitoring. 2001. "Russian Health Experts Present Latest 'Shocking Figures.'" March 1. Available http://www.cdi.org/russia/johnson/5141.cfm.

Belkina, Polina. 2003. "Consumer Trends in Russia." *BISNIS Bulletin*, May, pp. 1, 7. Available http://www.bisnis.doc.gov/BISNIS/bulletin/may03.pdf.

Bernshtein, Erlen. 2002. "Poverty Russian Style." *Moscow News*, September 25 to October 1. Available http://www.cdi.org/russia/johnson/6458.cfm.

Boustany, Nora. 2002. "From the Russian Duma, a Champion of Small Business Makes Her Case to Congress." *Washington Post*, June 19.

Buckley, Mary. 1989. *Women and Ideology in the Soviet Union.* Ann Arbor, MI: University of Michigan Press.

Cook, Linda J. 2002. "Institutional and Political Legacies of the Socialist Welfare State," in David Lane (ed.) *The Legacy of State Socialism and the Future of Transformation*, pp. 107–25. Lanham, MD: Rowman & Littlefield.

Demoscope Weekly. 2001, "Vnebrachnye deti." November 5–18. Available http://demoscope.ru/weekly/041/tema02.php.

Dunstan, John. 1980. "Soviet Boarding Education: Its Rise and Progress," in Jenny Brine, Maureen Perrie, and Andrew Sutton (eds.) *Home, School and Leisure in the Soviet Union*, pp. 110–41. London: George Allen & Unwin.

Folbre, Nancy. 1993. "Socialism, Feminist and Scientific," in Marianne A. Ferber and Julie A. Nelson (eds.) *Beyond Economic Man: Feminist Theory and Economics*, pp. 94–110. Chicago: University of Chicago Press.

Foley, Mark C. and Jeni Klugman. 1997. "The Impact of Social Support: Errors of Leakage and Exclusion," in Jeni Klugman (ed.) *Poverty in Russia: Public Policy and Private Responses*, pp. 189–210. Washington, DC: The World Bank.

Garrett, Laurie. 1998. "Shots in the Dark." Available http://www.newsday.com/news/russpak/mainday4.htm (April 9, 1998).

Goldman, Wendy Z. 1993. *Women, the State and Revolution: Soviet Family Policy and Social Life, 1917–1936.* Cambridge, UK: Cambridge University Press.

Golovachev, Vitalii. 2000. "Zhizn' I Koshelek. Skol'ko bednykh na rusi? Ezhemesiachnye dokhody 60 millionov nashikh grazhdan-nizhe prozhitochnogo minimuma." *Trud*, June 7.

Gorbachev, Mikhail. 1987. *Perestroika: New Thinking for Our Country and the World.* New York: Harper & Row.

——1989. "On the Basic Guidelines of the USSR's Domestic and Foreign Policy." *Pravda*, May 31. Trans. *Current Digest of the Post-Soviet Press* 41(25): 5.

Gorodetskaya, Natalya. 1995. "Boris Yeltsin Orders that Precious Metals Be Sold and Pensions Paid." *Segodnya*, November 21, p. 2. Trans. *Current Digest of the Post-Soviet Press* 47(47): 9.

Gorzev, Boris. 1996. "The Demographic Burden of Empire." *Moskovskie novosti*, March 17–24, p. 35. Trans. *Current Digest of the Post-Soviet Press* 48(13).

Gosudarstvennyi komitet rossiskoi federatsii po statistike. 1992. *Narodnoe khoziaistvo rossiiskoi federatsii 1992, Statisticheskii ezhegodnik.* Moscow: Respublikanskii informatsion-no-izdatel'skii tsentr.

Gosudarstvennyi komitet SSSR po statistike. 1987. *Narodnoe khoziaistvo SSSR za 70 let.* Moscow: Finansy i statistika.

Gosudarstvennyi komitet SSSR po statistike. 1991. *Narodnoe khoziaistvo SSSR v 1990 g.* Moscow: Finansy i statistika.

Gosudarstvennyi komitet statistiki. 1996. *Semiia v rossii, Statisticheskii sbornik.* Moscow: Finansy i statistika.

Government of the Russian Federation. 1994. *Russian Economic Trends* 3(2): 41.

Hartman, Arthur. 1992. "Life or Death for Russian Children." *New York Times*, February 25.

Harwin, Judith. 1996. *Children of the Russian State: 1917–1995.* Aldershot, UK: Avebury.

Itar-TASS. 1999a. "Children's Rights Not Observed in Russia." December 3. Johnson Russia List 3660. Available http://www.cdi.org/russia/johnson/arch.cfm.

Itar-TASS. 1999b. "Matrimony Rate on Decline in Russia." December 7. Available http://www.cdi.org/russia/johnson/archives.cfm.

Itar-TASS. 2002. "Russian Experts Say Only About One-Third of Infants Healthy." July 10. Available http://www.cdi.org/russia/johnson/6348-3.cfm.

Izvestiia. 1990. "Money for Children," August 4. Trans. *Current Digest of the Post-Soviet Press* 42(31): 30.

Kalashnikov, Sergei. 1999. "Living Standards in Russia." *Profil* (45). Available http://www.cdi.org/russia/johnson/archives.cfm.

Karpova, Oksana. 2002. "Wages to the Starving." *Vremya MN*, July 27. Available http://www.cdi.org/russia/johnson/6379.

Khudyakova, Tatyana. 1993. "Minimum Wage, Pensions, and Stipends Increased." *Izvestiia*, April 20, p. 4. Trans. *Current Digest of the Post-Soviet Press* 45(16): 29.

Kosareva, Nadezhda B., Andrei Tkachenko, and Raymond J. Struyk. 2000. "Russia: Dramatic Shift to Demand-Side Assistance," in Raymond J. Struyk (ed.) *Homeownership and Housing Finance Policy in the Former Soviet Bloc: Costly Populism*, pp. 151–215. Urban Institute. Available http://www.urban.org/UploadedPDF/costly-populism.pdf.

Lapidus, Gail Warshofsky. 1978. *Women in Soviet Society: Equality, Development, and Social Change.* Berkeley, CA: University of California Press.

Latsis, Otto. 1999. "Generation of Hope Asks for Help." *Novye Izvestiia*, January 21. Trans. *Current Digest of the Post-Soviet Press* 51(9): 6–7.

Le Cacheus, Jacques. 1996. "The Current Situation and Key Issues for the Long Term," in *The Changing Social Benefits in Russian Enterprises*, pp. 17–29. Paris: Organisation for Economic Co-operation and Development.

Lodahl, Maria. 2001. " The Housing Market in Russia: Disappointing Results." *Economic Bulletin* 38(6): 195–204. Available http://www.worldbank.org/wbi/banking/capmarkets/housing/pdf/Lodahl_2001.pdf.

Lokshin, Michael, Kathleen Mullan Harris, and Barry Popkin, 2000. "Single Mothers in Russia: Household Strategies for Coping with Poverty." *World Bank Working Paper No. 2300.* Available http://econ.worldbank.org/docs/1054.pdf.

Mace, David and Vera Mace. 1964. *The Soviet Family.* Garden City, NY: Doubleday.

Malakhova, Alla. 1999. "'Flowers of Life' Are Fading Before Our Eyes." *Novyie Izvestiia,* January 21. Trans. *Current Digest of the Post-Soviet Press* 51(9): 7–8.

Manning, Nick, Ovsey Shkaratan, and Natalya Tikhonova. 2000. *Work and Welfare in the New Russia.* Aldershot, UK: Ashgate.

Massey, Stephen. 2002. "Russia's Maternal and Child Health Crisis: Socio-Economic Implications and the Path Forward." *East–West Institute Policy Brief* 1(9). Available http://www.cdi.org/russia/johnson/6596-19.cfm.

Materialy ministerstva truda i sotsial'nogo razvitiia Rossiiskoi Federatsii k zasedaniiu komissii po voprosam zhenshchin, sem'ii i demografii pri prezidente Rossiiskoi Federatsii. 1999. "O problemakh narodonaseleniia v rossiiskoi federatsii," November 12.

Matthews, Mervyn. 1986. *Poverty in the Soviet Union: The Life-Styles of the Underprivileged in Recent Years.* Cambridge, UK: Cambridge University Press.

Mereu, Francesca. 2002. "Russia: Fighting 'Social Calamity' of Drug Addiction is Uphill Battle." *RFE/RL Newsline,* September 26. Available http://www.cdi.org/russia/johnson/6460.cfm.

Ministry of Taxation of the Russian Federation. 2003. *Tax Code of the Russian Federation.* Part 1 No. 146-F2 of July 31, 1998. Available http://www.garweb.ru/project/mns/en/law/garweb_law/10800200/10800200-047.htm (June 13, 2003)

Moscow News. 2000. "Social Reform to Phase Out Perks." June 21–27.

Moskoff, William. 1993. *Hard Times.* Armonk, NY: M. E. Sharpe.

Muravieva, Inna. 2002. "Two Russias: Speaking Different Languages and not Understanding Each Other." *Vek,* No. 30, September 6. Available http://www.cdi.org/russia/johnson/6427.ctm.

Nedelya. 1987. "The Kind of Family We Need." November 23–29, pp. 17–18. Trans. *Current Digest of the Soviet Press* 39(47): 25–26.

Nezavisimaya gazeta. 1992. "State Reports on the Condition of the Environment and the Population's Health Will Be Made Public Today," October 7. Trans. *Current Digest of the Post-Soviet Press* 44(41): 1–5, 20.

——. 2001. May 25. Available http://www.cdi.org/russia/johnson/5273.html##5.

Office of the Assistant Secretary for Planning and Evaluation, United States Department of Health and Human Services. 2001. "Trends in the Well-Being of America's Children and Youth." Available http://aspe.hhs.gov/hsp/97trends/pf2-3.htm (January 30, 2004).

Peterson, D. J. 1993. *Troubled Lands: The Legacy of Soviet Environmental Destruction.* Boulder, CO: Westview Press.

Protsenko, Alexander. 2002. "The Shadow Economy is Gaining Force." *Trud,* August 30. Available http://www.cdi.org/russia/johnson/6414.cfm.

Putin, Vladimir. 2001. Annual Address to the Federal Assembly. Available http://www.cdi.org/russia/johnson/5185.cfm.

Ransel, David L. 2000. *Village Mothers: Three Generations of Change in Russia and Tataria.* Bloomington, IN: Indiana University Press.

RFE/RL Newsline. 2001. "Non-Pharmacists Now Dispensing Medicines." May 22. Available http://www.rferl.org/newsline/2001/05/1-rus/rus-220501.asp.

——. 2001. "Health Minister Seeks Boost in Spending." May 30. Available http://www.rferl.org/newsline/2001/05/300501.asp.

——. 2001. "Improved Tax Collections May Make More Rate Cuts Possible." October 22. Available http://www.rferl.org/newsline/2001/10/1-RUS/rus-221001.asp.

——. 2001. "49 Percent of Russians Get Some State Benefits." November 5. Available http://www.rferl.org/newsline/2001/11/1-RUS/rus-051101.asp.

——. 2002. "Few Russians to Travel Abroad This Year." July 15. Available http://www.rferl.org/newsline/2002/07/150702.asp.

——. 2002. "Wage Arrears Soared in June." July 23. Available http://www.rferl.org/newsline/2002/07/230702.asp.

RIA Novosti, 2002. July 31. Available http://www.cdi.org/russia/johnson/6380.cfm.

Rodriguez, Alex. 2002. "Workers Fume as Russia Struggles to Pay Them." *Chicago Tribune*, August 4. Available http://www.cdi.org/russia/johnson/6385.cfm.

Shafran, Yelena. 1994. "Why Women in Russia are Afraid to Give Birth." *Izvestiia*, January 26. Trans. *Current Digest of the Post-Soviet Press* 46(4): 23.

Silverman, Bertram and Murray Yanowitch. 1997. *New Rich, New Poor, New Russia: Winners and Losers on the Russian Road to Capitalism.* Armonk, NY: M. E. Sharpe.

Startseva, Alla. 2001. "Pulling the Poor Out of Poverty." *Moscow Times*, June 26. Available http://www.cdi.org/russia/johnson/5324.html.

Tsentral'noe statisticheskoe upravlenie SSSR. 1985. *Zhenshchiny i deti v SSSR.* Moscow: Finansy i statistika.

UNICEF-MONEE. 1999. "Women, Families and Policies," Ch. 3 in *Women in Transition.* Regional Monitoring Report 6. Available http://eurochild.gla.ac.uk/Documents/monee/pdf/monee6/chap-3.pdf.

Waters, Elizabeth. 1992. "'Cuckoo-Mothers' and 'Apparatchiks': Glasnost and Children's Homes," in Mary Buckley (ed.) *Perestroika and Soviet Women*, pp. 123–41. Cambridge, UK: Cambridge University Press.

World Bank Group in Russia. 2002. "Social and Human Development." Available http://www.worldbank.org.ru/eng/group/strategy3/strategy042.htm.

Zakharov, Sergei. 1999. "Fertility, Nuptiality, and Family Planning in Russia: Problems and Prospects," in George J. Demko, Grigory Ioffe, and Zhanna Zayonchkovskaya (eds.) *Population under Duress: The Geodemography of Post-Soviet Russia*, pp. 41–58. Boulder, CO: Westview Press.

Zouev, Alexandre (ed.). 1999. *Generation in Jeopardy: Children in Central and Eastern Europe and the Former Soviet Union.* Armonk, NY: M. E. Sharpe.

WELFARE RULES, BUSINESS CYCLES, AND EMPLOYMENT DYNAMICS AMONG LONE PARENTS IN NORWAY

Randi Kjeldstad and Marit Rønsen

INTRODUCTION

In Norway, as in many other Western European countries, shifting macroeconomic conditions in the 1990s brought about a changing labor market. But whereas the employment rates of men and women below the age of 25 decreased during the Norwegian recession of the mid-1990s, the employment rates of women older than 25 and married mothers increased steadily. Today, the employment rate of married and cohabiting mothers with children younger than 16 is well above that of women in general *and* even that of men. The increasing participation of lone mothers has not, however, kept up with the increase in married mothers' participation, and during the last decades, a gap has emerged. The lower employment rate among lone mothers has been common through the 1990s for all Scandinavian countries, but this is not the general picture for Europe as a whole (Jonathan Bradshaw, Steven Kennedy, Majella Kilkey, Sandra Hutton, Anne Corden, Tony Eardley, Hilary Holmes, and Joanne Neale 1996; Anne Skevik 2001; Jonathan Bradshaw and Naomi Finch 2002). A common assumption is that the pattern particular to Scandinavia is an expression of a well-established social security system and quite generous economic support to lone parents. This is especially true of Norway, where lone mothers and fathers receive a special social security transitional allowance if they are not able to support themselves.

Recently, however, the so-called "work line" approach, which links economic transfers to efforts to become self-supporting, has become more prominent in Norwegian social policy. Incentives to encourage employment activity have been directed at lone parents, first in the early 1990s by making part-time work more economically attractive, and then in the late 1990s by reducing the maximum period over which benefits can be collected. Scholars of Norwegian social policy have drawn less attention to the fact that changing macroeconomic conditions, rather than work incentives, may have more strongly influenced the labor market attachment of lone parents.

In recent years, economic fluctuations have created periods of high unemployment in many countries, especially among lone parents (Bradshaw *et al.* 1996; Ulla Björnberg 1997; Björn Gustafsson, Ali Tasiran, and Håkan Nyman 1996;). In Norway, the national unemployment rate reached a peak in 1993 with 6 percent unemployment, but subsided to the "normal" level of about 3 percent during the last half of the decade. In contrast, the peak unemployment level of the 1980s was significantly lower, about 3.5 percent in 1983, with the "normal" level resting at just above 2 percent (Randi Kjeldstad and Marit Rønsen 2002).

BACKGROUND

Lone-parent families are significantly over-represented among low-income and poor families in most countries, and child poverty rates in one-parent families far exceed the rates in two-parent families (Bruce Bradbury and Markus Jäntti 2001). Employed lone parents are, as a rule, far better off than nonemployed ones, even in countries that offer fairly generous welfare benefits (Jan Lyngstad 2000; Jon Epland 2001; Majella Kilkey and Jonathan Bradshaw 2001). Accordingly, policy-makers generally regard employment as the core remedy to avoid the marginalization of lone parents and to reduce poverty among lone-parent families.

In Norway, lone-parent families have customarily been considered in particular need of support, and expectations of employment activity have been low (Sheila B. Kamerman and Alfred J. Kahn 1988; Lars Inge Terum 1993; Liv Johanne Syltevik 1998; Monica Strell 1999). The attitudes and policies prevalent in Norway contrast with those of Sweden and Denmark, where work-line policies have a longer tradition, and benefits to lone-parent families are part of public support for the jobless, the poor, and families with children (Barbara Hobson and Mieko Takahashi 1997; Birthe Siim 1997; Håkan Nyman 1998). Over the years, however, it has become less socially acceptable even for Norwegian lone parents to be without paid work, and the Norwegian society commonly accepts that lone mothers should hold jobs just as married mothers do (Anne Skevik 1996, 1998). Accordingly, Norwegian work-line policies of the 1990s reflect the new and stronger political priority afforded the role of the worker at the expense of the role of the caregiver, even for lone parents.

Yet measures taken to increase the employment of lone parents reflect limited assumptions about the factors that condition their labor market participation. Usually the expected determinants relate to the lone parent as *an individual*, to her human capital and social resources, and to how she chooses between work and care. Since most lone parents are mothers, assumptions about the characteristics of lone mothers dominate lone-parent policies, although their human capital and background resources differ substantially from those of lone fathers (Grete Dahl 1993; Randi Kjeldstad 1998, 2000). But, like other parents, lone parents of either sex are very heterogeneous. Today the great majority of Norwegian lone parents were formerly married or in a consensual union, and as a group their background characteristics are becoming increasingly similar to those of partnered parents. Still, they continue to be viewed as distinct from married or cohabiting parents; that is, as persons who possess low human capital, little social participation, and low motivation to accept paid work.

The principal means of encouraging lone parents to join the labor force in greater numbers are new and altered welfare regulations, which increase the economic incentives to take employment. The policy changes cover both supportive and coercive measures, but their main thrust is to secure the employment of lone parents by politically motivated changes in economic incentives. These new measures are assumed to be both transparent and unproblematic with regard to economic participation. Only rarely are policy measures aimed at increasing the employment of lone parents directed toward *the demand side* of the labor market, and policy-makers rarely question whether the demand for labor may systematically or periodically be unfavorable to the employment of lone parents. This lack of awareness is remarkable, especially since the general increase in female employment in Norway during the last three or four decades is predominantly assumed to be a result of changing demand as well as changing supply conditions (Kari Skrede and Kristin Tornes 1986; Kari Skrede 1994). Still, it is likely that incentives embedded in welfare regulation have encouraged greater labor force participation of lone parents. Research from other countries, especially the US and Great

Britain, has found that the benefit regime has a significant and substantial effect on lone mothers' labor supply (for the US see Bruce D. Meyer and Dan T. Rosenbaum 2001; for the UK, John F. Ermisch and Robert E. Wright 1991). Our analysis will consider both the demand and the supply sides of the labor market and focus on changing employment opportunities as well as changing welfare policies.

THE NORWEGIAN SOCIAL SECURITY SETTING

Since the end of the 1960s, financial support for Norwegian lone parents has mainly been regulated by the National Insurance Act. The entitlement presupposes that the parent who receives the support has never married or is separated or divorced, and clearly provides more of the day-to-day care for the child than the other parent.[1] The entitlement is lost if the parent (re)marries or has a child with a cohabitant. After July 1, 1999, the entitlement lapsed for all lone parents living in long-term consensual unions.

The Norwegian National Insurance scheme for lone parents covers a variety of benefits, including economic support for childcare and education for the parent, but the main benefit is the "transitional allowance," a subsistence benefit that constitutes an alternative to paid work. The benefit is income-tested and its level falls as earnings increase. A desire to encourage voluntary economic activity among lone parents motivated new and more lenient rules for income testing, first introduced in January 1990. They specifically made part-time work more remunerative.

Two subsequent amendments during the 1990s introduced cutbacks in the entitlements to social support, thus removing former options *not* to take employment. The first amendment, introduced in January 1998, significantly shortened the benefit period. Although transitional allowance has always been intended to provide temporary help, lone parents had formerly, in effect, been able to choose whether to be supported solely or partially by the benefit scheme until the youngest child was 10 years old. The 1998 change reduced the benefit period to a total of three years. Other new restrictions made the right to the benefit after the child had reached the age of 3 conditional on employment or educational activities. Thus, for the first time, lone-parent benefits were made conditional on a certain amount of labor market activity. At the same time, the *level* of benefit was raised from US$840 to US$955 per month[2] for all lone-parent families receiving the full benefit. The last change in July 1999 removed the entitlement to transitional allowance for lone parents living in long-term cohabitation, defined as a relationship that had lasted more than twelve of the previous eighteen months.

Besides changes in the National Insurance benefits, the 1990s also saw the introduction of the "follow-up arrangement for lone parents," a new county-level policy intended to stimulate the active participation of lone parents in society. The arrangement relies on locally appointed "mediators," who assist parents in their contact with various public institutions and provide motivation for various social activities, such as education and employment. It targets all recipients of lone-parent benefits, but participation is voluntary. Different counties introduced the scheme at various times during the 1990s.

Unlike the aims of predominantly "work-line" policies for lone parents, a principal objective of recent general Norwegian family policies has been to reduce the time pressures on working mothers and fathers. Several measures have been introduced to enable parents to spend more time with their children and to facilitate more flexible adjustments between work and family. The most important is the cash-for-care reform introduced in August 1998, which grants a cash payment to parents who do not use publicly subsidized daycare; parents who use part-time care receive a smaller payment. Initially, only parents of children aged between 12 and 24 months were eligible for the benefit, but since January 1999, parents of children aged 24 to 36 months have also been included in the program. The benefit, a monthly, tax-free payment of US$440 (see note 2), is roughly equivalent to the state subsidy for a place in a daycare center. Parents who claim the benefit are not obligated to stay at home and care for the children themselves, and they may buy any other form of childcare, as long as it is not publicly subsidized.

LONE PARENTS ON THE NORWEGIAN LABOR MARKET[3]

Norwegian *Labor Force Surveys* (LFS) display great differences in the employment rates and trends of lone and partnered parents during recent decades. The most distinct difference is the steadily growing employment rate of married and cohabiting mothers throughout most of the period, in contrast to the employment rate of lone mothers, which remained, by and large, unchanged from 1980 until the mid-1990s. Since then, a steady increase in employment among lone mothers has matched the earlier trends for their married and cohabiting counterparts. Despite this catch-up, by the turn of the century a gap still existed between the employment rates of the two groups of mothers: 68 percent of single mothers held paid employment, compared to 81 percent of nonsingle mothers (Figure 1). But since the proportion of employees temporarily absent from work because of vacation, parental leave, and illness (either their own or their children's) is, as a rule, significantly higher for married mothers (about 10 percentage points in the 1990s (Kjeldstad and Rønsen 2002)), the proportions of actual workers in the two groups differ considerably less. In 1999, 56 percent of lone mothers versus 61 percent of married mothers were actually at work. In addition, employed lone mothers work full-time more often than do

Percent

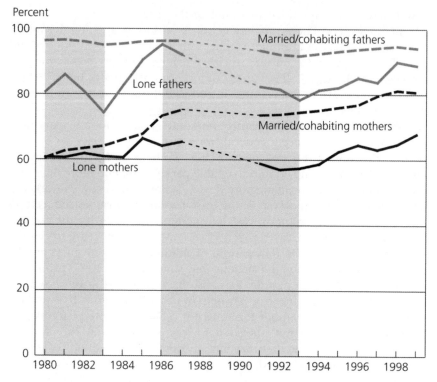

Figure 1 Employed single and married/cohabiting mothers and fathers, 1980–99[1]
(percent)
[1]Shaded areas indicate periods of recession with unemployment peaks in 1983 and
1993. *Source:* Norwegian *Labour Force Surveys*, Statistics Norway.

married mothers, and are more often engaged in educational activities
(Kjeldstad and Rønsen 2002). Accordingly, the assumption that today's
lone mothers are much more detached from economic activity than other
mothers and have a marginal position in society requires revision.

The employment rate of lone fathers has evolved in much the same way
as that of lone mothers. As with mothers, the employment rate of lone
fathers was lower than that of married or cohabiting fathers throughout the
1980s and 1990s. This statistic clearly indicates that being a lone parent is a
decisive factor conditioning labor market attachment for both genders.

The unemployment trends depicted in Figure 2 reveal the same pattern.
Lone mothers had by far the highest unemployment rate throughout the
period, with a rate twice that of married mothers. The same is true for lone
as compared to married fathers during most of the period. According to
LFS definitions, unemployed persons are nonemployed persons who are
available and actively seeking work. The high unemployment rates of lone
parents, then, demonstrate that lone parents of both genders, to a larger

Percent

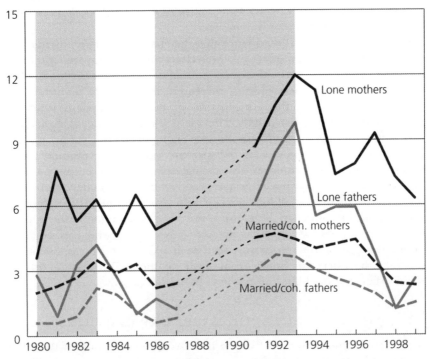

Figure 2 Unemployed single and married/cohabiting mothers and fathers as percent of the labour force, 1980–91[1]

[1]Shaded areas indicate periods of recession with unemployment peaks in 1983 and 1993. *Source*: Norwegian *Labour Force Surveys*, Statistics Norway.

extent than married or cohabiting parents, are involuntarily excluded from the labor market. Further substantiating this conclusion is the fact that underemployment rates – that is, the proportion of part-time workers who are actively seeking more work – are systematically higher among lone parents than among married and cohabiting ones. In 1999, 26 percent of part-time working lone mothers were underemployed compared to 10 percent of non-lone mothers who were working part-time (Kjeldstad and Rønsen 2002).

As would be expected, there is a close relationship between changes in the demand for labor and the changing employment and unemployment trends among lone parents. At the bottom of the recession in 1983 and even more so in the 1993 recession, there are significant peaks in the unemployment rate and corresponding dips in the employment rate of lone parents. Although a similar pattern also appears in the employment rates of married and cohabiting parents, the fluctuations are generally much smaller, indicating that lone parents experience greater problems in the labor market during spells of high unemployment. This finding applies to lone fathers as well as to lone mothers, but lone mothers have a consistently higher unemployment level.

In contrast, there is little evidence that the changes in welfare benefits to lone parents exerted an effect on their labor force attachment. Although no data exist for 1988–90, subsequent annual statistics indicate that neither lone mothers nor lone fathers increased their employment activity immediately following the introduction of the more lenient rules for income testing of benefits in 1990. There is also little evidence that the 1998 restrictions brought about significant changes in the labor market attachments of lone parents, as the increase among lone mothers could be merely the continuation of an existing trend, and the employment of lone fathers actually dropped.[4] So far, however, our analysis has been based on statistics comprising all lone parents with children under the age of 16. These limits may obscure the picture, since the amendments (introduced in 1990 and 1998, see earlier) affected only parents who had children under the age of 10.[5] Moreover, to date it has also been impossible to separate the effects of policy from those of the business cycle. In the multivariate analysis below we disentangle these factors.

INDIVIDUAL LABOR MARKET TRANSITIONS

Large cross-sectional surveys like the LFS give good snapshots of the labor market at certain points in time, but tell little about the processes that lie behind the observed outcomes. For example, changes in the numbers of employed persons from one survey to another result from both the numbers of persons who began working and from the number who quit working during the period; that is, they reflect transitions both into and out of employment. To get a better understanding of individual adaptations and the functioning of the labor market, it is important to study such dynamics as we do in the last part of our article.

In particular, we hope to throw more light on some of the issues that remain unclear after examining the general trends based on the Norwegian LFS. Our primary research questions are: (i) Will the differences in labor market behavior between single and nonsingle parents remain even when we control for dissimilarities in their personal characteristics; that is, will the differences be significant also in a multivariate analysis? (ii) Which processes are creating the large differences in the observed aggregate statistics? Is, for example, the higher unemployment rate among lone parents caused by a higher risk of becoming unemployed, or do lone parents have greater problems finding jobs when outside the labor market, or both? (iii) What are the effects of changes in social policies, especially those directed explicitly at lone parents, but also of general family policy reforms such as the cash-for-care benefit? (iv) Finally, how important are changing business cycles? Are lone parents really more vulnerable than other parents during economic downswings, and if so, is their vulnerability the result of a higher risk of exclusion from, or a lower chance of admission into, the labor market?

DATA, EMPIRICAL MODEL, AND MODELING STRATEGY

To address these questions, we analyze transitions in the Norwegian labor market during the 1990s, using a longitudinal dataset extracted from a large database covering the whole population of Norway. The database contains information on individual life events based on several administrative registers. These sources of data have been linked together to form complete histories of demography, employment, education, and social security for the period 1992–98. We use a sample of mothers and fathers who, by January 1, 1992, were 16–49 years old and had at least one child below the age of 18.[6] The sample consists of a 5 percent draw of married or cohabiting mothers and fathers, a 25 percent draw of lone mothers, and all lone fathers (about 21,500). The total sample includes 108,730 individuals.[7]

As a point of departure, we distinguish between the following activities: (i) employment, (ii) unemployment, and (iii) home work (at home without paid work, supported by social security or by a partner). According to register information these activities are sometimes overlapping. This may be true, but it may also result from lags in the registers. Still, we have defined three mutually exclusive activities, as follows. A person who is registered as completely unemployed is defined as unemployed.[8] If not unemployed, but registered as employed or on sick or parental leave, the person is defined as employed. If neither of these activities is recorded, and the person is not registered as a student, we have defined him or her as mainly occupied with home work. From each of the three activity states there can be a transition to one of two other activity states, as depicted in Figure 3.[9]

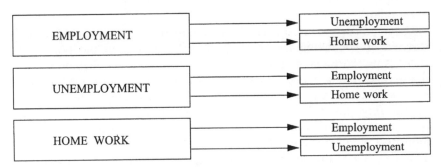

Figure 3 Activity states and transitions.

We use a discrete multivariate hazard rate model: in discrete time, the hazard rate is the conditional probability that an event will occur at a particular time to a particular individual (for example, that a person who is employed will become unemployed), given that the individual has not experienced the event before (see, for example, Paul D. Allison 1984). In our case, an ongoing spell of a specific activity may end in one of two alternative events; that is, we have a competing risk model. Besides depending on the duration of the current spell, the hazard rate varies with personal, policy, and labor market characteristics.[10]

The first policy change during the period covered by our register data occurred in January 1998 and shortened considerably the duration of transitional allowance for lone parents (from roughly 10 to 3 years, as discussed earlier). At the same time, the allowance for eligible parents (basically mothers with children younger than 3) was raised. For lone parents with no children younger than about 10, there was no change. The indicator of change in lone-parent (LP) benefits thus reflects three different outcomes: no change, shorter duration, or higher benefits. The second policy change, the cash-for-care reform, affected the economic opportunities of single as well as nonsingle parents and was introduced toward the very end of the analysis period (August 1998). As the benefit is a fixed amount per child for all parents, the cash-for-care benefit indicator is merely a dummy reflecting benefit eligibility, which during the period covered by our analysis only comprised parents of 1 year olds (12 to 24 months).[11] Finally, to identify a possible impact of the local "follow-up arrangement" for lone parents, we have included a dummy variable reflecting whether the lone parent lives in a county included in the program.

Business cycles and changing demand for labor are represented in the model by the local unemployment rate, expressed as the annual average percentage in the municipality of residence. This variable may, however, also pick up other geographical differences, and to adjust for that situation, we include several regional dummies in the model. As the regional effects are probably mainly of national interest, we will not present or comment upon them further here.

The main personal characteristic used to identify our groups of lone and married or cohabiting parents is partnership status. In the population register, two partners of opposite sexes are registered as cohabiting only if they have common biological children. This means that some lone mothers or fathers may have a cohabitant, but the cohabitant is then not the biological parent of the child(ren).[12] Other important personal characteristics are age, education, and employment experience, which are used as indicators of human capital resources. Education refers to the highest level attained prior to the current month. Employment experience is based on annual updates on the total number of years with work income above the

70

minimum limit required for pension payments, and age is measured as current year minus birth year. The number of children and age of the youngest child reflect differences in care responsibilities. Age of youngest child is age during the current month, if the child is born after 1992, and age at the end of the year otherwise. Number of children is updated in the month of a new birth or in January the year after an older child has turned 18.

In addition to the covariates already mentioned, the model also includes duration of the ongoing activity spell. This variable is typical of hazard rate models and represents the time process under analysis. It is measured in months from the beginning of the spell.[13] In addition to duration we also include dummies for spell order, as an individual may experience more than one spell of a particular activity during the analysis period.[14]

To assess the effect of partnership status, the model is initially estimated jointly for lone and married or cohabiting parents with partnership status included among the covariates. This method gives us an estimate of the differences between lone and non-lone parents, and a direct test of whether there is in fact a significant difference after controlling for other dissimilarities. The results are presented separately for mothers and fathers (Table 1). We further expect that the effects of other covariates will vary across partnership status, and therefore also estimate the model for lone and married or cohabiting parents separately. These results are reported in full, showing the effects of each independent variable on the various labor market transitions of each of the four parental groups (Tables 2–5).

FINDINGS

Table 1 provides the immediate answers to two of our research questions. First, the results confirm that there are indeed substantial differences in the labor market behavior of single and nonsingle parents, even when we control for other dissimilarities between the groups. The impression that both lone mothers *and* lone fathers are particularly vulnerable in the labor market remains. Second, the difference in behavior is seen to relate to processes leading both in and out of the labor market. Relative to the reference group of married and cohabiting parents (coefficients = 0), lone mothers and fathers are found to have a considerably higher risk of becoming unemployed when employed (25 and 20 percent higher, respectively: odds ratios = $\exp(0.221)$ and $\exp(0.185)$); and when unemployed, they are less likely to re-enter employment (9 and 27 percent less likely, respectively: odds ratios = $\exp(-0.098)$ and $\exp(-0.309)$).[15] In addition, the large positive and significant coefficients for transitions to home work from both employment and unemployment show that lone parents are more likely than other parents to quit the labor market altogether. When at home, single parents also have lower employment

71

Table 1 Estimated effects of partnership status on labor market transitions among mothers and fathers using a discrete hazard rate model (logit specification). Standard errors in parentheses

	From employment		From unemployment		From home work	
	To unemployment	*To home work*	*To employment*	*To home work*	*To employment*	*To unemployment*
Mothers						
Lone	**0.221** (0.025)	**0.274** (0.021)	−**0.098** (0.023)	**0.362** (0.029)	−**0.184** (0.019)	**0.243** (0.026)
Married/cohabiting[a]	0	0	0	0	0	0
Fathers						
Lone	**0.185** (0.033)	**0.357** (0.039)	−**0.309** (0.030)	**0.310** (0.055)	−**0.211** (0.036)	**0.311** (0.053)
Married/cohabiting[a]	0	0	0	0	0	0

[a]Reference category.
Note. The model also includes all the other covariates in Table 2. Coefficients in bold are significant at the 5 percent level or below.

72

Table 2 Determinants of labor market transitions among lone mothers. Estimated effects using a discrete hazard rate model (logit specification). Standard errors in parentheses.

	From employment		From unemployment		From home work	
	To unemployment	To home work	To employment	To home work	To employment	To unemployment
Welfare reforms						
Change in LP benefits[a]						
Shorter duration	**0.213** (0.076)	**−0.526** (0.079)	**0.135** (0.068)	**−0.419** (0.075)	**−0.425** (0.065)	**0.291** (0.064)
Higher benefits	−0.002 (0.138)	**−0.405** (0.123)	0.165 (0.135)	−0.218 (0.130)	**−0.628** (0.123)	−0.040 (0.108)
Local follow-up arrangement[b]	−0.038 (0.048)	−0.020 (0.039)	−0.079 (0.042)	0.076 (0.042)	**0.151** (0.032)	**0.203** (0.037)
Cash-for-care benefit[b]	−1.821 (1.001)	0.564 (0.304)	0.064 (0.392)	**0.671** (0.328)	−0.110 (0.295)	**−0.996** (0.393)
Business cycle						
Local unemployment rate	**0.055** (0.011)	0.015 (0.009)	**−0.093** (0.010)	−0.020 (0.011)	**−0.048** (0.008)	**0.063** (0.009)
Human capital resources						
Own age	−0.015 (0.022)	**0.046** (0.019)	**−0.073** (0.020)	−0.003 (0.020)	**−0.037** (0.016)	**0.062** (0.017)
Own age sq.[c]	0.003 (0.003)	−0.001 (0.003)	**0.005** (0.003)	0.003 (0.003)	**−0.005** (0.002)	**−0.013** (0.002)
Education[d]						
Lower secondary	**−0.092** (0.043)	**−0.166** (0.037)	**0.098** (0.039)	**−0.214** (0.037)	**0.100** (0.031)	**0.082** (0.033)
Upper secondary	**−0.283** (0.043)	**−0.448** (0.038)	**0.288** (0.039)	**−0.411** (0.041)	**0.462** (0.032)	**0.104** (0.037)
University, short	**−0.897** (0.061)	**−0.887** (0.050)	**0.463** (0.055)	**−0.602** (0.073)	**0.733** (0.043)	−0.099 (0.067)
University, long	**−1.149** (0.184)	**−1.100** (0.138)	**0.659** (0.150)	**−0.794** (0.237)	**0.989** (0.118)	−0.132 (0.234)
Unknown	−0.191 (0.129)	−0.222 (0.102)	0.127 (0.117)	−0.222 (0.087)	−0.082 (0.083)	**−0.200** (0.074)
Employment experience	**−0.079** (0.009)	**−0.129** (0.008)	**0.122** (0.008)	**−0.182** (0.008)	**0.166** (0.006)	**−0.052** (0.007)
Employment exp. sq.[c]	0.003 (0.004)	**0.019** (0.003)	**−0.035** (0.003)	**0.047** (0.004)	**−0.038** (0.003)	**0.011** (0.004)

(continued overleaf)

73

Table 2 (continued)

	From employment		From unemployment		From home work	
	To unemployment	To home work	To employment	To home work	To employment	To unemployment
Care responsibilities						
Number of children[e]						
2	−0.035 (0036)	0.025 (0.031)	0.020 (0.033)	0.010 (0.036)	**0.160** (0.026)	0.017 (0.032)
3 or more	−**0.158** (0.070)	0.026 (0.055)	0.114 (0.064)	0.041 (0.061)	**0.189** (0.045)	−0.049 (0.052)
Age youngest child	−**0.032** (0.005)	−**0.083** (0.004)	**0.035** (0.005)	−**0.050** (0.005)	**0.052** (0.004)	**0.033** (0.004)
Model-specific covariates						
Spell order[f]						
2nd	**0.527** (0.038)	**0.386** (0.034)	**0.048** (0.033)	**0.128** (0.036)	**0.421** (0.027)	**0.623** (0.033)
3rd or later	**0.763** (0.047)	**0.676** (0.044)	**0.169** (0.039)	**0.177** (0.041)	**0.576** (0.034)	**0.922** (0.038)
Duration	−0.005 (0.003)	−0.000 (0.002)	−**0.024** (0.004)	−**0.074** (0.004)	−**0.059** (0.002)	−**0.067** (0.002)
Duration sq.[c]	−**0.002** (0.001)	−**0.001** (0.000)	**0.002** (0.001)	**0.011** (0.001)	**0.006** (0.000)	**0.008** (0.000)
Intercept	−**4.062** (0.364)	−**4.365** (0.312)	−**1.509** (0.328)	−**1.104** (0.311)	−**2.926** (0.252)	−**4.810** (0.274)
Model statistics						
−2 log L	53,017	66,886	44,470	37,645	76,701	59,604
DF	27	27	27	27	27	27
No. of person-months	882,261	882,261	99,910	99,910	378,851	378,851

Notes: [a]Reference category: no change. [b]Yes = 1/No = 0. [c]The variable is squared and divided by 10. [d]Reference category: Primary. [e]Reference category: 1 child. [f]Reference category: 1st. Note: The model also includes regional dummies which are not reported, as they are mainly of national interest. Coefficients in bold are significant at the 5 percent level or below.

74

Table 3 Determinants of labor market transitions among lone fathers. Estimated effects using a discrete hazard rate model (logit specification). Standard errors in parentheses.

	From employment		From unemployment		From home work	
	To unemployment	To home work	To employment	To home work	To employment	To unemployment
Welfare reforms						
Change in LP benefits[a]						
Shorter duration	0.403 (0.237)	−0.258 (0.272)	−0.207 (0.237)	**−0.851** (0.404)	−0.349 (0.249)	0.303 (0.270)
Higher benefits	0.518 (0.464)	−0.400 (0.590)	0.511 (0.492)	−1.031 (1.029)	0.234 (0.479)	−0.226 (0.743)
Local follow-up arrangement[b]	−0.101 (0.097)	−0.010 (0.1001)	−0.038 (0.088)	0.144 (0.118)	0.115 (0.093)	0.166 (0.109)
Cash-for-care benefit[b]	−8.595 (151.2)	−7.742 (125.5)	0.688 (0.958)	1.991 (1.483)	−8.126 (192.1)	58.084 (7.881e11)
Business cycle						
Local unemployment rate	**0.138** (0.016)	0.002 (0.020)	**−0.036** (0.015)	−0.010 (0.027)	**−0.038** (0.018)	**0.105** (0.024)
Human capital resources						
Own age	−0.018 (0.043)	−0.027 (0.047)	**−0.166** (0.037)	−0.003 (0.049)	**−0.081** (0.041)	**0.115** (0.045)
Own age sq.[c]	0.002 (0.006)	0.011 (0.006)	**0.016** (0.005)	0.006 (0.007)	−0.002 (0.005)	**−0.017** (0.006)
Education[d]						
Lower secondary	−0.104 (0.065)	**−0.176** (0.077)	−0.027 (0.058)	−0.101 (0.091)	**0.215** (0.071)	−0.029 (0.085)
Upper secondary	**−0.338** (0.064)	**−0.423** (0.074)	**0.252** (0.057)	−0.171 (0.092)	**0.373** (0.069)	−0.124 (0.088)
University, short	**−1.017** (0.097)	**−1.012** (0.102)	**0.234** (0.088)	**−0.547** (0.140)	**0.858** (0.094)	−0.098 (0.130)
University, long	**−1.661** (0.191)	**−1.483** (0.164)	**0.666** (0.184)	−0.494 (0.277)	**0.868** (0.158)	**−0.924** (0.314)
Unknown	−0.122 (0.168)	−0.215 (0.166)	−0.117 (0.143)	−0.177 (0.144)	0.208 (0.170)	0.040 (0.140)
Employment experience	**−0.113** (0.020)	**−0.069** (0.022)	**0.098** (0.016)	−0.025 (0.017)	**0.078** (0.019)	**−0.067** (0.016)
Employment exp. sq.[c]	**0.023** (0.006)	−0.006 (0.006)	**−0.012** (0.005)	**−0.015** (0.006)	0.007 (0.005)	**0.016** (0.006)

(continued overleaf)

75

Table 3 (continued)

	From employment		From unemployment		From home work	
	To unemployment	To home work	To employment	To home work	To employment	To unemployment
Care responsibilities						
Number of children[e]						
2	−0.016 (0.057)	−0.070 (0.067)	−0.028 (0.052)	−0.093 (0.085)	−0.089 (0.061)	−0.037 (0.078)
3 or more	−0.172 (0.122)	0.075 (0.123)	0.161 (0.109)	0.170 (0.146)	−0.085 (0.113)	−0.029 (0.134)
Age youngest child	−0.000 (0.006)	**−0.024** (0.007)	0.002 (0.006)	−0.010 (0.009)	**−0.020** (0.007)	−0.013 (0.008)
Model-specific covariates						
Spell order[f]						
2nd	**0.940** (0.060)	**0.830** (0.071)	**0.183** (0.051)	**0.172** (0.083)	**0.448** (0.065)	**0.789** (0.078)
3rd or later	**1.204** (0.074)	**0.953** (0.097)	**0.295** (0.064)	**0.484** (0.095)	**0.678** (0.084)	**1.038** (0.095)
Duration	**−0.019** (0.005)	−0.003 (0.005)	**−0.038** (0.006)	**−0.031** (0.008)	**−0.057** (0.005)	**−0.118** (0.008)
Duration sq.[c]	**−0.002** (0.001)	**−0.002** (0.001)	0.003 (0.001)	0.004 (0.002)	**0.006** (0.001)	**0.012** (0.001)
Intercept	**−4.118** (0.718)	**−4.123** (0.842)	0.150 (0.630)	**−2.855** (0.893)	−1.063 (0.702)	**−4.734** (0.801)
Model statistics						
−2 Log L	22,422	18,077	16,967	8,123	14,296	9,309
DF	27	27	27	27	27	27
No. of person-months	422,457	422,457	31,058	31,058	56,797	56,797

Notes: [a]Reference category: no change. [b]Yes = 1/No = 0. [c]The variable is squared and divided by 10. [d]Reference category: Primary. [e]Reference category: 1 child. [f]Reference category: 1st. Note: The model also includes regional dummies which are not reported, as they are mainly of national interest. Coefficients in bold are significant at the 5 percent level or below.

Table 4 Determinants of labor market transitions among married or cohabiting mothers. Estimated effects using a discrete hazard rate model (logit specification). Standard errors in parentheses.

	From employment		From unemployment		From home work	
	To unemployment	To home work	To employment	To home work	To employment	To unemployment
Welfare reforms						
Cash-for-care benefit[b]	−1.097 (0.279)	−0.186 (0.133)	−0.017 (0.150)	0.376 (0.171)	−0.588 (0.117)	−1.182 (0.292)
Business cycle						
Local unemployment rate	0.090 (0.009)	0.024 (0.008)	−0.120 (0.009)	−0.038 (0.012)	−0.010 (0.007)	0.107 (0.012)
Human capital resources						
Own age	−0.116 (0.022)	−0.046 (0.018)	−0.031 (0.021)	0.027 (0.026)	−0.111 (0.016)	−0.026 (0.025)
Own age sq.[c]	0.016 (0.003)	0.012 (0.002)	0.001 (0.003)	−0.001 (0.004)	0.006 (0.002)	−0.003 (0.004)
Education[d]						
Lower secondary	−0.038 (0.044)	−0.106 (0.036)	0.025 (0.041)	−0.230 (0.052)	0.148 (0.032)	0.075 (0.051)
Upper secondary	−0.283 (0.045)	−0.336 (0.037)	0.168 (0.042)	−0.261 (0.054)	0.291 (0.033)	0.057 (0.055)
University, short	−1.068 (0.060)	−0.615 (0.041)	0.391 (0.056)	−0.368 (0.085)	0.572 (0.038)	−0.143 (0.082)
University, long	−1.140 (0.145)	−0.854 (0.087)	0.585 (0.130)	−0.343 (0.203)	0.849 (0.086)	0.321 (0.191)
Unknown	0.084 (0.113)	−0.070 (0.089)	−0.245 (0.107)	−0.245 (0.096)	−0.143 (0.080)	0.193 (0.088)
Employment exp.	−0.030 (0.010)	−0.091 (0.008)	0.074 (0.008)	−0.203 (0.010)	0.157 (0.006)	−0.060 (0.010)
Employment exp. sq.[c]	−0.017 (0.004)	0.006 (0.003)	−0.020 (0.004)	0.058 (0.005)	−0.038 (0.003)	0.014 (0.005)
Care responsibilities						
Number of children[e]						
2	−0.014 (0.037)	0.042 (0.030)	−0.089 (0.034)	0.023 (0.047)	0.106 (0.028)	−0.104 (0.047)
3 or more	−0.139 (0.049)	0.087 (0.037)	−0.072 (0.046)	0.024 (0.061)	0.153 (0.035)	−0.212 (0.060)
Age youngest child	−0.067 (0.005)	−0.113 (0.004)	0.032 (0.004)	−0.033 (0.007)	0.042 (0.003)	0.015 (0.006)

(continued overleaf)

77

Table 4 (continued)

	From employment		From unemployment		From home work	
	To unemployment	To home work	To employment	To home work	To employment	To unemployment
Model-specific covariates						
Spell order[f]						
2nd	**0.504** (0.036)	**0.388** (0.029)	**0.069** (0.032)	**0.100** (0.044)	**0.308** (0.026)	**0.637** (0.045)
3rd or later	**0.875** (0.044)	**0.653** (0.039)	0.054 (0.040)	**0.218** (0.053)	**0.494** (0.034)	**1.032** (0.053)
Duration	−0.005 (0.003)	0.001 (0.002)	−**0.010** (0.003)	−**0.044** (0.005)	−**0.059** (0.002)	−**0.071** (0.003)
Duration sq.[c]	−**0.003** (0.000)	−**0.001** (0.000)	0.000 (0.001)	**0.006** (0.001)	**0.006** (0.000)	**0.007** (0.001)
Intercept	−**2.626** (0.354)	−**3.099** (0.289)	−**1.874** (0.333)	−**2.223** (0.412)	−**1.319** (0.253)	−**3.232** (0.388)
Model statistics						
−2 log L	58,247	91,450	44,155	25,871	84,666	32,774
DF	24	24	24	24	24	24
No. of person-months	1,325,344	1,325,344	92,743	92,743	358,505	358,505

Notes: [a]Reference category: no change. [b]Yes = 1/No = 0. [c]The variable is squared and divided by 10. [d]Reference category: 1 child. [e]Reference category: Primary. [f]Reference category: 1st. Note: The model also includes regional dummies which are not reported, as they are mainly of national interest. Coefficients in bold are significant at the 5 percent level or below.

Table 5 Determinants of labor market transitions among married or cohabiting fathers. Estimated effects using a discrete hazard rate model (logit specification). Standard errors in parentheses.

	From employment		From unemployment		From home work	
	To unemployment	To home work	To employment	To home work	To employment	To unemployment
Welfare reforms						
Cash for care benefit[b]	0.062 (0.222)	−0.506 (0.319)	−0.098 (0.288)	0.131 (0.464)	−0.489 (0.299)	0.041 (0.511)
Business cycle						
Local unemployment rate	**0.159** (0.010)	**0.093** (0.013)	**−0.073** (0.009)	−0.026 (0.020)	0.018 (0.010)	**0.134** (0.018)
Human capital resources						
Own age	−0.024 (0.027)	0.039 (0.030)	**−0.101** (0.023)	**−0.086** (0.036)	**−0.054** (0.027)	−0.040 (0.035)
Own age sq.[c]	0.003 (0.004)	0.001 (0.004)	**0.007** (0.003)	**0.014** (0.005)	−0.005 (0.004)	0.004 (0.005)
Education[d]						
Lower secondary	**−0.105** (0.044)	−0.086 (0.056)	−0.035 (0.041)	**−0.174** (0.084)	**0.232** (0.053)	0.016 (0.087)
Upper secondary	**−0.456** (0.042)	**−0.479** (0.053)	**0.212** (0.039)	**−0.213** (0.083)	**0.310** (0.051)	−0.122 (0.085)
University, short	**−1.110** (0.063)	**−0.596** (0.064)	0.101 (0.060)	−0.089 (0.114)	**0.636** (0.061)	**−0.367** (0.123)
University, long	**−2.074** (0.138)	**−0.987** (0.094)	**0.252** (0.122)	−0.354 (0.219)	**0.716** (0.091)	**−0.689** (0.215)
Unknown	−0.187 (0.114)	−0.088 (0.116)	−0.065 (0.098)	**0.296** (0.120)	**0.224** (0.105)	−0.046 (0.124)
Employment experience	**−0.112** (0.013)	**−0.104** (0.014)	**0.107** (0.011)	**−0.063** (0.015)	**0.082** (0.012)	**−0.103** (0.015)
Employment exp. sq.[c]	**0.024** (0.004)	**0.009** (0.004)	**−0.015** (0.003)	0.005 (0.005)	0.003 (0.004)	**0.023** (0.005)
Care responsibilities						
Number of children[e]						
2	−0.049 (0.036)	−0.078 (0.045)	0.038 (0.034)	0.062 (0.071)	−0.030 (0.042)	−0.032 (0.074)
3 or more	−0.008 (0.046)	0.016 (0.054)	−0.036 (0.042)	0.135 (0.083)	−0.089 (0.050)	0.088 (0.084)
Age youngest child	−0.003 (0.004)	**−0.018** (0.005)	−0.001 (0.004)	0.002 (0.008)	**−0.027** (0.005)	0.001 (0.009)

(continued overleaf)

Table 5 (continued)

	From employment		From unemployment		From home work	
	To unemployment	To home work	To employment	To home work	To employment	To unemployment
Model-specific covariates						
Spell order[f]						
2nd	**0.888** (0.038)	**0.907** (0.047)	−0.045 (0.034)	**0.275** (0.069)	**0.317** (0.043)	**0.509** (0.074)
3rd or later	**1.266** (0.043)	**1.161** (0.058)	**0.150** (0.039)	**0.359** (0.080)	**0.538** (0.056)	**0.904** (0.084)
Duration	**−0.029** (0.003)	**−0.011** (0.003)	**−0.034** (0.004)	0.001 (0.008)	**−0.053** (0.004)	**−0.112** (0.007)
Duration sq.[c]	−0.000 (0.000)	0.000 (0.000)	0.001 (0.001)	−0.001 (0.002)	**0.004** (0.001)	**0.011** (0.001)
Intercept	**−4.143** (0.419)	**−5.948** (0.504)	**−0.416** (0.371)	**−1.712** (0.597)	**−1.486** (0.434)	**−2.284** (0.577)
Model statistics						
−2 log L	54,730	43,328	35,105	11,447	28,868	10,950
DF	24	24	24	24	24	24
No. of person-months	1,415,046	1,415,046	50,995	50,995	84,357	84,357

Notes: [a]Reference category: no change. [b]Yes = 1/No = 0. [c]The variable is squared and divided by 10. [d]Reference category: 1 child. [e]Reference category: Primary. [f]Reference category: 1st. Note: The model also includes regional dummies which are not reported, as they are mainly of national interest. Coefficients in bold are significant at the 5 percent level or below.

entry rates than nonsingle parents, but unemployment entry rates are higher. Hence, lone parents more often seek paid work by registering as unemployed, which implies that they are not more inactive in all respects.[16]

To answer the more comprehensive question about the determinants of labor market transitions among lone and married/cohabiting parents, we turn to Tables 2–5. Regarding welfare reforms, we would expect the shortening of the duration of lone-parent benefits to strengthen labor market attachment, while higher benefits should have the opposite effect. Some of the results corroborate these expectations. For example, among lone mothers, a shorter duration of benefits reduces exits from both employment and unemployment to home work, speeds up employment entry among those who are unemployed, and encourages job-seeking through unemployment registration among those who are at home. Also as expected, a higher benefit level is associated with lower employment entry rates among home workers. Contrary to expectations, however, are the findings that a shorter benefit period leads to higher employment exit rates to unemployment and lower employment entry rates from home work, and that higher benefits lead to lower employment exit rates to home work. One reason for the somewhat unexpected results may be the very brief observation period, as the changes in the benefit scheme were first introduced toward the end of our analysis period (January 1998). In addition, special temporary arrangements meant that the changes would not necessarily have an immediate effect.

The local "follow-up arrangement" for lone parents is mainly directed at nonactive (neither employed nor studying) parents. Hence, we primarily expect an effect on home workers. This expectation is confirmed by the results, which show that the program had the intended effect on mothers, strengthening their labor market attachment through higher employment entry and more unemployment registration.

Generally, lone-parent policies hardly affect fathers at all. The only exception is the large negative and significant effect of a shorter benefit period on transitions from unemployment to home work, similar to that also observed for lone mothers. The lack of impact of welfare policies on fathers is further emphasized by the results for the cash-for-care benefit that was introduced at the end of our analysis period. This reform applied to all parents – single and nonsingle alike – who had children of eligible age, which at the time were only 1 year old (12 to 24 months). Nevertheless, we do observe some negative effects on the labor supply of mothers. Among married and cohabiting mothers, the negative effects operate both in the form of lower employment and unemployment entry rates when at home, as well as in higher exit rates to home work when unemployed. Among lone mothers, only transitions between unemployment and home work are affected, raising entry into and lowering exits from home work. The cash-for-care entitlement further reduces unemployment entry among employed married and cohabiting mothers, and a similar effect is also noticeable among lone mothers, although it is not statistically significant. This may suggest that unemployment played a larger role in the coping strategies of both single and nonsingle mothers before the cash-for-care reform was introduced.

When we turn to the impact of business cycles and changing demand for labor, as reflected through the local unemployment rate, we find – as expected, and for all parental groups – that recession increases the unemployment risk among those who are employed and reduces re-entry rates into employment among those who are already unemployed.[17] Yet, home-working parents in all groups are also more inclined to seek employment during recessions by registering as unemployed, which is less expected. This finding probably shows that jobs are harder to obtain by ordinary means during economic downswings. There is no evidence that lone parents are at greater risk of losing their jobs and leaving the labor market during slumps, however. On the contrary, the estimated positive effects of rising local unemployment on employment exits to either unemployment or home work tend to be higher (although not significantly so) among married and cohabiting parents than among lone parents.[18] Among home-working parents, the employment entry rate declines, and significantly so, only for lone mothers and fathers when the local unemployment rate rises.[19] Possible discrimination against lone parents by employers thus appears primarily manifest in hiring rather than firing.

The other covariates included in our model are important as control variables and also prove to have significant effects. Human capital resources, in particular, are strong determinants of labor market transitions among mothers as well as fathers, and the effects for single and nonsingle parents appear to be quite similar. The more education and employment experience a parent has, the stronger the attachment to the labor market. This is expressed through lower exit rates out of, and higher (re)entry rates into, employment. Among both groups of mothers (single and nonsingle), we see strong negative effects of education and employment experience on transitions from unemployment to home work, implying that mothers with more human capital resources are less likely to quit the labor force completely. Moreover, employment experience exerts a strong negative effect on transitions from home work to unemployment in all groups, probably indicating that it is easier for parents with longer experience to find a job without registering at the unemployment office. The square term of employment experience has in most cases the opposite sign, indicating that the effect declines (becomes less positive or less negative) as employment experience increases.

The general pattern for care responsibilities is, not surprisingly, that mothers are affected more than fathers, and that age of the youngest child has a greater effect than number of children. Among both lone and married/cohabiting mothers, employment exit rates decrease and employment entry rates increase as the youngest child grows older. Similarly, a higher age of youngest child makes home-working mothers more inclined to seek a job by registering as unemployed, and unemployed mothers less inclined to quit the workforce to stay at home. The age-of-youngest-child effect is thus quite similar for single and nonsingle mothers. The number of children, on the other hand, seems to affect married and cohabiting mothers more than lone mothers. Common for both groups is the finding that having more children encourages a closer attachment to the labor market, increasing employment entry from home work and decreasing employment exits to unemployment. Among married and cohabiting mothers there is, however, also evidence in the opposite direction: mothers with several children are more likely to quit employment for home work, less likely to re-enter employment when unemployed, and less likely to seek work by registering as unemployed when at home. The mixed pattern is not entirely unexpected, since children require extra time as well as extra money, the former predicting a lower female labor supply, and the latter, a higher one. The finding is also in line with research results from other countries. In a comparative study of the US and Germany, Sonja Drobnic (2000) finds, for example, that number of children has no effect on the employment behavior of American mothers, while in Germany a larger family lowers full-time exit rates and increases employment entry among married mothers. According to Drobnic, this may indicate that the employment activity of married mothers in Germany is largely driven by the financial needs of their families.

The remaining model covariates, duration and spell order, are important for model specification, but are of less interest in this analysis. From Tables 2–5, we note that the estimates are generally as expected, with a negative effect of duration and a positive effect of spell order in most transitions.

SUMMARY AND DISCUSSION

This article has explored the labor force attachment of Norwegian lone parents over time, in the sense of calendar time using cross-sectional data from the LFS, as well as over individual lifetimes, using individual longitudinal data from linked administrative registers covering the period 1992–98. Married and cohabiting parents serve as benchmarks in both approaches, and we highlight gender differences by analyzing fathers as well as mothers.

A basic framework for the analysis is that conditions on both the supply and the demand side of the labor market determine the labor market adaptations of single as well as married or cohabiting parents. Common supply-side determinants are human capital resources and care responsibilities, along with the budget restrictions set by different economic and financial opportunities, including welfare transfers. The demand side is modeled using the local unemployment level as an indicator of shifting labor demand.

Our main concern in this article is the role of changing welfare regulations and fluctuating business cycles. Based on the descriptive analysis, we conclude that favorable economic conditions might be more important for the successful incorporation of lone parents in the labor market than work-incentive policies on the supply side. The multivariate analysis corroborates this assumption to some extent, as the estimated effects of changes in social policies partly point in opposite directions and are generally less significant than the effects of changing labor market conditions.[20] Lone fathers, for instance, are hardly affected at all by policy changes. Among lone mothers, however, we find some evidence of effects in the expected direction: cuts in the benefit period encourage a closer attachment to the workforce by reducing exit rates to home work from employment and unemployment, raising unemployment registration rates among home workers, and speeding up the return to work among those who are unemployed. Also as expected, a higher benefit level reduces employment entry among home workers. Other policy effects are small and insignificant and in some cases, even contrary to expectations. The somewhat ambiguous pattern may have partly resulted from a very short observation period and transitory arrangements, implying that policy changes would not necessarily have immediate effect. In addition, we have not been able to analyze all reforms during the 1990s, as our longitudinal data do not cover the period surrounding the 1990 change that made part-time work more profitable. A previous analysis of the 1990 reform concluded, however, that the effect on the labor supply of lone mothers was fairly limited (Marit Rønsen and Steinar Strøm 1993).

The effect of rising unemployment in the local labor market is, on the other hand, unambiguous, implying a looser labor market attachment among all parents, single as well as nonsingle, and mothers as well as fathers. A remaining crucial question is whether lone parents are particularly vulnerable during times of recession, for example as a result of discrimination from employers in hiring or firing. Based on the multivariate analysis we cannot conclude that lone mothers or fathers are more at risk than other parents of losing their jobs and leaving the labor market during business cycle slumps. If, however, they are already outside the labor market when a downturn occurs, lone parents do have lower employment entry rates than other parents. Possible discrimination by employers is thus primarily connected to the hiring process rather than the firing process. Similar adverse effects of local economic conditions on lone parents have also been found in the US by Lingxin Hao and Mary C. Brinton (1997). Further, research from Germany, cited in Drobnic (2000), indicates that one reason lone parents may have greater difficulties in finding jobs is that employers often assume they will be more frequently absent from work and less willing to work long hours than partnered parents.

We conclude, therefore, that both welfare policy and business cycles matter. This result is also consistent with US research on the impact of the 1996 welfare reform (see, for example, Rebecca M. Blank 2001, 2002). However, to date, the general impression for Norway is that favorable economic conditions have played a larger role than stringent social policies in increasing the employment activity of lone parents and reducing welfare expenditures. Measures directed toward the demand side of the labor market should therefore also be part of policies that promote the successful integration of lone parents into the labor market. Such policies become particularly important during times of recession and surplus labor demand, when lone parents may face stronger barriers to employment entry than other parents.

ACKNOWLEDGMENTS

The authors would like to thank the Norwegian Research Council and Statistics Norway for research funding, as well as the editors and anonymous referees of *Feminist Economics* for helpful comments on earlier drafts of this article.

NOTES

[1] Widows and widowers are, in principle, entitled to the same benefits, but in most cases they are also eligible for additional earmarked benefits.

[2] According to the NOK/US$ exchange rate of December 2003.

[3] The figures are based on tables from a specially prepared LFS dataset comprising mothers and fathers with children under the age of 16, covering the period 1980– 99. The years 1988–90 have been excluded due to a major change in the method of registering children in 1988 and to inadequate data for 1989 and 1990. Through 1980–87 "lone parents" are defined as mothers and fathers living alone (with no co-resident partner) with one or more children under the age of 16 in the household, regardless of biological relationship. Through 1991–99 "lone parents" comprise mothers and fathers living alone with one or more biological or adopted children under the age of 16. This change of definition is due to changes in survey design and has no significant effects on the statistics presented here.

[4] Newly released employment figures for 2000 and 2001 show a continuation of these trends; a slow increase in the employment rate of lone mothers and a decrease among lone fathers (Ragni Hege Kitterød and Randi Kjeldstad 2004).

[5] When split into groups according to age of youngest child, employment figures show an increase among lone mothers with children between 3 and 10 years of age, and a decrease among lone mothers with children under 3 years of age from 1998 to 1999 (Kjeldstad and Rønsen 2002). This could reflect the early effects of the 1998 regulatory changes, but there may also be other interpretations (Kjeldstad and Rønsen 2002). The decrease in the group with children less than 3 years may, for example, also partly be an effect of the cash-for-care reform introduced in August 1998.

[6] Hence, parents who had their first child during 1992–98 are not included in our sample. If included, this group would only constitute about 12 percent of the total sample of parents. The parents in our sample will, on average, be somewhat older and have more and older children than the new parents of the 1990s. A higher average age of both parents and children implies higher participation rates and lower labor market vulnerability, especially among lone parents. These and other observable characteristics are controlled for in the model and should not bias the results, as long as age and other determinants have the same effects in the new parental group. One source of bias for which we cannot control is the possible difference in unobservable characteristics between old and new first-time parents. The new mothers of the 1990s might, for example, have higher participation rates than their forerunners – "all else" being equal, including age – both because they generally belong to younger cohorts with stronger labor market attachment than older cohorts, and because they become mothers at a time of higher labor market participation. Their exclusion then is likely to impart a downward bias to the coefficients on participation for mothers in general, and possibly more so for lone mothers. Given the size of the group of parents not included, however, this bias is likely to be fairly small.

[7] We use a sample instead of the whole population, as the dataset would otherwise be too large for efficient model estimation. This is because all mothers and fathers constitute more than 1.2 million individuals, and they are followed up to 84 months (Jan. 1992 to Dec. 1998). Since person-months are the unit of analysis, this would easily yield a dataset of tens of millions of records.

[8] Being based on unemployment registration, the definition of unemployment in the multivariate analysis is stricter than in the LFS, where an individual does not have to register as unemployed to be defined as unemployed. The only criterion in LFS is that the person is available for, and actively seeking, work.

[9] Transitions to education from any other state are censored at the time of that event. We have also estimated transitions to and from education, but the results are not presented here.

[10] Using a logit specification, the discrete hazard rate function can be expressed as $\log(P_{jkt}/P_{j0t}) = \beta_{jk}X_t$, where P_{jkt} is the conditional probability that event k occurs during spell j at time t, P_{j0t} is the probability that no event occurs at time t during spell j, β_{jk} is a vector of coefficients associated with spell j and event k, and X_t is a vector of policy, labor market, and personal covariates that, in our model, all vary with time. Individuals experiencing an event other than k during spell j are treated as censored at the time of the other event.

[11] Unfortunately, it is not possible to control for other important elements of the economic opportunity structure of parents, since this would require more information on wages, income, tax, and benefits than we have in our data.

[12] This definition is thus less restrictive than in the LFS, where partnership status is based on the respondent's own information at the time of interview. Further, the maximum age of children is 17 years in the register data and 15 years in the LFS.

[13] We have specified duration as a continuous variable with a square term to catch possible nonlinearity. It may also be specified as a categorical variable, but since the duration itself (the baseline hazard) is not our primary interest, and early investigations showed that other estimates were not affected much by the choice of specification, we chose the more parsimonious continuous formulation.

[14] With repeated spells, there are multiple observations from the same individual, implying that there may be resemblance between successive spells. Including an indicator of spell order will pick up such interdependence, but will generally not adjust for it. Correlated observations lead to standard error estimates that are biased downward and test statistics that are biased upward. Incorporating methods that correct for these problems is not straightforward, and will not be attempted here.

[15] For categorical variables like partnership status, the coefficient represents the difference in log-odds between a specific group and the reference group.

[16] More detailed analyses show that lone parents, and in particular lone mothers, are also more inclined to take up education. (These results are not yet published, but can be obtained from the authors on request.)

[17] Since the local unemployment rate is a continuous variable, its coefficient expresses the change in the log-odds when the variable increases with one unit (here: 1 percentage point). For example, among employed lone mothers an increase in the local unemployment rate of 1 percentage point raises the log-odds of exiting to unemployment by 0.055.

[18] Even if the coefficients are estimated to be significant for one group and non-significant for another, the difference in effects between groups is not necessarily significant. Here, the difference in the estimated effects on employment exits is significant only for fathers and for transitions to home work. These conclusions are based on confidence intervals computed from standard errors as shown in Tables 2–5.

[19] The difference in the estimated effects on employment entry among home workers is significant for both mothers and fathers.

[20] Less significant in the sense that more of the policy effects are nonsignificant, and when significant, the corresponding p-values (the smallest significance level for which the hypothesis of no effect can be rejected) are generally higher than the p-values corresponding to the business cycle estimates. It is not possible to evaluate the relative importance of these variables by comparing the numerical size of their coefficients, as the policy indicators are categorical variables and the business cycle indicator is a continuous variable (see also notes 15 and 17, above).

REFERENCES

Allison, Paul D. 1984. *Event History Analysis. Regression for Longitudinal Event Data.* Sage University Paper Series on Quantitative Applications in the Social Sciences, 07-046. London: Sage.

Björnberg, Ulla. 1997. "Single Mothers in Sweden: Supported Workers Who Mother," in Simon Duncan and Rosalind Edwards (eds.) *Single Mothers in an International Context: Mothers or Workers?*, Bjorberg, Ulta pp. 241–67. London: UCL Press.

Blank, Rebecca M. 2001. "Declining Caseloads/Increased Work: What Can We Conclude About the Effects of Welfare Reform?" *Federal Reserve Bank of New York Economic Policy Review* 7(2): 25–36.

——2002. "Evaluating Welfare Reform in the US." *Journal of Economic Literature* 40(4): 1105–66.

Bradbury, Bruce and Markus Jäntti. 2001. "Child Poverty Across Twenty-Five Countries," in Bruce Bradbury, Stephen P. Jenkins, and John Micklewright (eds.) *The Dynamics of Child Poverty in Industrialised Countries*, pp. 62–91. Cambridge, UK: UNICEF/Cambridge University Press.

Bradshaw, Jonathan, Steven Kennedy, Majella Kilkey, Sandra Hutton, Anne Corden, Tony Eardley, Hilary Holmes, and Joanne Neale. 1996. *Policy and the Employment of Lone Parents in 20 Countries. The EU Report.* European Observatory on National Family Policies. York, UK: Social Policy Research Unit, University of York.

—— and Naomi Finch. 2002. *A Comparison of Child Benefit Packages in 22 Countries.* Department for Work and Pensions Research Report No. 174. Leeds, UK: Corporate Document Services.

Dahl, Grete. 1993. "Enslige forsørgere" ["Lone Parents"], in *Sosialt Utsyn* [*Social Survey*], pp. 313–23. Oslo: Statistics Norway.

Drobnic, Sonja. 2000. "The Effects of Children on Married and Lone Mothers' Employment in the United States and (West) Germany." *European Sociological Review* 16(2): 137–57.

Epland, Jon. 2001. *Barn i husholdninger med lav inntekt: Omfang, utvikling, Årsaker* [*Children in Low Income Households: Extent, Development, Causes*]. Rapport 2001/9. Oslo: Statistics Norway.

Ermisch, John F. and Robert E. Wright. 1991. "Welfare Benefits and Lone Parents' Employment in Great Britain." *The Journal of Human Resources* 26(3): 424–56.

Gustafsson, Bjørn, Ali Tasiran, and Håkan Nyman. 1996. "Lone Parent Families and Social Security – The Case of Sweden." Paper for the Third International Research Seminar on Issues in Social Security, Sigtuna, Sweden.

Hao, Lingxin and Mary C. Brinton. 1997. "Productive Activities and Support Systems of Single Mothers." *American Journal of Sociology* 102(5): 1305–44.

Hobson, Barbara and Mieko Takahashi. 1997. "The Parent–Worker Model: Lone Mothers in Sweden," in Jane Lewis (ed.) *Lone Mothers in European Welfare Regimes. Shifting Policy Logics*, pp. 121–39. London: Jessica Kingsley.

Kamerman, Sheila B. and Alfred J. Kahn. 1988. *Mothers Alone–Strategies for a Time of Change.* Boston, MA: Auburn House.

Kilkey, Majella and Jonathan Bradshaw. 2001. "Making Work Pay: Policies for Lone Parents," in Jane Millar and Karen Rowlingson (eds.) *Lone Parents, Employment and Social Policy: Cross-National Comparisons*, pp. 211–32. Bristol: Policy Press.

Kitterød, Ragni Hege and Randi Kjeldstad. 2004. *Foreldres Arbeidstid 1991–2001.* [*Parents' Working Hours 1991–2001*]. Rapport 2004/6. Oslo: Statistics Norway.

Kjeldstad, Randi. 1998. *Enslige forsørgere: forsørgelse og levekår før og etter overgang til en ny livsfase* [*Single Parents: Social and Economic Adjustment Before and After Transition to Single Parenthood*]. Social and Economic Studies 100. Oslo: Statistics Norway.

——2000. "Employment Strategy Policies and Lone Parenthood: The Case of Norway." *Social Politics: International Studies in Gender, State and Society* 7(3): 343–71.

Kjeldstad, Randi and Marit Rønsen. 2002. *Enslige foreldre på arbeidsmarkedet 1980–1999. En sammenligning med gifte mødre og fedre* [*Single Parents on the Labor Market 1980–1999. A Comparison with Married Mothers and Fathers*]. Statistical Analyses 49. Oslo: Statistics Norway.

——Anne Skevik. 2004. "Enslige forsørgere: en sosialpolitisk kategori utgått på dato?" ["Single Parents: An Outdated Social Policy Category?"], in Anne Lise Ellingsæter and Arnlaug Leira (eds.) *Velferdsstaten og familien* [*Welfare State and the Family*], pp. 231–60. Oslo: Gyldendal norsk forlag.

Lyngstad, Jan. 2000. "Inntekt og levekår for enkeltgrupper" ["Income and Living Conditions, Various Groups"]), in Anders Barstad (ed.) *På vei mot det gode samfunn* [*Towards the Good Society*]. Notater 2001/21, pp. 248–79. Oslo: Statistics Norway.

Meyer, Bruce D. and Dan T. Rosenbaum. 2001. "Welfare, the Earned Income Tax Credit, and the Labor Supply of Single Mothers." *Quarterly Journal of Economics*, August: 1063–114.

Nyman, Håkan. 1998. "An Economic Analysis of Lone Motherhood in Sweden." *Economiska Studier utgivna av Nationaleconomisks institusjonen Handelshøgskolan vid Gøteborgs universitet 89.* Gøteborg.

Rønsen, Marit and Steinar Strøm. 1993. "Arbeidstilbudet blant enslige mødre og gifte kvinner" ["The Labor Supply of Single and Married Mothers"]. *Norsk Økonomisk Tidsskrift* 108: 115–47.

Siim, Birthe. 1997. "Dilemmas of Citizenship in Denmark: Lone Mothers Between Work and Care," in Jane Lewis (ed.) *Lone Mothers in European Welfare Regimes: Shifting Policy Logics*, pp. 140–70. London: Jessica Kingsley.

Skevik, Anne. 1996. *Holdninger til enslige forsørgere* [*Attitudes Towards Lone Parents*]. INAS-notat 1996/4. Oslo: Institute for Applied Social Research.

——1998. *Children's Right, Father's Duty, Mothers' Responsibility: Policies and Attitudes towards Lone Parents.* Skriftserie 1998/2. Oslo: NOVA.

——2001. *Eneforsørgede eneforsørgere. Aktiveringspolitikk for enslige forsørgere i seks land på 1990-tallet* [*Self-supporting Lone Parents. Activating Politics for Lone Parents in Six Countries During the 1990s*]. NOVA-Rapport 2001/13. Oslo: Institute for Applied Social Research.

Skrede, Kari. 1994. "Hva er det kvinnene vil? Kvinners utdanning og yrkesliv" ["What Do Women Want? Women's Education and Employment"], in Ivar Frønes and Andreas Hompland (eds.) *Den nye barne-og familieboka* [*The New Family and Child Book*], pp. 67–79. Oslo: Norwegian University Press.

Skrede, Kari and Kristin Tornes (eds.). 1986. *Den norske kvinnerevolusjonen. Kvinners arbeid 1975–1985* [*The Norwegian Women's Revolution. Women's Work 1975–1985*]. Oslo: Norwegian University Press.

Strell, Monica. 1999. "Lone Mothers in Norway: Variations in Understanding and Decisions About Mothering and the Ideal of Paid Work." Paper for Economic and Social Research Council seminar "Parents, Children and Workers: Rationalities, Contexts and Decisions." April 16, South Bank University, London.

Syltevik, Liv Johanne. 1998. "Changing Welfare Policy for Lone Mothers in Norway – A Transition from Relational to Individualised Lone Motherhood?" Paper for seminar on "Current European Research on Lone Mothers," April 24–25, Gøteborg University.

Terum, Lars Inge. 1993. *Stønad, samliv og sjølvforsørging. Om korleis eineforsørgarane brukar overgangsstønaden frå folketrygda* [*Support, Self-Support and Life Together. How Lone Parents Use the Transitional Allowance*]. INAS-report 1993/1. Oslo: Institute of Applied Social Research.

FAMILY ECONOMY WORKERS OR CARING MOTHERS? MALE BREADWINNING AND WIDOWS' PENSIONS IN NORWAY AND THE UK

Anne Skevik

INTRODUCTION

The publication of Jane Lewis's (1992) much-quoted article on variations in welfare state commitment to the male-breadwinner model of family economies inspired both empirical research and conceptual debates. A problem that remains, however, is how that variety of models can be applied to studies of lone motherhood. To date, attempts to study differences in national policies toward lone mothers through the lens of "strong/weak male-breadwinner assumptions" have raised more questions than they have solved. For instance, Jane Lewis and Barbara Hobson's (1997) discussion of the treatment of lone mothers in European countries noted a number of important differences between the countries they considered "male-breadwinner" countries. They concluded that "policy logics based on assumptions about male breadwinning tend to treat lone mothers as *either* workers *or* mothers" (Lewis and Hobson 1997: 9), and noted that many strong male-breadwinner countries had swung toward the "worker" option in the 1990s. Their conclusion raises a series of questions: are all lone mothers treated similarly, or is the category subdivided by characteristics such as marital status, age and number of children, or ethnicity? What accounted for the apparent swing in the 1990s, and was this swing uniform?

The aim of this article is to understand, by means of a detailed historical study, the background of this "swing" in two countries that Lewis (1992) characterized as strong male-breadwinner countries, namely Norway and the UK (see also Diane Sainsbury 1996). The timing, as well as the extent, of family policy changes in these two countries has been rather different, as I will show below. Why was this so? If the countries had such similar cultural and institutional starting points, why did Norway move away from these positions so much more rapidly than the UK? This complex question can obviously be answered in many different ways. I shall explore one specific hypothesis, namely that there are important variations within the traditional view of the family that affect the position of lone mothers. A country can be both traditional and skeptical about encouraging mothers to work outside the home, without conforming to the male breadwinner model in which "married women [are] excluded from the labour market, firmly subordinated to their husbands for the purposes of social security entitlements and tax, and expected to undertake the work of caring ... at home without public support" (Lewis 1992: 162). In this paper, I argue that Norway and the UK have been traditional in different ways, so that their starting points were more and less resistant to change, respectively.

The idea of different versions of the traditional family models is not new. Birgit Pfau-Effinger (1999) has proposed a paradigm of the male breadwinner/female caregiver model that is particularly useful for this study. Although she does not discuss lone motherhood in any detail, her approach still provides insights of great interest for our purposes here. Pfau-Effinger proposes replacing the male-breadwinner model with the broader concept of "gender cultural models." Her gender cultural models have four dimensions: (1) the social ideal of the spheres through which women and men should be integrated into society (public/private); (2) the construction of dependencies between men and women; (3) the construction of the relationship between generations; and (4) the main social sphere for caring (Pfau-Effinger 1999: 62). She suggests that these dimensions are grounded in five gender models, two of which are versions of the male-breadwinner model: the family economic gender model and the male-breadwinner/female-home-carer model. The family economic gender model depicts the cooperation of men and women within a family business (farm or craft): both sexes contribute substantially to the family economy, thus ensuring that men and women are fundamentally dependent on each other. Mothers (and fathers) work at home, but motherhood is not construed as a long phase of life in which special tasks of caring absorb most of women's capacity for work. Children are treated as members of the family economic unit – that is, as workers – as soon as they are physically able to contribute. Within the male breadwinner/female-home-carer model there is a strict division of public and private spheres, with men and women seen as complementarily competent for one of these spheres: men are breadwinners who earn an income in the public sphere, while women are primarily responsible for the work in the private household, including childcare. This model construes children as needing comprehensive and enduring care, to be provided by the mother.

What happens in each of these models when the male breadwinner or the male partner in the family business is not in the picture? What, in other words, happens to lone mothers? Before I turn to this question, I will outline some of the recent policy changes that show the mounting differences between Norway and the UK. Rather than presenting a systematic comparison of contemporary policies or practices, my aim is to provide background for the claim that Norway has moved more rapidly away from the traditional model than the UK.

FAREWELL TO THE MALE BREADWINNER? NORWAY AND THE UK

As both Arnlaug Leira (1989, 1992) and Diane Sainsbury (1999) have shown, Norway has lagged among the Nordic countries in enabling women to reconcile work and care. Progress in this area occurred mainly in the late 1980s and early 1990s (Arnlaug Leira 2002). The absolute number of nursery places doubled between 1985 and 2000, bringing the estimated coverage for children aged 3 – 5 up to 80 percent (Statistics Norway 2002), and most nurseries offer full-time daycare. School-starting age was lowered from 7 to 6 years in 1997, and since 1999 all municipalities have been obliged to provide daycare facilities before and after school hours. Moreover, while parental leave in 1986 was 18 weeks with full wage replacement, by 2003 parents could take up to 42 weeks of leave with full wage replacement, or 52 weeks with 80 percent replacement (Charlotte Koren 1997). Four of those weeks were reserved for the father.

All of these programs were part of a conscious policy to encourage the dual-breadwinner family. Partly as a reaction against this emphasis on dual breadwinning, the cash-for-childcare benefit was introduced in 1998. This benefit is payable to parents of children between 1 and 3 who do not use public childcare: they can use the benefit to "free" either parent from employment for two years – that is, as a subsidy for home-based care – or to pay for private childminding (Arnlaug Leira 1998; Anne-Lise Ellingsæter 1999).

In the UK, little occurred to promote the reconciliation of work and care until the election of a Labour government in 1997. This government's Childcare Strategy, implemented in 1998, built on a promise to provide free, part-time education places for two and a half hours per day for all 3- and 4-year-olds (school-starting age is 5 years). By 2001, 90 percent of English children under 5 had places in early education. However, early education is offered part-time, and fits poorly with parents' employment (Hilary Land 2002; Naomi Finch 2003; Jane Lewis 2003). The additional care that must be found is almost entirely private, and frequently incurs very high costs to the family. Subsidies introduced in 1999, covering 70 percent of such costs, up to a ceiling, for registered and approved childcare, are available to low-income families in which both parents or a lone parent work more than sixteen hours per week. Still, only 13 percent of parents with dependent children use formal childcare services to cover all their (extra-family) childcare needs, a fact explained mainly by the high costs (Finch 2003: 21). Labour increased paid maternity leave from fourteen to twenty-six weeks in April 2003: this is paid at a 90 percent replacement rate for six weeks, then at a fixed rate of £100 per week. Since April 2003, fathers have been entitled to two weeks' paternity leave around the birth of the child, paid at £100 per week. In addition, fathers have the right to thirteen weeks of unpaid parental leave before the child turns 6, which was introduced in 1999 in response to a directive from the European Union.

Both Norway and the UK have relatively high proportions of lone parents: 22 percent of all families with children in the UK (Jonathan Bradshaw and Naomi Finch 2002: 26) and 20 percent in Norway (Statistics Norway 2003). Norwegian lone mothers have higher employment rates than their British counterparts (68 versus 50 percent in 1999/2001, see also Bradshaw and Finch 2002: 31), but in both countries lone mothers are less likely to be in employment than married/cohabiting mothers, unlike in many other European countries. Both countries thus see room for improvement, and in the late 1990s both redesigned their policies for lone parents around the principle of labor-market activation. Before 1998, lone parents in Norway could receive benefits for as long as they had children under 10 with no work requirement. Under the 1998 reform, lone parents may receive benefits only for a limited time after the break-up of their relationship or the birth of their youngest child (whichever happened later). This period can last a maximum of three years, or five years if the parent is undertaking full-time education, all of which must be before the youngest child turns 8. Work-related activity is required if the youngest child is older than 3 (Randi Kjeldstad 2000; Anne Skevik 2001b). The UK Labour government's effort to increase employment among lone parents has mainly taken the form of low-wage subsidies, plus the work-oriented "New Deal for Lone Parents" (Alan Marsh 2001). Since 2001, all lone mothers receiving benefits have had to attend work-focused interviews. As of yet, however, the New Deal has not imposed work requirements for lone parents with children under 16, or 19 if the child is in full-time education.

All in all, although both countries are moving away from traditional male-breadwinner assumptions, changes occurred ten to twenty years earlier in Norway and (as of 2003) have gone much further. However, the cash-for-childcare reform, which enables parents to care for children at home, illustrates that the emphasis on the dual-breadwinner family remains more controversial in Norway than in neighboring Sweden and Denmark. Thus, while it is somewhat anomalous to identify Norway as a "male-breadwinner" country, Norway does not conform to a clear-cut dual-breadwinner model, either.

SINGLE/DIVORCED/WIDOWED MOTHERS AND THE MALE-BREADWINNER REGIME

Lone mothers are often used as a test case in discussions of women's citizenship in the welfare state (e.g. Bettina Cass 1992; Barbara Hobson 1994; Lewis and Hobson 1997; Majella Kilkey 2000). Since lone mothers are solely responsible for providing both cash and care, they represent an extreme in the tensions between paid work and care. Thus, how welfare policies treat such mothers is sometimes taken as the quintessential test case of how states construct the relationship between work and care for all women (Kilkey 2000: 70). While this argument is plausible in studies of current arrangements, it has less validity in historical studies.

"Lone mothers" is a relatively new social category, comprising single (unmarried), separated, divorced, and widowed mothers. Historically, clear distinctions have been drawn between these groups. Socially and legally, it made a dramatic difference whether or not the woman was married when giving birth. Unmarried mothers risked being treated as the *opposite* of good, responsible, married mothers. Similarly, separation and divorce carried a certain stigma, with public reactions varying from pity to suspicion (Anne Skevik 2001a). The least stigma attached to widowed mothers, who had fallen into their situation innocently. They had done as prevailing morals dictated – married and had children by their husbands – and then suffered the terrible blow of losing their partners. We can assume that the policy-makers of the past protected widowed mothers and their children more than any other category of lone-mother family and wished to help them to continue living according to prevailing standards of a good family life. Thus, political constructions of widows' opportunities and responsibilities *can* be taken as quintessential examples of constructions of motherhood in general.

Today, this emphasis on widowed mothers may seem odd: after all, these make up only a small minority of all lone mothers. Although we will never have precise information about the marital status of lone mothers in

95

previous decades, widowed mothers must have been less of a minority in, say, 1950 – in the wake of the enormous death toll of World War II – than they were in 2000. Using widowed mothers as an analytical category in historical studies is therefore less peculiar than employing a similar research design might be for contemporary studies. The main reason for focusing on widowed mothers in this article is to strip away the more complicated issues that arise from other paths into lone motherhood, to focus as clearly as possible on the relationship between entitlements and work obligations.

Countries differ in how markedly they separate widowed mothers from other categories of lone mothers/lone parents. In this respect, Norway and the UK represent different ends of a continuum. In the UK, widows are the only category of lone mothers who are entitled to a separate class of rights-based benefits. Unmarried, separated, and divorced mothers who cannot provide for themselves have to rely on means-tested benefits (known as Income Support since 1986), combined with whatever support they can get from their children's father. In Norway, unmarried mothers were given practically the same benefit entitlements as widows even in the earliest benefit scheme (see below), while other categories of lone parents became eligible for these entitlements in 1980[1] (Skevik 2001b: 92). Lone parents who lose their benefit entitlements, or who find that their benefit entitlements are too low to make ends meet, can apply for means-tested social assistance. The same applies to widows in the UK. Thus, in neither country are the widow's benefits compared here those of the last resort; rather, their function is to "lift" certain categories of recipients out of the residual social-assistance schemes. Both countries provide means-tested social assistance as a safety net for those who do not qualify for categorical benefits. As Ivar Lødemel (1997) argues, welfare state modernization in Norway consisted to a large extent of giving vulnerable groups entitlements under the national insurance scheme. National assistance, which derived from nineteenth-century poor relief, remained a punitive and stigmatized scheme for the "least deserving" sections of the population. This policy contrasts with the approach in the UK, where policy-makers broke with the Poor Law tradition and developed social assistance into a quasi-universal system that catered to the needs of far larger sections of the population. Thus, means-tested benefits play a far more important role in the UK social welfare system than they do in Norway, but these means-tested benefits are less residual – that is, better regulated, and with stronger entitlements – than their Norwegian counterparts.

TWO MODELS OF WIDOWS' BENEFITS

In designing benefits for widowed mothers, policy-makers must answer three key questions. First, what should be the entitlement criteria? The deceased spouse's contribution or the surviving family's needs? Or, should the surviving spouse and children be given individual entitlements based on their status as "bereaved"? Second, how long should the benefits be paid? Should the benefits period depend on the widowed parent's age, the age of the children, the surviving parent's income potential, the presence or absence of new partners, or other criteria? And third, should the benefit arrangement be gender-neutral, or do only women need survivors' benefits?

These three questions loosely correspond to Pfau-Effinger's (1999) outline of relevant dimensions of the different gender models, as introduced above. The question of entitlement criteria is related to the public/private dimension, in which the crucial question is, can women and children – who live their lives in the "private" sphere – receive "public" entitlements? Or must such entitlements be mediated through the breadwinner? (See also Carole Pateman 1989: 118; Sainsbury 1999.) Determining the duration of benefits relates to the dimension of the relationship between generations: how long do children require their parent's comprehensive care – and can children at some point be seen as an economic resource for the family? Finally, the question of gender equality is echoed in Pfau-Effinger's dimension of dependency between women and men: if policy-makers assume that wives are dependent on their husbands, they will introduce benefits restricted to women. If they assume interdependence, survivors' benefits will be gender-neutral.

Depending on the answers to these three questions, we can outline two sets of principles, both of which start from traditional assumptions about family life and gender roles. One takes the public/private distinction as a starting point, assuming that married men will be breadwinners while their wives are home-based dependents. In the purest form of this model, benefits depend solely on the deceased breadwinner's contributions. Contributions and entitlements are linked together in the public sphere, while the widow's needs and situation otherwise belong in the private one, and therefore do not matter. The working husband and father pays his social security contributions as a form of insurance, and his contributions cover his wife and children in the event of the breadwinner's death. The right to a widow's pension will be an *automatic derived right* for the dependents of insured men: married women are protected from the risk of losing their breadwinners.

A slightly modified adaptation of the same principles places more weight on the surviving family's situation: benefit entitlements are still derived, but not automatic. The male-breadwinner/female-home-carer model is pre-mised on the assumption that a home needs a home-based woman to care for it. If the husband dies and there are no children in the marriage, then the woman no longer has a family home to care for, and she is no longer needed in this role. In this situation, there is no reason why the woman should not go out to work and earn her own money. But if there are dependent children in the home, the mother's presence is still needed. Even if the family breadwinner is gone, the home carer should remain – for as long as the household includes dependent children. The assumption of a strict division of roles remains; thus, a widowed mother – like a married one – stays at home and cares for her family. This model views children as dependents with a comprehensive and lasting need for care, supervision, and guidance rather than as potential resources for the family. Widowed mothers are thus protected as family carers, while childless widows have no such entitlements. We may call this a "caring mother" model of widow's benefits, emphasizing as it does women's caring obligation within the home and their ongoing relationships with children.

A different model of widows' benefits arises from an alternative recognition of the home-based mother, which emphasizes the work involved in running a household and raising young children. This "family economic gender model" principle for widows' benefits places little importance on the public/private distinction, since both men and women frequently work in family businesses. The contribution record of a deceased spouse will therefore not be a decisive factor. And, since in this model husbands and wives depend on each other's efforts, survivors' benefits will normally be gender-neutral. Who gets the benefit and for how long will depend, essentially, on how much work there is to do in the household. In the "family economic gender model," marriage is a partnership with a pragmatic division of work. However, in the phase of life when young children are present, motherhood absorbs much of the woman's capacity. As the children grow up, they require less attention and provide more help, and the mother can increasingly turn her attention to other tasks.

According to this scenario, widow's benefits will then depend on whether or not policy-makers deem it necessary that the widow continue her work in the household full-time. If her domestic workload is small, she will be expected to work outside the home. Thus, widows are supported in their own right as workers in the family economy – that is, as contributors to social welfare who receive no direct payment for their work. This is the family economy worker model of widow's benefits.

The different models carry within them different potential for change. The purest version of the male-breadwinner/female-home-carer model, emphasizing the contributions of the deceased provider, will have distributional effects that are hard to defend. This model is probably unsustainable in its pure form. The "caring mother" model maintains strong assumptions about a gendered division of work; it essentially claims that motherhood is not compatible with paid employment. A mother is a mother until the youngest child leaves the home, and after this point – usually late in her life – it may be unreasonable to expect her to fully join the labor force. This view of family and gender roles is incompatible with a dual-earner pattern, and it will probably resist moving in that direction. The "family economy worker" model is more dynamic, in that it assumes the mother is a worker – except that she works at home. If the domestic workload decreases, this model dictates that mothers take their capacity to work to the market. This view of the family is much less likely to oppose legislative or social impetus toward dual-breadwinner households. Making such households the norm is only a matter of reorganizing women's workdays.

I have argued that Norway has moved away from the male-breadwinner model faster and more consistently than the UK has. Using the analytical framework sketched out here, we might assume that Norway has seen widowed mothers as family workers – for as long as there was considerable work to do in the household – while widowed mothers in the UK to a larger extent have been defined by their roles as wives and mothers. To explore this assumption, I will trace the historical development of social protection of widowed mothers in the two countries.

THE UK: A MOTHER HAS OTHER DUTIES

The first statutory widow's pension in the UK was the 1925 Widows', Orphans', and Old Age Pension Act. This pension was based on a pure male-breadwinner model, as the following quotation from Neville Chamberlain, then minister of health and a Conservative party member, makes clear:

> You ought to consider in this matter not merely the woman, you should consider in the first place the man. It is the man who is going to make the contribution, it is the man who is effecting the insurance; and surely the first thing a man thinks about is that you should make provision for his widow. (Chamberlain, introducing the bill. HC debates, 18 May 1925, col. 89, quoted in Susan Pedersen 1993: 175–6)

The 1925 Act thus gave entitlements to every widow of an insured man, regardless of her age, her income from earnings, and whether or not she had children. The pension entitlement ended if the widow found a new breadwinner, either through remarriage or cohabitation. The level of the pension was low, however, as the wish to protect widows had to be balanced against other concerns. In effect it was little more than a base upon which self-help – including savings, benefits from trade unions or private charities, private insurance, or family support – could be built (Joan C. Brown 1989: 28). (For a more detailed account of the 1925 scheme, see Pedersen 1993: 167.)

William Beveridge, the British economist and politician, criticized the 1925 scheme when, in 1941, he began to outline an encompassing social insurance scheme for Great Britain. His work culminated in the report he prepared for the British government (Cmnd. 6404 (1942)), which became by far the most important document in postwar debates on social insurance and made Beveridge known as the "founding father" of the British welfare state (Howard Glennerster 1995: 19) On the one hand, Beveridge was very clear about the role of a married woman: she should be provided for by her husband, in exchange for the work she did by keeping his home and raising his children (Cmnd. 6404 (1942): para. 107). On the other hand, Beveridge assumed that women would work outside the home before they married, and he had no objections to the employment of single women. These beliefs colored his attitude toward widows: those without children, like unmarried childless women, should not have the right to a pension. His starting point for thinking about widows follows:

> There is no reason why a childless widow should get a pension for life; if she is able to work she should work. On the other hand, provision much better than at present should be made for those who, because they have the care of children, cannot work for gain or cannot work regularly. (Cmnd. 6404 (1942): para. 153)

Beveridge argued that widowed mothers' rights to benefits should end when their youngest child turned 16 and, according to the definition set by the National Insurance, ceased to be a child. The mother should then go out to work, Beveridge believed, unless she had reached the age limit for old-age pension (60 years). On this point, the government went one step further than Beveridge. The Ministry of National Insurance worried about the consequences for the family if the mother was forced to seek employment with a 16-year-old in the house, even if the child was no longer considered a dependent. The White Paper the government issued following the Beveridge report proposed three distinctly different benefits for widows: widow's allowance, widowed mother's allowance, and widow's pension (Cmnd. 6550 (1944)).

Widow's allowance was to be payable to all widows for thirteen weeks following the death of the husband. Widowed mothers' allowance should be payable to widows with children under 16, while widows' pension should be available for widows who would find it hard to find paid employment because of age (older than 50) or disability. A recipient of a widowed mother's allowance should, however, qualify for a widow's pension at the age of 40, to avoid withdrawing her benefit while she had adolescent children. In this way, widowed mothers usually secured lifelong pensions, provided their husbands had made sufficient contributions to the National Insurance. They would receive widowed mothers' allowances for as long as they had dependent children, then be transferred to widow's pensions. Both forms of assistance would be reduced if the recipient had earnings above a low ceiling. A widowed mother's allowance consisted of a "widow's element" and an additional stipend for each dependent child.

What, then, did mothers do at home that was so important that they had to be supported throughout their lives to enable them to stay there? "Married women must be regarded as occupied on work which is vital though unpaid, without which their husbands could not do their paid work and ... the nation could not continue," Beveridge asserted (Cmnd. 6404 (1942): para. 107). Beveridge was, however, extremely vague about what these "vital unpaid services" were. In closing the section about "recognition of housewives as a distinct insurance class" he declared: "In the next thirty years housewives as mothers have vital work to do in ensuring the adequate continuance of the British race and of British ideals in the world" (Cmnd. 6404 (1942): para. 117). This is the only mention in this section of the report of what housewives are actually expected to do. There is no explicit mention in the Beveridge report of practical work related to children's needs or other domestic chores, nor is there any discussion of how this vital unpaid work might vary between different classes nor over the life course. The Minister of National Insurance, in introducing the White Paper based on the Beveridge report, emphasized more strongly women's ongoing relationship with children:

> I reduced [the qualifying age for widow's pension] to 40 because I believe it is important ... that mothers should be enabled, without undue anxiety, to stay at home and look after the family during the period of adolescence. (HC debates, 6 February 1946, quoted in Cmnd. 9684 (1956): para. 42)

This way of thinking clearly saw children as dependents with continuous need for their mother's care, not as people with an increasing capacity to look after themselves and even help out in the household. With the adjustments made to Beveridge's draft by the politicians following him, widowed mothers were in all but a few cases secured a lifelong pension. The targeting of this measure was arguably somewhat clumsy – widows who were younger than 40 when their youngest children turned 16 lost out – but a lifelong pension was nevertheless the intention. With the introduction of a lifelong pension, the mother was, in principle, enabled to stay at home and look after her family until all children had married and left home. This provision reinforces the impression left from Beveridge's outline: that the role of housewife was not linked to actual tasks – such as the workload in the family household – but rather was an intrinsic function, that of wife and mother. Wives and mothers belonged in the private sphere, and while it was assumed they would be occupied with some private tasks, these were of little public interest. Policy-makers themselves had no legitimate interest in determining when a mother should be required to leave the private sphere. What mattered, essentially, was the late husband's contributions to National Insurance and the presence of children from the marriage.

Some modifications to this scheme were made in 1956 (Cmnd. 9684 (1956); Skevik 2001a: 203). The most important of these was that the widow's element of the pension became payable until the child turned 18, provided the child resided with the mother. Simultaneously, the qualifying age for widow's pension increased from 40 to 50. The lower age limit had been introduced in order to allow the widow to stay at home with her children even after the youngest child had turned 16 – by increasing the age limit for children to 18, the government left no reason to qualify the widowed mother for a lifelong benefit. The aim was the same, but the targeting measure more refined.

Aside from these changes, little happened until 1964, when a Labour government took office with a strong commitment to social policy improvements (Glennerster 1995). One of the first acts of the new government was to upgrade most pensions to combat poverty among pensioners. For widows in receipt of National Insurance benefits, however, the main "upgrade" would be the abolition of the earnings rule (Kathleen Kiernan, Hilary Land, and Jane Lewis 1998: 165). Widows would retain their full pension regardless of how much money they made from employment. Although the aim of reducing poverty among widows was widely accepted, the reform was criticized for muddling the principles on which the widow's pension and widowed mother's allowance were based. The logic of the 1946 scheme was that entitlement to widow's pension should be a compensation for low earnings capacity. Low earnings capacity was defined as a straightforward function of age (widow's pension) and motherhood (widowed mother's allowance). After 1964, widow's benefits became *fixed-level, categorical* benefits payable in full to widowed women whose husbands had a contribution record, and who met one out of two additional criteria: they were over 50, or they had children under 16 or 18 in full-time education.[2] For widows who fulfilled these criteria, earnings capacity – or indeed actual earnings – did not matter. The new system clearly provided these widows a strong incentive to work outside the home, yet judging from the debate, this effect was unintended. Apparently, the politicians were indifferent about how the widowed mothers reconciled paid and unpaid work – the 1964 reform was motivated solely by anti-poverty concerns.

From 1964 to 2001, there were few changes to widows' benefits in the UK.[3] In April 2001, the entire system was made gender-neutral and the benefits renamed accordingly: Bereavement Allowance replaced Widow's Pension; Bereavement Payment replaced Widow's Payment; and Widowed Parent's Allowance replaced Widowed Mother's Allowance. Unlike Widow's Pension, Bereavement Allowance is payable for only fifty-two weeks. The abolition of a lifelong pension for widows is in tune with the New Labour government's welfare-to-work strategy. This strategy has, however, not yet reached widowed parents, who can still receive benefits as long as they have children under 16, or under 19 in full-time education.

The main argument for granting men rights as widowers was that working women also paid contributions into National Insurance – contributions that were lost to the family when the woman died. Neither men nor women receive any specific entitlements if the late spouse did not have a sufficient contribution record. In such cases they will have to apply for means-tested income support, like other lone parents with little or no income from work.

NORWAY: "IT MUST BE MORE SATISFACTORY TO HAVE PAID EMPLOYMENT"

Norway did not introduce a national widow's benefit until 1964. Previously, many municipalities paid out benefits to widows, and some widows were covered by their late husbands' work-related pension schemes, but many widows went entirely without benefit rights (Skevik 2001a). One might think that this later timing of the national benefit scheme in itself would lead to Norway applying more "modern" principles than the UK, but this was not necessarily so: the ideology of housewifery was still strong in Norway in the early 1960s. Women had high employment rates in the wartime UK, which might have challenged the traditional ideology of women's duties expressed in the Beveridge report. Moreover, Norway in 1964 was still a rural society with a high proportion of its workforce in the primary industries (agriculture, fishing, forestry), while the UK was fully industrialized and urbanized even in 1946. As late as 1960, 43 percent of the Norwegian population lived in rural areas (Kari Skrede 1986). In small family businesses, such as farms, both men and women worked together in the common enterprise, with children contributing to the extent their age and ability allowed. This would influence the ways in which mothers' employment outside the household was seen. Norway in 1964 was not necessarily more "modern" than the UK in 1946 – but it was different.

In Norway, the Family Pension Committee (appointed in 1959) played a role similar to that of the Beveridge committee in the UK with regard to widows' and mothers' benefits. They thoroughly discussed the matter and presented a proposal, which was modified somewhat by the Ministry of Social Affairs. The late timing of these benefits in Norway implied that a larger work was already in progress: the unified National Insurance Scheme was implemented in 1967, only three years after the widows' and mothers' pensions were established. Benefits for widows were integrated into the National Insurance Scheme, again with some modifications. Thus, in Norway, three models of protection for widowed mothers were presented in rapid succession: the 1962 proposal of the Family Pension Committee; the 1964 Widows' and Mothers' Pension Act; and the provisions for widows under the National Insurance Scheme. It is worth noting that a pure widow's pension was never suggested: all three proposals made widows and unmarried mothers their target group. They argued that those two groups would have similar needs, since neither could rely on help from the child's other parent. This characteristic set them apart from separated and divorced parents, who would be entitled to alimony if the marriage had severely reduced their earnings capacity. Since the interest here is in widows, I will deal only very briefly with the benefits for unmarried mothers (but see Skevik 2001a: 107).

The first outline of a widow's and mother's benefit was presented by the Family Pension Committee's report of 1962. This committee strongly emphasized that the pension should not be an alternative to paid employment:

> In the Committee's assessment ... the dominant view has been that it must be a more satisfactory solution for the lone woman, if possible, to have paid employment so that she can support herself, than to enter a situation in which she is lastingly dependent on public support. ... Among other things, it will give more personal satisfaction to solve work-related tasks and come into contact with other people, than to risk feeling isolated and lonely. (Family Pension Committee report, p. 17, translated by author)

The Family Pension Committee argued that no woman should be awarded a lifelong benefit on the basis of widowhood alone. The local social security board should assess her benefit requirement on a discretionary basis, taking into account the woman's situation and qualifications, as well as the local labor markets, before awarding the benefit. In principle, neither mothers nor older widows should have an automatic right to a lasting benefit. There were, however, circumstances in which paid employment would not be a good, or even a realistic, solution. These would include if the woman was old and had not been in employment for very many years, or if the woman had young children. In these cases, some form of benefit should be available.

The committee therefore proposed a new set of *means-tested* benefits payable to widows and unmarried mothers. Widows with young children and unmarried mothers who qualified would be awarded a "provisioning benefit." This should be payable as long as the family included children under 7. Older widows (over 60) should be awarded a widow's pension. Widows younger than 60 who did not have children under 7 should not be entitled to any benefit, but be expected to provide for themselves and their children on their own. In addition, the committee proposed an education benefit to help the women in question increase their qualifications and thereby increase their chances in the labor market. In the latter two respects, this scheme differed substantially from what existed in the UK.

The Ministry of Social Affairs agreed with the committee that for many widows, the problem was one of lack of employment experience. However, the ministry rejected the committee's emphasis on means-testing, arguing that Norwegian social policy tried to avoid such testing. The benefits proposed by the committee were maintained, but they were to be earnings-tested (that is, reduced for current earnings) rather than means-tested (tested against assets and other property). In addition, the ministry introduced a lump-sum payment, called the "one-time-allowance" (*engangsstønad*), payable to widows immediately after bereavement and to unmarried mothers after delivery, and a "helping allowance" to offset childcare costs. The latter benefit was to be flat rate and payable to widows and unmarried mothers who needed childcare because they had taken up employment or education. Like the education benefit, it was intended to be an incentive to enter the labor market.

The government argued that given the "current rights and opportunities for women in the labor market," there was no reason to introduce an unconditional right to support (Ot. prp. no. 34 (1963–64): 9). Widows who fully supported themselves and their families were not to receive a widow's pension. In principle, the government intended that the pension also not be paid to widows who were seen as *able* to support themselves, with earnings capacity rather than actual earnings the central criterion. Because each application was to be assessed by the local board, no upper or lower age limits were introduced – neither for the widow nor for her children. To protect low-earning widows, the pension was graded in four levels: nil, one-third, two-thirds, and the full pension. The full pension would equal that received by old-age pensioners, a fixed amount determined in relation to estimated living costs. This would be payable to widows with no earnings at all, while lower levels of pension would be paid to widows with some earnings.

When the Labour government's White Paper was presented to the Storting (the Norwegian legislative assembly) in 1963, the heavy emphasis on labor market participation caused anxiety. The standing committee on social security had no concrete objections to the government's proposal, but strongly emphasized that the social security boards should exercise their decision-making authority with flexibility. Within the Storting, there was a striking lack of political conflict. The idea of protecting widows and unmarried mothers was uncontroversial, as were the principles of the pension.

Yet although the general impression is one of unanimity, many representatives in the Storting were concerned about the relationship between the benefit entitlement and the duty of widows to provide for themselves. This concern translated into words of caution to the local social security boards. A number of speakers used the opportunity to praise housewives and to emphasize both the value of their work and their impression that these women were both active and enterprising. Never-theless, this was mainly a symbolic battle, since the Storting voted unanimously in favor of a benefit arrangement that was clearly oriented toward employment (Liv Syltevik 1996: Skevik 2001a).

The interesting thing about the symbolic battle for the housewives' honor, followed by a unanimous vote to encourage paid employment, was that politicians apparently saw no contradiction between the two principles. Precisely because housewives were seen as hardworking and enterprising, one could assume they would be eager to take up paid employment as soon as their situation allowed. Encouraging employment for women did not imply that the housewife's role was not important. Rather, it was based on the assumption that work in the home did not require the full attention of the woman forever. As soon as the children grew older, housework could be performed as a part-time job – indeed, the woman might be bored if she had no other outlets for her energies.

The 1964 widow's and mother's pension was met with enthusiasm in the Storting, and it was passed without fundamental controversies. Shortly after its implementation, however, reports started coming in from the social security boards, pointing out the perceived injustices in the new system. The main criticism was that widows working outside the home were excluded from the pension because of the inflexible rules of earning capacity. This was presented as a class issue: compared with better-off women, poor women were more likely to work outside the home while married. When the husband died, the often weary and overworked widow was forced to continue in her job. Widows from higher social strata, on the other hand, who often had other nonemployment income, could live comfortably on their widow's pension. Adding to this was the view of the four-step grading system for widow's pensions as far too inflexible and unreasonable, creating poverty traps. Finally, widowers had no entitlement under the 1964 scheme, something that was perceived as unfair.

The National Insurance Scheme, introduced in 1967, gave widowers the same rights as widows. Moreover, it replaced the previous flat-rate pensions with a system of basic pensions plus earnings-related supplements. Integrating widow's pension into this framework implied granting a maximum pension depending on the earnings of the deceased. If the deceased did not have earnings that entitled him or her to the earnings-related pension, the surviving spouse would still be entitled to the basic pension. The government emphasized this in order to drive home the important principle that a bereaved person's social rights to benefits were essentially individual, not derived; though the level at which they were paid would depend on their deceased partner's contribution. Following the principle of individual rights, also, children were given a separate entitlement to a children's pension (Anne Skevik 2003). Moreover, as the National Insurance was centralized and relied on codified rules, the power of the social security boards was taken away. The 1967 system left little room for discretion and required clarification of the principle of income testing. Earnings lower than half the basic pension would be disregarded entirely. For earnings above this level, the pension would be withheld at a 40 percent rate. These rules tapered pensions off gradually and strongly reduced the possibility that widows, widowers, and their children would be trapped in poverty.

The question of how long parents should be supported to stay at home remained. The 1967 Act simply stated that benefits to cover daily expenditure (that is, the widow's pension) should be available to surviving spouses who were "temporarily unable to provide for themselves due to care for children or [lack of qualifications]" (National Insurance Act 1996). It appears that this rule was interpreted liberally. In 1980, governmental regulations stipulated that lone parents could continue to receive full benefits until their children finished third grade, "provided that the child is by then sufficiently self-reliant in practical matters such as dressing, eating etc." (Governmental guidelines 10/1980, quoted in Lars Inge Terum 1993: 41). This decree, the government argued, was nothing more than a codification of existing practice. Thus, eligibility criteria were always explicitly linked to the domestic workload, and the debate focused on finding the right time, in terms of children's ages and development, to draw the line. The education benefit and the childcare benefit (formerly the helping allowance) were maintained in the 1967 system, to ease widows' transition into employment.

DISCUSSION

This discussion of the historical development of benefits for widowed mothers in Norway and the UK has highlighted important differences.

- In the UK, entitlements for widows depend entirely on the deceased spouses' contributions, while in Norway such benefits are the individual rights of surviving spouses. The contributions of deceased spouses affect only the level at which benefits are paid. Widowed mothers (later, widowed parents) in the UK receive benefits with additions for children, while orphans in Norway have a separate right to children's pensions.
- Widowers had no specific entitlements in the UK before 2001, while the Norwegian system has been gender-neutral since 1967.
- The right to benefits to cover daily expenditures in Norway has always depended on the youngest child's age, and has at no time continued beyond the child's tenth year. In the UK, entitlements remain until the youngest child is 16 or, in some cases, 19; prior to 1956, receipt of widowed mother's allowances led most mothers directly to lifelong pensions.
- From its inception in 1964, the Norwegian system has included benefits to encourage employment (an education benefit and a childcare

benefit). Such provisions have been much more limited in the UK, though financial support for childcare has improved since 1999 (see Lewis 2003: 224 for details).

- Widows and widowed mothers in Norway are not, in principle, entitled to wage replacement benefits if they provide for themselves through employment or are deemed able to do so. In the UK, the widowed mother's earnings capacity – or even her actual earnings – is not relevant.

It would be useful in this context also to compare levels of benefits. After all, entitlements are of little value if they provide only pocket money. Such a comparison would, however, require a separate study, given the wide variations in how benefits are determined: by ages of claimants (in the UK), by the earnings of the deceased (in Norway), by the number of children, and by other factors. Moreover, even if a widow must supplement her rights-based benefit with a means-tested benefit, she will face different benefit regimes in the two countries, given the different structures of the two social assistance schemes (see, for example, Lødemel 1997). Applying for means-tested supplements might not be the same process in Norway as in the UK, and again, the supplement awarded might vary widely. I will therefore not explore the question of benefit levels here (for a comparison of family benefits across different countries, see Bradshaw and Finch 2002).

My last three bullet points above (covering, respectively, the right to benefits for daily expenditures in Norway, the Norwegian emphasis on employment, and the Norwegian stress on earnings capacity) illustrate how Norway's policies assumed adults would provide for themselves through their own earnings. Exemptions from this duty to work for pay had to be justified. Widowed mothers could justify such an exemption by showing that family work was so demanding it precludes work outside the home. Yet as soon as the family workload decreased – when the children grew older – this justification was no longer valid, and the widowed mother had to start looking for employment.

In the UK, on the other hand, some categories of the population have been exempt by default from the duty to provide for themselves. No widowed mother had to justify why she should not work outside the home. Beveridge described a mother's role as "vital though unpaid work," while others among his contemporaries – including the Minister for National Insurance – explicitly linked this role to children's continued need for maternal care. Mothers should be enabled to be full-time mothers until their youngest children took up employment or turned 18 (later 19); that is, until the child could be defined as an adult. Of course, a teenage child is normally able to dress herself and eat independently, and can be left unsupervised for a few hours. Thus, when policy makers conceive of the mother's continued presence in the home as important, they cannot believe the child's demand for practical help takes up most of the day, as would be the case with a toddler. Rather, the policy-makers seem to imply the mother is needed to provide support and security for, and to exert a certain control on, the potentially rebellious teenager.

That the UK and Norway have established such different entitlements for widows implies that their policy-makers hold opposing views on children's abilities to help in the household. Having teenagers in the house can be quite work-intensive: they have clothes that must be cleaned and mended, they must be fed (in the case of some boys, almost unstoppably), and they tend to forget essentials like wiping their feet and tidying up after themselves. UK politicians therefore did not need to worry that a widowed mother of teenagers would lack for duties around the house. But teenage children can also be helpful. A mother can reasonably expect their aid with cooking and cleaning, looking after younger siblings, and other everyday activities. Norwegian politicians seem to have assumed that when a child completes third grade, he or she requires less help and can increasingly become a resource for the parent. When the children became old enough to manage day-to-day activities on their own, the mother was expected to take up employment outside the household.

My analysis seems to run counter to the standard descriptions of the two countries in much social policy literature, inspired by the influential work of Gösta Esping-Andersen (1990). According to this literature, Norway and the UK are, respectively, "social-democratic" and "liberal." But it was the UK that "decommodified" widows' labor by guaranteeing benefits for very long periods, sometimes for the rest of their lives (before 2001). Norway, by contrast, expected commodification and put in place a pension system with far stricter eligibility criteria – although the rules were implemented relatively liberally. Once again, as other scholars have also pointed out, Esping-Andersen's (1990) framework seems to have little explanatory power when it comes to the actual integration of women in welfare states[4] (see also Lewis 1992; Julia O'Connor 1993; Ann S. Orloff 1993; Diane Sainsbury 1994). But what of the current scholarship on the male-breadwinner model, which has had an explicit emphasis on family organization and gender roles?

The Norwegian model of widow's benefits conforms to the "family economy worker" model outlined above, which is in turn associated with the family economic gender model (Pfau-Effinger 1999). Norwegian benefits for surviving spouses were developed for the widows (and since 1967, widowers) of self-employed workers in the primary industries, who still made up a large proportion of the population by the 1960s. The gender-neutrality, which was introduced early on, indicates that men and women were seen as interdependent within marriage. Women's work meant as much to the family's welfare as men's. That the benefit ended no later than when the youngest child finished third grade, indicates – as

109

outlined above – that older children were seen as a resource to the family at least as much as an added workload. In rural households, children have always had duties and carried at least some of their own weight. And finally, the fact that entitlements to survivor's benefit was an individual right that did not depend on the deceased spouse's contributions demonstrates that the rights of those working in the private sphere were not mediated through the spouse working in the public sphere: home-based workers and their children had separate entitlements (see also Skevik 2003).

The UK model for widow's benefits seems more in tune with the "caring mother" model, associated with Pfau-Effinger's male-breadwinner/female-home-carer model. The image of the typical recipient of these benefits is not a farming woman, but the wife of a deceased blue- or white-collar worker, caring for the family home. That until 2001, a widow's benefit was available only to women highlights an image of female dependence rather than one of mutual co-dependence within marriage. The 2001 reform must also be seen as a sign of the growing recognition of the dual-earner family in the UK, as well as an overall policy effort to make benefits gender-neutral. The reform is an indication of the move away from traditional male-breadwinner assumptions in the UK, but does not challenge the basic argument made here.

That the benefit is available as long as there are dependent children in the household suggests two points: first, that UK policy-makers assume that women as mothers belong by default to the private sphere; second, that they view children primarily as dependents with a continuous need for care more than as economic resources to the family. Finally, there is no individual right to a bereaved person's benefit in the UK; widow's entitlements have always depended on the late husband's contributions to National Insurance. This requirement signals a strict division between the public and private spheres, according to which social rights are bestowed only upon those who earn an income in the public sphere. Other people, including both widowers and widows of men with an insufficient contribution record, are limited to claiming benefits under the heavily means-tested Income Support scheme.

The analysis also suggests that the male-breadwinner model is a somewhat blunt instrument for making sense of how different welfare states treat women in different situations. There are variations within the traditional male breadwinner model that the uniform concept overlooks. The multifaceted approach Pfau-Effinger (1999) suggests seems more promising as an analytical tool, but must be developed further to enable researchers to better grasp the treatment of (different categories of) lone mothers. My identification of the divergent models for widowed mother's benefits in Norway and the UK indicates the need to differentiate between two traditional models: both assume that mothers will work in the home, but for different reasons and with different inbuilt dynamics. Differentiating between systems that view women as "caring mothers" and "family economy workers" helps us make sense of the different trajectories of change: both Norway and the UK began by basing their welfare programs on traditional approaches to family life, but these traditionalisms were of different natures. The Norwegian transformation toward a dual-breadwinner regime, including the more radical activation policies for lone parents, underscores an essential difference: that being a wife and mother had never been seen as fundamentally incompatible with being a worker, even if for short periods of time family duties might become sufficiently time-consuming to preclude employment.

In Norway, eligibility for benefits has historically depended on the amount of work to be undertaken at home, largely defined by children's ages and capabilities, as well as the availability of high-quality childcare. Policy-makers saw paid employment for women in practical terms, as a matter of women organizing their working days to accommodate their jobs and their families. In the UK, the architects of the welfare state viewed paid employment as incompatible with a woman's essential support role, whether as wife or mother, and this perception has rendered the country's institutions far more resistant – albeit not immune – to change.

ACKNOWLEDGMENTS

This article is based on research undertaken as part of my doctoral project, funded by the Norwegian Ministry of Social Affairs and NOVA – Norwegian Social Research, and draws on material presented in Chapter 6 of my dissertation (Skevik 2001a). I thank the special issue editors as well as two anonymous referees for comments on earlier drafts.

NOTES

[1] The different constructions of the categories are in themselves interesting features of the two social security systems. While the UK developed differentiated policies for unmarried, separated, divorced, and widowed mothers and fathers, Norway had a far more unified policy toward all categories of lone parents. While the construction of the categories is not the topic here, I have written extensively about this elsewhere (Skevik 2001a: Ch. 4).

[2] The age limit for children in full-time education was later increased to 19 years.

[3] The most important changes occurred with the 1986 Social Security Act, which increased the qualifying age for widow's pension to 55 years. Also, this Act replaced widow's allowance with a lump-sum payment of £1,000 called Widow's Payment (Skevik 2001a: 208).

[4] His point about the "red–green" class coalition – the influence of the farmers' organizations – in the formative phase of the Nordic welfare states does, however, resonate the argument made here.

REFERENCES

Bradshaw, Jonathan and Naomi Finch. 2002. *A Comparison of Child Benefit Packages in 22 Countries.* London: Department for Work and Pensions.

Brown, Joan C. 1989. *In Search of a Policy. The Rationale for Social Security Provision for One Parent Families.* London: National Council for One Parent Families.

Cass, Bettina. 1992. "Caring Work and Welfare Regimes: Policies for Sole Parents in Four Countries," in Sheila Shaver (ed.) *Comparative Perspectives on Sole Parents Policy: Work and Welfare,* SPRC Reports and Proceedings, No. 106. University of New South Wales, Australia.

Cmnd. 6404 (1942). *National Insurance and the Allied Services. The Beveridge Report.* London: HMSO.

Cmnd. 6550 (1944). *Social Insurance Part 1.* London: HMSO.

Cmnd. 9684 (1956). *Report of NIAC on the Question of Widow's Benefits.* London: HSMO.

Ellingsæter, Anne-Lise. 1999. "Dual Breadwinners between State and Market," in Rosemary Crompton (ed.) *Restructuring Gender Relations and Employment: the Decline of the Male Breadwinner,* pp. 40–59. Oxford: Oxford University Press.

Esping-Andersen, Gösta. 1990. *The Three Worlds of Welfare Capitalism.* Cambridge, UK: Polity Press.

Finch, Naomi. 2003. *Family Policies in the UK.* Report for the project "Welfare Policy and Employment in the Context of Family Change", presented at the meeting June 5–6, 2003, in Reykjavik, Iceland.

Glennerster, Howard. 1995. *British Social Policy since 1945.* Oxford: Blackwell.

Hobson, Barbara. 1994. "Solo Mothers, Social Policy Regimes and the Logics of Gender," in D. Sainsbury (ed.) *Gendering Welfare States,* pp. 170–87. London: Sage.

Kiernan, Kathleen, Hilary Land, and Jane Lewis. 1998. *Lone Motherhood in Twentieth-Century Britain.* Oxford: Clarendon Press.

Kilkey, Majella. 2000. *Lone Mothers between Paid Work and Welfare. The Policy Regime in Twenty Countries.* Aldershot, UK: Ashgate.

Kjeldstad, Randi. 2000. "Employment Strategy Policies and Lone Parenthood: The Case of Norway." *Social Politics* 7(3): 343–71.

Koren, Charlotte. 1997. *Trygd og omsorgsarbeid.* Report Series 17/97. Oslo: NOVA.

Land, Hilary. 2002. *Meeting the Child Poverty Challenge: Why Universal Childcare is Key to Ending Child Poverty.* London: The Daycare Trust.

Leira, Arnlaug. 1989. *Models of Motherhood. Welfare State Policies and Everyday Practices.* Report Series 07/89. Oslo: Institute of Social Research.

——. 1992. *Welfare States and Working Mothers.* Cambridge, UK: Cambridge University Press.

——. 1998. "Caring as Social Right: Cash for Child Care and Daddy Leave." *Social Politics* 5(3): 362–78.

——. 2002. *Working Parents and the Welfare State. Family Change and Policy Reform in Scandinavia.* Cambridge, UK: Cambridge University Press.

Lewis, Jane. 1992. "Gender and the Development of Welfare Regimes." *Journal of European Social Policy* 2(3): 159–73.

——. 2003. "Developing Early Years Childcare in England 1997–2002: The Choices for (Working) Mothers." *Social Policy and Administration* 37(3): 219–38.

—— with Barbara Hobson. 1997. "Introduction," in Jane Lewis (ed.) *Lone Mothers in European Welfare Regimes: Shifting Policy Logics*, pp. 1–20. London: Jessica Kingsley.

Lødemel, Ivar. 1997. *The Welfare Paradox. Income Maintenance and Personal Social Services in Norway and Britain, 1945–1966.* Oslo: Scandinavian University Press.

Marsh, Alan. 2001. "Helping British Lone Parents Get and Keep Paid Work," in Jane Millar and Karen Rowlingson (eds.) *Lone Parents, Employment and Social Policy: Cross-National Comparisons*, pp. 11–36. Bristol: Policy Press.

National Insurance Act of 1996, Royal Council 17. (June 1996), no. 12.

O'Connor, Julia S. 1993. "Gender, Class and Citizenship in the Comparative Analysis of Welfare Regimes: Theoretical and Methodological Issues." *British Journal of Sociology* 44(3): 501–18.

Orloff, Ann S. 1993. "Gender and the Rights of Citizenship: The Comparative Analysis of Gender Relations and the Welfare State." *American Sociological Review* 58(3): 303–28.

Ot. prp. no. 34. 1963–64. *1. Om lov om enkje-og morstrygd, 2. Om lover om endringer i lov om alderstrygd, lov om syketrygd og lov om forsørgertrygd for barn.*

Pateman, Carole. 1989. *The Disorder of Women.* Cambridge, UK: Polity Press.

Pedersen, Susan. 1993. *Family, Dependence and the Origins of the Welfare State. Britain and France 1914–1945.* Cambridge, UK: Cambridge University Press.

Pfau-Effinger, Birgit. 1999. "The Modernization of Family and Motherhood in Western Europe," in Rosemary Crompton (ed.) *Restructuring Gender Relations and Employment: The Decline of the Male Breadwinner*, pp. 40–59. Oxford: Oxford University Press.

Sainsbury, Diane (ed.). 1994. *Gendering Welfare States.* London: Sage.

Sainsbury, Diane. 1996. *Gender, Equality and Welfare States.* Cambridge, UK: Cambridge University Press.

——. 1999. "Gender and Social-Democratic Welfare States," in Diane Sainsbury (ed.) *Gender and Welfare State Regimes*, pp. 75–114. Oxford: Oxford University Press.

Skevik, Anne. 2001a. *Family Ideology and Social Policy. Policies towards Lone Parents in Norway and the UK.* Report Series 7/01. Oslo: NOVA.

——. 2001b. "Lone Parents and Employment in Norway," in Jane Millar and Karen Rowlingson (eds.) *Lone Parents, Employment and Social Policy: Cross-National Comparisons*, pp. 87–106. Bristol: Policy Press.

——. 2003. "Children of the Welfare State: Individuals with Entitlements, or Hidden in the Family?" *Journal of Social Policy* 32(3): 423–40.

Skrede, Kari. 1986. "Gifte kvinner i arbeidslivet," in Lars Alldén, Natalie Rogoff Ramsøy, and Mariken Vaa (eds.) *Det norske samfunn*, pp. 145–67. Oslo: Gyldendal Norsk Forlag.

Statistics Norway. 2002. *Yearbook of Annual Statistics.* Oslo: Statistics Norway.

Statistics Norway. 2003. *Fem av seks barn bor med søsken.* Online. Available http://www.ssb.no/emner/02/01/20/barn/ (September 2003).

Syltevik, Liv. 1996. "Fra relasjonelt til individualisert alenemoderskap. En studie av alenemødre som mødre, lønnsarbeidere og klienter i velferdsstaten." Doctorate thesis submitted at the University of Bergen.

Terum, Lars Inge. 1993. *Stønad, samliv og sjølforsørging.* Report Series 01/93. Oslo: INAS.

THE COMMODIFICATION OF LONE MOTHERS' LABOR: A COMPARISON OF US AND GERMAN POLICIES

Lisa Giddings, Irene Dingeldey, and Susan Ulbricht

INTRODUCTION

Recent policy shifts in the United States (US) and in Germany have altered the terrain for lone mothers. Within different social contexts and through differences in budget priorities and political landscapes, these policies have generated different incentives for labor market behavior, especially among lone mothers. For example, in the US, welfare reform has imposed work requirements and limits on lifetime benefits for welfare recipients, while the Earned Income Tax Credit (EITC) has created monetary incentives to encourage labor market participation among lone mothers. In contrast, Germany now offers lone mothers a particular combination of benefits and financial resources that indirectly encourages labor market abstinence among lone mothers.

To analyze these policy shifts, we draw on Gøsta Esping-Andersen's use of the concept of commodification: to distinguish policy regimes by the extent to which people's economic survival is dependent on the sale of their labor power (1990: 21). Using feminist critiques of this analysis, we then attempt an alternative conceptualization of the differences between the US and German welfare state regimes. To contextualize this analysis, we compare and contrast the degree to which lone mothers have relied on the sale of their own labor power for survival in the United States and Germany over time by examining two dramatically different periods in the two countries: the US pre- and post-welfare reform (1996) and Germany pre- and post-unification (1990).

THEORETICAL BACKGROUND

In *The Three Worlds of Welfare Capitalism*, Esping-Andersen (1990) develops a typology of welfare-state regimes based on the concept of commodification of labor. The level of such commodification indicates the degree to which individuals must rely on the sale of their labor power for economic survival. According to Esping-Andersen, the "blossoming of capitalism came with the withering away of 'pre-commodified' social protection. ... When ... labor power also became a commodity, peoples' rights to survive outside the market [were] at stake" (1990: 35).

To be "precommodified" is to survive economically outside of the labor market. In the Middle Ages, for example, individuals were precommodified in the sense that they relied on social institutions such as the family, church, or lord for their economic survival. Post-industrial individuals, in contrast, depend "entirely on the cash nexus" and are stripped of the institutional layers that "[guarantee] social reproduction outside [of] the labor contract" (Esping-Andersen 1990: 22).

The commodity status of labor lies at the heart of nineteenth-century debates over the "social question" (or *Arbeiterfrage*, in Germany) and, ultimately, the creation of the modern welfare state. This question acknowledges that an individual's labor power is a unique commodity. In contrast to other commodities that are bought and sold as and when required, workers (the owners of labor power) must survive and reproduce both themselves and the society in which they live. Further, labor market power is vulnerable to the business cycle and can be destroyed by even minor social contingencies, like illness. As a result, pressures for the decommodification of labor evolve to protect labor from the vagaries of the free market.

The decommodification of labor pertains to the extent to which individuals are economically supported once they can no longer participate in the labor market, whether because of old age, illness, or forced unemployment–factors beyond the individual's control that limit the ability to garner a wage. In contrast to the notion of precommodification of labor, decommodification of labor implies an attachment to the labor force at some point in the worker's past (Esping-Andersen 1990: 37). The development of modern welfare states reflects the variety of policies enacted to decommodify labor. The debate about to what degree labor should be decommodified centers on "what degree of market immunity would be permissible; i.e. the strength, scope, and quality of social rights" (Esping-Andersen 1990: 37).

Many feminist critiques note that the typology of welfare states is only partly applicable to women and their welfare because the concept of decommodification of labor implies a prior commodification of labor. Other welfare-state typologies (Jane Lewis and Ilona Ostner 1994; Diane Sainsbury 1994, 1996) examine whether and how strongly welfare-state institutions offer *married* women as "home carers" a form of precommodified status, including social rights in pensions and health systems that are derived from their husbands' labor market positions and records.

Lone mothers (particularly never-married mothers) are a unique case to integrate into this typology, because, unlike the home carer, they lack the presumed male breadwinner. Absent a male breadwinner (or absent an indirect link to a deceased or divorced male breadwinner), never-married and divorced lone mothers[1] do not have access to any precommodified status – either their own, or that of a husband. One means of characterizing welfare states is by the degree to which they offer policies to substitute for the male breadwinner.

Our task is to call attention to the different types of commodification of lone mothers' labor in the US and Germany and to show how these differences influence the labor market participation rates of lone mothers. In doing so, we also distinguish the different levels of social protection that follow labor market participation, and we thus delineate varying rights to decommodification. We hypothesize that the increasing labor market participation rates among lone mothers in both countries result from very different policies and incentive structures; these structures are themselves related to the types of commodification of labor (and access to the decommodification of labor). Reinforcing the differences between the US and Germany are the varying institutional and demographic traits of lone mothers in the two countries.

To characterize a country's degree of commodification of labor, we distinguish between incentive structures that "enable" labor market participation and those that "enforce" it. Enabling structures are the "carrots" designed to encourage labor market participation; these include, for example, policies that reduce the cost of participating in the market. Thus, enabling policies might improve the supply and quality of childcare facilities or provide financial support during a defined period of leave for childbirth. Such policies provide temporary protection for survival outside

117

of the market, if necessary, and help mothers, particularly lone mothers without access to a male breadwinner, to balance work and family.

In contrast, enforcing structures are the "stick," characterized by requiring participants to work in order to obtain welfare benefits and by eventually withdrawing welfare benefits entirely. Under the logic of a workfare system, the labor market is the source of emancipation for individuals. The workfare system assumes that jobs are available for all those who want them and that the labor market will provide individuals with the ability ultimately to secure their own welfare, independent of the state. This system links access to social benefits with employment. Unlike other European-style welfare-state programs, however, the workfare system itself provides no access to decommodification; that is, little or no protection for survival outside of the market. The burden of protecting oneself from the vagaries of the market is on the individual: save money for retirement because the state will not provide enough for you to survive.

There are striking differences between the US and Germany in how the state enables and enforces the commodification of lone mothers' labor as well as in how it provides access to the decommodification of their labor. Policies based on the principle of the adult-worker model (as in the former East Germany, hereafter the German Democratic Republic or GDR) regarded lone mothers as workers and gave them more or less the same rights and protection as all other workers, enabling the commodification of lone mothers' labor. Policies based on the principle of the male-breadwinner model (as in the former West Germany, hereafter the Federal Republic of Germany or FRG) regarded all mothers, including lone mothers, as being primarily responsible for childcare. However, for a mother without a male breadwinner, the consequence was lifelong welfare dependence. For lone mothers in the FRG, one incentive therefore to take employment, and thereby escape such dependence, was to be able to access the pension and healthcare benefits of employment upon retirement. Here the commodification of lone mothers' labor can be considered to be voluntary, as it would be possible to survive, albeit with a lower level of benefits, without participating in the labor market.

Workfarism in the US commodifies lone mother's labor without providing access to the decommodification of labor, because benefits are not provided as a social right but instead derive primarily from labor market engagement. US workfare policies may acknowledge that many lone mothers have little or no education or experience and therefore access only to low-paid employment; as a result, the US state governments that implement the federal policy may provide some training and income transfers for childcare. However, in practice, these benefits are limited and often do little to help women secure their basic needs in any permanent way. In workfare as practiced in the US, given the context of insecure, low-wage employment, often without access to adequate healthcare or old-age pensions, the chance of obtaining adequate economic security is small for many lone mothers. To make matters worse, low-quality and precarious childcare works against lone mothers' chances of success in the labor market. The workfare system provides a massive degree of underprotection from the vagaries of the market and family life even while "enforcing" the commodification of lone mothers' labor. The following sections compare and analyze the policies directed at lone mothers in East and West Germany before and after unification, and in the US before and after the 1996 welfare reforms.

EVIDENCE OF COMMODIFICATION

East Germany, pre-unification – the GDR

Prior to the East German transition from a planned to a market economy, the political and public discourse concerning lone mothers focused on the image of "super women" (Martina Klett-Davies 1997). The aim of family policy in the GDR was to achieve continuous full-time employment for all women, including lone mothers. As a result, women juggled full-time work and the bulk of the domestic responsibilities, as well as political commitments that added up to more than a day's worth of work. As Table 1 indicates, women in the former GDR were much more likely to be employed than in West Germany during the same era (Deutsches Institut für Wirtschaftsforschung 1990). They also worked longer hours, were more likely to work full-time, and had fewer and shorter career breaks (Deutsches Institut für Wirtschaftsforschung 1990; Heike Trappe 1995). This situation was particularly true for lone mothers. By 1988, 89 percent of lone mothers were working full-time (Uwe-Jens Walther 1992), compared to 81 percent of all mothers and 77 percent of all women in the former GDR at the start of the transition in 1991 (Gerhard Bäcker, Reinhard Bispinck, Klaus Hofemann, and Gerhard Naegele 2000). As Figure 1 shows, these trends continued into the 1990s, when only approximately 15 percent of employed mothers in

Table 1 Female labor force participation rates: Germany

	FRG	GDR
1970	46	
1980	50	86
1990	58	85
1991	58	86

Source: DIW (1990); Elke Holst and Jürgen Schupp (1990); Walther (1992); Trappe (1995); Bäcker *et al.* (2000); Stefan Hradil (2001); Engstler and Menning (2003).

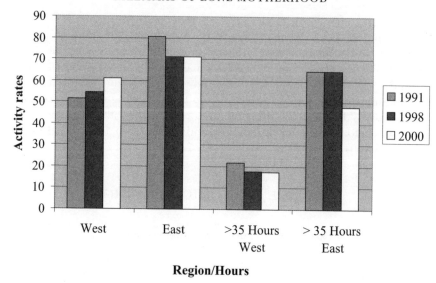

Source: DIW (1990); Holst and Schupp (1990); Walther (1992); Trappe (1995); Bäcker, Bispink, Hofemann, and Naegele (2000); Engster and Menning (2003).

Figure 1 German mothers' activity rates by region and hours worked.

the East worked less than 35 hours per week (Heribert Engstler and Sonja Menning 2003).

The high employment rates among mothers in the GDR resulted from steps taken during the 1970s, when the state instituted expansive neo-natal social policies. The goal was to increase birth rates without reducing female labor market participation (Gabriele Niepel 1994; Trappe 1995). The impetus for this spate of family-friendly policies was a declining birth rate and consequent fear of a future labor shortage. Some East German mothers criticized these policies as "mommy politics" (*Muttipolitik*), because they were based on the assumption that women were the primary caregivers and responsible for the home, and therefore applied only to women (Lynn Duggan 1995: 177). The policies included extended time off each week, shortened working hours, and paid time off to care for sick children; a few policies applied to men as well, including extended credit to married couples, whose loans would be reduced if they had children, and reduced rents.

These policies particularly favored lone mothers, who were guaranteed social protection and support by the constitution. For example, children of lone mothers received priority access to public daycare. When a child was sick or when daycare could not be provided, lone mothers were guaranteed paid leave (Jutta Gysi and Wulfram Speigner 1983; Gesine Obertreis 1986). In 1974, the state expanded the availability of nurseries and kindergartens, lowering the cost of childcare for all parents. The government provided childcare at no cost; parents paid only a minimal amount for meals. In 1976, the *Babyjahr* (or "Baby Year") was introduced, which allowed a lone mother to take a year of paid leave from work with her job guaranteed upon her return. Married mothers could take advantage of this regulation only after the birth of a second or subsequent child. Some researchers, noting that between 1980 and 1996, the proportion of births to unmarried women rose from 23 percent to 42 percent of the total, suggest that this policy encouraged cohabitation rather than marriage (Charlotte Hohn 1992: 9; Trappe 1995: 210). As a result of the *Babyjahr,* out-of-wedlock births in the GDR were not unusual, and they were not socially stigmatized (Oliver Razum, Albrecht Jahn, and Rachel Snow 1999).

The GDR exhibited a highly generalized commodification of all mothers' labor in the sense that nearly all women, including lone mothers, were required to participate in the labor market on a full-time basis. Political measures taken during central planning encouraged mothers, particularly lone mothers, to participate in the labor force with no social stigma attached to their situation. By providing childcare, financial support during a defined period of maternity leave, and the right to return to a particular occupation, this policy regime enabled commodification of all mothers' labor.

West Germany, pre-unification – the FRG

In contrast to the GDR, a public discourse on lone mothers was almost nonexistent in the FRG during the 1980s. Lone parents and their children were thought of as incomplete families and were socially stigmatized. Compared to other European countries (and in particular to the former GDR), the FRG displayed low rates of out-of-wedlock births (Razum, Jahn, and Snow 1999). Cultural norms followed the breadwinner model and dictated that mothers of children under the age of 3 stay at home to take care of their children (Ilona Ostner 1997). Mothers of older children were expected to work only part-time. Without requiring any extra contributions, the public insurance system gave full protection for healthcare to nonworking spouses and children, and the pension system gave rights to widows and orphans. Benefits for mothers were linked to marriage rather than to participation in the labor market (Irene Dingeldey 2001). Social policies for lone mothers in the FRG mirrored social norms by encouraging them to stay at home with their younger children, with the state substituting for the father/husband as the breadwinner in case of need.

During the 1980s, a childrearing benefit (*Erziehungsgeld*) was introduced for all mothers. The benefit was income-based, and granted for the first two years after birth (during parental leave). It supplemented existing parental leave benefits and had rapidly declining income limits after the first six months. For those relying on social transfers (social assistance or unemployment), the childrearing benefit was more generous. For all mothers on social assistance, primarily lone mothers, there were strong financial incentives to stay at home in the first two years (in some regions the benefit was even given for a third year). For mothers with older children, social institutions continued to reinforce the social norm. Childcare institutions (kindergarten was provided for children 3 years old and above) and schools (for children 6 years old and above) operated on a part-time basis. As late as 1990, while kindergartens were attended by 73 percent of eligible children, preschool was provided to 2 percent of children younger than 3 years old, and after-school care was provided for just 3 percent of school-aged students (Bäcker *et al.* 2000: 212). Furthermore, parents were expected to interrupt their work and join their children for the *Mittagesse*, or midday meal. In short, both financial and social incentives encouraged mothers to place childrearing over participation in the labor market.

As Table 1 shows, the labor force participation rate of women in the former FRG was 46 percent in 1970 (Bäcker *et al.* 2000). Among mothers, the activity rate was 40 percent in 1972, with only 21 percent working more than 35 hours per week (Engstler and Menning 2003). From 1970 to 1990, female labor force participation in the West increased substantially, to 52 percent in 1991 (Figure 1) (Bäcker *et al.* 2000). A majority of lone mothers worked full-time, and they were more likely to be in paid employment than either married or cohabiting mothers (Klett-Davies 1997). About 57 percent worked full-time in 1988 (Elke Holst and Jürgen Schupp 1990; Walther 1992).

The policy regime in the former FRG upheld the prevailing social norms by providing no enabling or enforcing strategies to commodify lone mothers' labor. Policies that supported the breadwinner model strongly encouraged lone mothers to remain out of the labor market. While the former GDR attempted to integrate women into the labor force by adopting enabling policies that made motherhood compatible with full-time employment, the former FRG "based its family policy on the assumption of a stark gender division of labor, with one lifetime breadwinner per family and a second parent who temporarily leaves the labor force to raise children" (Duggan 1995: 175–6). Nevertheless, most lone mothers worked. While the benefits provided by the state under the substitute-breadwinner model allowed lone mothers to attain a precommodified status, they provided no rights to other benefits associated with decommodification of labor, like old-age pensions or social security. Long periods of receiving benefits could therefore create lifelong dependence on social assistance. The fear of becoming dependent motivated many FRG women to rely only temporarily on social assistance (Wolfgang Voges and Ilona Ostner 1995) and instead opt to participate in the labor market. They sought to eventually obtain individual pension rights and access to future decommodification of their labor power.

Unified Germany

The labor market participation rate of women in general, and mothers in particular, is still substantially higher in the East than in the West. However, trends show that mothers' labor market participation rates are increasing in the West and decreasing in the East (Statistisches Bundesamt, Mikrozensus 1994, 1998). By 1991 (the start of the transition), the activity rate among mothers in the West was 52 percent, with slightly more than 20 percent working more than 35 hours per week (Figure 1). The largest increase was in those working part-time. In the East, activity rates among mothers remained greater than 80 percent, with 64 percent working more than 35 hours per week (Figure 1).

By 2000, the activity rates of mothers in the East and West had grown closer. In the West, the activity rate of mothers increased to 61 percent, with 18 percent working more than 35 hours per week; the corresponding figures in the East were 71 percent and 48 percent, respectively (Engstler and Menning 2003). By 2000, 26 percent of all couples with children under the age of 15 were dual income, with the mother working part-time in 33 percent of such couples (Irene Dingeldey and Silke Reuter 2003).

The decline in labor force participation rates in the East did not result from a shift in mothers' attitudes toward attaining a precommodified status for their labor, but rather from several factors associated with the East's transition from planned economy to a mixed one, as well as unification with the West. After unification, work was no longer mandated by the state. In addition, social norms retained their bias toward the male-breadwinner model (with policies reflecting these norms) and the state failed to adopt the East's enabling policies. As a result, East German women in unified Germany lost a degree of economic independence. "Like West German women, East German women ... increasingly [had to] decide between career and motherhood; if their choice [was] motherhood, they [had to] decide between sporadic employment and none at all" (Duggan 1995: 189).

In unified Germany, lone mothers on social assistance had no obligation to work as long as their youngest child was under the age of 3. In most cases, lone mothers were not seriously expected to work until their children were 12 years old. Social policies such as childrearing benefits (*Erziehungsgeld*), parental leave (*Erziehungsurlaub*), and social assistance (*Sozialhilfe*) encouraged mothers to remain out of the labor market. Lone mothers could combine social assistance and childrearing benefits, reaching a level of income similar to that of working women in low-income groups. By the late 1990s, about 15 percent of all lone parents relied on social assistance. The numbers were higher in the West (17 percent of all lone parents) than in the East (8 percent) (Statistisches Bundesamt 2001: 24).

While financial benefits encouraged mothers to stay at home, the increasing costs of childcare (particularly from the perspective of mothers from the former GDR) reinforced the incentive for mothers to care for their own children. Most childcare costs were socialized in the former GDR, and mothers expected such support in unified Germany as well (Trappe 1995). In contrast to this expectation, not only did the state childcare subsidies vanish, but so did the availability of state-run childcare. Even though coverage remained higher in the East than in the West, fewer places were available in childcare facilities, and when they did exist they were no longer as inexpensive as they had been in the GDR.

In addition, influenced by the above factors, the decline in employment among women reflected the extremely high rates of overall unemployment in the East after unification. At the start of the transition, unemployment in the East reached as high as 25 percent of the workforce in some areas; by 1991, it remained at almost 14 percent, nearly double the level in the West. Empirical evidence suggests that lone mothers were hit harder than married mothers by rising unemployment and cuts in childcare (Statistisches Bundesamt, Mikrozensus 1994, 1998).

Despite strong incentives to stay at home, most lone mothers combined employment and motherhood in unified Germany, as had been the case in the former FRG (Trappe 1995; Klett-Davies 1997). In 1999, 24 percent of lone parents with children younger than 6 years of age were working full-time, and 24 percent were working part-time (Eurostat 2002). In 2001, the labor force participation rate of lone mothers was higher (66 percent) than that of married mothers (64 percent). Because the combination of social assistance and child subsidies provides only a basic income for lone mothers, many choose to participate in the labor force in order to gain access to pension and health benefits upon retirement. Participation now provides access to the decommodification of labor in the future. Some researchers also argue that women who live in the former GDR consider economic independence and full-time participation in the labor market a "matter of course" (Michael Braun, Jacqueline Scott, and Duane A. Alwin 1994; Marina A. Adler 1997). Therefore, despite social support that could provide access to a precommodified status, women in the West would prefer working to lifelong welfare dependence.

United States, pre-welfare reform

Political and public discourse around what has come to be known as "welfare" in the United States has always been contentious, and particularly disdainful stereotypes have developed over time about the marital and racial status of mothers relying on state transfers. Social norms based on the Protestant work ethic, as well as on moral codes concerning out-of-wedlock births, blame lone women for their poverty and, as a result, recent policies prescribe work, personal responsibility for one's economic welfare, or marriage as the only acceptable ways to escape poverty.[2]

Brief history

Both centralized (federal) and decentralized (state) support for mothers in the United States originated in the early 1900s.[3] Between 1911 and 1920, forty states legislated "mothers' pensions" for all mothers, regardless of marital status, that allowed them to stay home and care for their children rather than work outside the home. At the federal level, the Social Security Act of 1935 created the Aid to Dependent Children program (what was to become the Aid to Families with Dependent Children or AFDC program), which incorporated the state pensions for mothers. The federal program created racial divides in the distribution of benefits to women, as Southern congressmen formed a powerful voting bloc and were able to retain the rights to establish eligibility criteria and benefit levels, ensuring that most of the initial beneficiaries throughout the country were white, widowed women with young children. Benefit levels in the South (where the majority of black women then resided) were much lower than elsewhere (Jill Quadagno 1994).

In 1939, changes in the federal program created new divisions. New legislation shifted white widows from AFDC to old-age insurance (both black and white widows were eligible for social security by the age of 62, but this shift allowed young white widows to access the insurance earlier), and the remaining beneficiaries of AFDC were mainly never-married and deserted mothers (Quadagno 1994). This created a dual system of social insurance and means-tested public assistance, in which social insurance was linked to contributory participation, while AFDC was reserved for those who could not claim access through marriage or legitimate paternity to a (deceased) male breadwinner. The new dual system provided much more generous provisions as a uniform entitlement under the insurance program and a punitive, vulnerable, and highly variable system of benefits under AFDC. Furthermore, it created a "de facto separation of the welfare income transfer program from the world of work and labor market policies" (Hugh Helco 2001).

The mid-1960s saw a dramatic increase in the number of welfare recipients and a shift in the social perception of welfare. From 1966 to 1967 alone, the number of welfare recipients grew from 7.8 to 8.4 million (Quadagno 1994). This increase resulted in part from a burgeoning welfare rights movement (an offshoot of the civil rights movement), in which African-American women, many of whom now lived in Northern urban areas, began claiming the entitlements they had been denied (Linda

Gordon 2002). As more black women began claiming welfare, the media began to portray welfare negatively, and politicians engaged in more generalized efforts to force mothers into employment. According to Martin Gilens (1999), media coverage of the War on Poverty, a series of domestic programs that President Lyndon Johnson initiated in the mid-1960s, and the urban riots put racialized images into the public domain that encouraged viewers to associate poverty, welfare, and race. In 1967, the US Congress enacted the Work Incentive Program (WIN) as an amendment to the nation's welfare law (Thomas B. Edsall and Mary E. Edsall 1991). The amendment imposed the first federal work and training requirements and froze federal funds for AFDC cases caused by out-of-wedlock births or desertion (Quadagno 1994).[4]

Increased work requirements for welfare recipients and shifts in social attitudes toward welfare continued through the 1980s. By now, the male-breadwinner model had broken down (Helco 2001). Real male wages in the US began to decline during the late 1970s and many families needed two incomes to make ends meet. An increasing percentage of women (more than 60 percent by 1980), and particularly of married mothers, were participating in the labor market, while at the same time the public began to give up the notion that welfare mothers should be exempted from work so they could raise their children on a full-time basis (Steven M. Teles 1996, quoted in Lawrence M. Mead 2001: 203).

The Omnibus Budget Reconciliation Act of 1981 strengthened existing work provisions for welfare recipients (Gwendolyn Mink 1998: 41). By the mid-1980s, state policies aimed at enhancing employability created programs that pushed women to get job-training and begin job-hunting (Randy Albelda and Chris Tilly 2001). The Family Support Act (FSA) of 1988 included the Job Opportunity and Basic Skills program, which made welfare eligibility conditional on a lone mother's participation in a work, education, or training program (Mink 1998: 41). While the FSA recognized that lone mothers needed education, training, and childcare in order to move out of welfare, the Act placed greater work expectations on lone mothers than it did on married mothers, and it did not address the labor market inequalities that left the majority of lone mothers in poverty (Mink 1998). As a result, although poor lone mothers were required to hold jobs, many had no means to achieve economic independence through such jobs (Mink 1998: 42).

In 1988, the median welfare payment for a family of three was $388 per month, or 34 percent of the poverty line the government had established for that year (see note 8, below). Given inadequate wages for low-skilled workers in combination with low welfare benefits, many lone mothers either combined welfare and work or cycled between the two in order to make ends meet (Roberta Spalter-Roth, Heidi Hartmann, and Linda Andrews 1992). Studies of former AFDC recipients found that over one-fourth of women who received AFDC during a twenty-four-month period in the late 1980s also had had some form of employment or were actively seeking employment at the time they received welfare (Spalter-Roth, Hartmann, and Andrews 1992). By the end of the 1980s, the rhetoric of workfare (especially concerning lone mothers) was completely inscribed in the US welfare system, with the assumption that women could and should perform paid work and that doing so would provide economic independence.[5]

By the 1990s, both federal and state plans to reform welfare had moved from enhancing employability to requiring work (Albelda and Tilly 2001). At the state level, eligibility rules were stepped up to include increased sanctions that reduced or even eliminated welfare assistance for noncompliance. The new rules also included less substantive training and education, as well as harsh "behavior modification" rules (Albelda and Tilly 2001) including "family caps," which withheld compensation for children born while the mother received welfare, and a program called "learnfare," which reduced compensation if a child missed school.[6] On the eve of welfare reform in the US, lone mothers were entitled to cash benefits from the government; however, their labor was not precommodified in that they were unable to survive economically outside of the labor market.

United States, post-welfare reform

The Personal Responsibility and Work Opportunity Reconciliation Act (PRWORA) of 1996 introduced dramatic changes to welfare provisioning in the US. The new law included five major components: block-grant funding, the elimination of a cash welfare entitlement, work requirements, sanctions, and time limits on the receipt of welfare benefits during one's lifetime (Avis Jones-DeWeever, Janice Peterson, and Xue Song 2003). Under the new law, the Temporary Aid to Needy Families (TANF) program replaced AFDC. TANF consists of a block grant provided to states to distribute to low-income families. Unlike AFDC, the TANF program does not require states to provide aid to all families eligible under state income standards. As a result, states are now free to determine the conditions and amounts of cash public assistance they will provide to poor families (Mark Greenberg, Jodie Levin-Epstein, Rutledge Hutson, Theodora Ooms, Rachel Schumacher, Vicki Turetsky, and David Engstrom 2000, quoted in Jones-DeWeever, Peterson, and Song 2003; US House of Representatives 2000).

The two programs also differ in work requirements. Whereas AFDC contained expectations about work requirements, TANF made work requirements a legal obligation by requiring adult recipients to work after twenty-four months of receiving benefits, or when a state decided the recipient was ready to work, whichever came first. Although work requirements differed across states, some states (including New York,

127

Massachusetts, California, Florida, Tennessee, Texas, and Wisconsin) compelled some mothers to work outside of the home almost immediately upon receipt of benefits (Mink 1998: 62).

In order to impose stringent work requirements, the designers of TANF sketched a broad definition of who was capable of working, excluding only disabled adults and parents with disabled children or children under the age of 1. Further, they explicitly defined which activities counted as work rather than leaving this up to the states. The definition did not include most education or long-term training activities that would better prepare individuals for the labor market.[7] The federal legislation mandated that states require substantial increases in labor market participation from those applying for welfare benefits, beginning with 25 percent of the caseload of lone parents (the requirements are higher for two-parent families) in 1997 and increasing to 50 percent of lone parents by 2002. Additionally, the number of required work hours for all parents receiving benefits increased from twenty hours per week in 1997 to thirty in 2000.

Lastly, TANF forced states to impose serious financial penalties on participants who failed to comply with the program requirements (Jason A. Turner and Thomas Main 2001). While federal law required states to, at a minimum, partially reduce benefits for families that failed to satisfy the work requirements, most states implemented stricter sanctions than those mandated by the federal government. By 2000, nearly all states had imposed time limits for receiving cash payments, but relatively few had developed limits that were more stringent than the federal limit. The federal law provided childcare funding at a higher level than had the old AFDC program; however, women leaving welfare were now only assured subsidies for one year.

Effects of welfare reform on labor force participation rates

Two of the main goals of the 1996 welfare reform Act were to raise employment among poor households and to discourage dependence on federal support. Strong evidence suggests that these goals were met. In particular, empirical evidence indicates that the labor force participation rate among lone mothers with children younger than age 18 increased sharply between 1995 and 1997 (Ron Haskins 2001), and studies have consistently shown that most families who left welfare found work (Patricia Loprest 1999; Jared Bernstein and Mark Greenberg 2001; Ron Haskins, Isabel Sawhill, and Kent Weaver 2001). One survey conducted by the Institute for Women's Policy Research found that from December 1995 to February 2000, the percentage of low-income parents who reported working rose from 60 to 69 percent (Jones-DeWeever, Peterson, and Song 2003).[8] The increase in paid employment was largest for lone mothers, with the percentage of those who reported working at some time during the

Table 2 Labor force participation rates for mothers in the US

	Total			With children under 6 years		
	Married	Lone	Other lone	Married	Lone	Other lone
1970	39.7	n.a.	60.7	30.3	n.a.	52.2
1980	54.1	52.0	69.4	45.1	44.1	60.3
1985	60.8	51.6	71.9	53.4	46.5	59.7
1990	66.3	55.2	74.2	58.9	48.7	63.6
1995	70.2	57.5	75.3	63.5	53.0	66.3
2000	70.6	73.9	82.7	62.8	70.5	76.6

Source: US Bureau of Labor Statistics (1988: Bulletin 2307) and unpublished data; US Census Bureau (2002a). Note "lone" indicates that the mother has never been married, "married" indicates that a husband is present, "lone other" indicates that the mother is widowed, divorced, or separated.

survey rising from from 58.5 percent to 68.1 percent (Jones-DeWeever, Peterson, and Song 2003).

These figures stand in marked contrast to historical labor force participation rates among different categories of women. Table 2 presents labor force participation rates for mothers in the US based on marital status. From the 1980s to the mid-1990s, married mothers consistently garnered higher labor force participation rates than never-married mothers. By 1995, 70 percent of married mothers participated in the labor market as compared to 58 percent of never-married mothers. However, by 2000, a larger percentage (74) of never-married mothers than married mothers (71) participated in the labor force (US Census Bureau 2002).

Empirical evidence also shows that the number of people receiving cash public assistance declined after welfare reform was enacted. In 1994, the national welfare caseload reached its highest point, with 5 million families on the welfare rolls. When the US Congress passed the welfare reform Act in August of 1996, caseloads had already declined to 4.4 million families. By June of 1999, there were 2.5 million families receiving cash public assistance. This translates into a 50 percent decline in the caseload since 1994 (US House of Representatives 2000; Mark Greenberg and Michael Laracy 2000).

While welfare reform led to an increase in employment among low-income lone mothers, and lowered the number of people relying on welfare, it is uncertain whether such changes actually improved their economic well-being. The reform policy was enacted during a time of unprecedented economic growth. Furthermore, the policy was enacted along with two other programs intended to benefit low-wage workers; the Earned Income Tax Credit and an increase in the federal minimum wage. As a result, it is difficult to determine which policies (or combination of policies) caused the decline in welfare rolls. Poverty rates initially declined. According to Jones-DeWeever, Peterson, and Song, more than 60 percent of lone mothers were in poverty in June of 1996, a number that fell to 53 percent by February 2000 (2003: 30). However, the overall poverty rate in the US rose during the following two years to just over 11 percent in 2001 and to 12 percent in 2002. Furthermore, evidence indicates that those leaving welfare for employment typically find jobs that pay below-poverty wages and offer few employer-provided benefits such as health insurance, sick leave, or vacations (Greenberg and Laracy 2000; Greenberg *et al.* 2000; Ladonna Pavetti 2000; US House of Representatives 2000; Bernstein and Greenberg 2001. See also Karen Christopher 2004, this issue).

ENABLING VERSUS ENFORCING POLICIES AND THE PROMISE OF DECOMMODIFICATION

Labor force participation rates among lone mothers have increased in both the unified Germany and in the United States. In 2001, the labor market participation rate of lone mothers in unified Germany was 66 percent as compared to 74 percent of lone mothers in the US in 2000 (Table 2). In Germany, lone mothers can survive without selling their labor, but they *choose* to work in order to escape poverty and to access rights to the future decommodification of their labor. In the US it is not a choice. Lone mothers *must* sell their labor in order to temporarily access welfare benefits even though most will not achieve ultimate economic independence.

One main difference in the ways in which the two countries treat lone mothers is the degree to which the state enables or enforces commodification of labor. That is, do state policies encourage and enhance lone mothers' participation in the labor market, by the provision of childcare, paid parental leave, and/or job guarantees? Or, does the state enforce labor force participation by using punitive measures, rather than addressing barriers to employment?

Unified Germany

Unified Germany is characterized by policies that reduce the relative privileges of lone mothers in employment and provide a general improvement of social rights for home carers, including lone mothers. Because lone mothers can survive on welfare benefits – that is, in a precommodified status without selling their labor – yet increasingly participate in the labor force anyway, Germany can be described as having a voluntary commodification of labor. Unlike the former GDR, social policies in the unified Germany do not enable mothers to participate in the labor market. In fact, social policies actively discourage mothers' participation by providing few childcare benefits for very young children and even less after-school care for older children. However, welfare benefits for women outside the labor market do not provide access to future decommodification in terms of pensions or long-term health benefits. So, while lone mothers have immediate financial incentives to stay at home with their children, they have long-run financial incentives to participate in the labor market in order to access some degree of decommodification in the future.

The United States

Welfare reform enforces the commodification of lone mothers' labor in the United States, providing ultimately very limited support outside of the labor market. Ladonna Pavetti and Dan Bloom describe a paternalistic state that ties the receipt of benefits to expectations for labor market participation and the cumulative time limit. The goal of the sanctions is to "instill in clients a realization that the choices they make have consequences" (2001: 246). In addition, alongside welfare reform, the US Congress introduced two additional policies directed toward low-wage labor: an increase in the minimum wage and an updated version of the Earned Income Tax Credit. Like welfare reform, both of these policies are linked directly with labor market participation, that is, one can only access benefits if one works.

Once commodified, lone mothers' labor is unlikely to become decommodified, given supply-and-demand factors in the low-wage labor market as well as the effects of welfare reform. According to Jones-DeWeever, Peterson, and Song, both supply and demand factors lead low-income women into "unstable, low-wage – often stereotypically 'female' – jobs that hinder their efforts to achieve economic self-sufficiency through market work" (2003: 9). Supply factors include a lack of skills and education necessary to move into higher-paying, stable jobs. Recent research by the Institute for Women's Policy Research shows that welfare leavers are most likely to have only the skills needed for low-paying, stereotypically "female" jobs in service and clerical occupations (Cynthia Negrey, Stacie Golin, Sunhwa Lee, Holly Mead, and Barbara Gault 2001). Welfare reform exacerbates this problem by requiring lone mothers to "work first," rather than acquire skills while on public assistance.

Furthermore, the constraints of caregiving and the high cost of childcare and out-of-school care worsen the problem for lone mothers, making it even more likely that they will start and remain in unstable, low-income work. On the demand side, occupational segregation by sex and race limits the opportunities available to welfare leavers to the lowest-paying occupations and industries (Heidi Hartmann, Katherine Allen, and Christine Owens 1999).

In the post-welfare-reform United States, there exist few universal policies that provide access to the decommodification of low-wage labor. While workers may have access to Social Security upon retirement, these benefits are low. Also, many benefits that could protect people when they leave employment (even temporarily) such as unemployment insurance, healthcare, and family leave, are tied to employment for a period of time and may be voluntarily provided by employers only to some employees. Few welfare leavers have access to such benefits, because they work too few hours, or are unable to sustain the job for the required period before receiving benefits. Whereas in unified Germany lone mothers have a strong social safety net in the form of a set of benefits allowing them to access a sort of precommodified status, low-income lone mothers in the US do not have the same protection. And while German mothers may choose to participate in order to access the future decommodification of their labor, many poor lone mothers in the US – even those with jobs – have no such promise of future decommodification, given the insecure and insufficient nature of the work that is available.

THE CARROT OR THE STICK?

Given similar recent trends in labor force participation rates among lone mothers in the US and Germany within starkly different political contexts, the obvious question is: why does the US use the stick whereas Germany employs the carrot? What are the implications of these strategies for the commodification of lone mothers' labor? Will the commodification of their labor lead to improved economic well-being and the future decommodification of labor? Several important differences between the United States and Germany might account for the varied political approaches to lone mothers and their effects. We focus on differences in the low-wage labor market and in the demographic characteristics of lone mothers in the US and in Germany.

Earnings and the character of the low-wage labor market

Because of the tradition of centralized collective bargaining and the extensive social security system, a low-wage employment sector comparable to that in the US never developed in Germany. Although there is no legal minimum wage, a minimum income level is indirectly set by collective agreements and social transfers. These collective agreements fix the wage category and the level of earnings for the majority of all wage and salary earners. Traditionally, all employees of an employer bound by a collective agreement receive the wage set in the collective wage negotiations. The traditional goal of trade unions' negotiation strategies has been to achieve an income sufficiently high for a main breadwinner to support a family. The social-safety net contributes to setting a minimum wage level that (for individuals or couples) is significantly higher than social transfers (Holger Buch and Peter Rühmann 1998: 111).

Those working in part-time employment or "marginal" work also earn low wages on average, but not as low as those paid for comparable jobs in the United States. Marginal, part-time employment is defined as employment that generates income below 400 euros per month. Such employment requires only a 25 percent flat rate payment of tax and social security contributions for employees in the industry and 12 percent for employees in private households, which is less than half of the usual deductions. Those employed in the marginal sector have no individual rights to unemployment insurance or healthcare and only since the mid-1990s have negligible rights to old-age pensions. It is an employment status attractive only to individuals who have alternative access to the social security system via the employment status of the head of the household, namely students and married women.

Those earning low wages (either through the collective bargaining agreement or through part-time work) are predominantly female. In the early 1990s, a study found that only 11 percent of full-time male workers in Germany held low-wage employment, compared with about 30 percent of full-time female workers. Of women who worked part-time, more than one-third earned low wages (Shirley Dex, Paul Robson, and Frank Wilkinson 1999: 508). In addition, branches in the service sector that were particularly "feminized" paid low wages. In 1995, among all full-time employed persons who earned less than 50 percent of average, full-time wages, 21 percent were male and 79 percent female. Nearly 80 percent of these individuals were unskilled, and 70 percent worked in the service sector (Claus Schäfer 2000: 544).[9] In 1997, of the 1.5 million women working in marginal part-time jobs, 75 percent were married and 61 percent had children. Lone mothers were more likely to obtain jobs that provided a living wage and made up just 9 percent of those in marginal employment (Schäfer 2000).

Differences in the types of low-income employment available to lone mothers in the US and Germany may relate to the differences in policy approaches in the two countries. Because lone mothers in Germany can obtain rights to the future decommodification of their labor through participation in employment, there is no need for German policy to force them into employment. In contrast, faced with a low-wage labor market with low levels (if any) of present and future benefits, lone mothers in the US must be forced off state support. At first glance, however, this seems shortsighted, ultimately providing only a few, if any, real opportunities for economic independence.

The United States

A significant problem with work requirements and the eventual elimination of welfare benefits to lone mothers in the US is that these provisions do not necessarily lead to economic independence and material well-being. There is mixed evidence on the effect of TANF on short-term earnings. Some studies have shown an association between an increase in work and an increase in annual earnings in the 1990s, although total earnings remain low (Judith M. Gueron and Edward Pauly 1991: 74). Jones-DeWeever, Peterson, and Song (2003) found that among low-income lone parents in the post-welfare-reform US, monthly earnings increased roughly $100 per month. Within this group, lone mothers experienced lower increases in average monthly earnings than did single fathers included in the study (Jones-DeWeever, Peterson, and Song 2003: 21).

Substantial evidence indicates that the workfare policies of the 1980s and 1990s in the US encouraged work but left parents no better off financially (Gueron and Pauly 1991; Norma B. Coe, Gregory Acs, and Keith Watson 1998; Richard Bavier 2000; Maria Cancian, Robert Haveman, Daniel R. Meyer, and Barbara Wolf 2000; Dan Bloom and Charles Michalopoulos 2001). Poor women in the US with low educational attainments and limited work experience most often find low-wage jobs, such as in clerical work, retail sales, food service, and cleaning, that provide limited or no employment benefits and few opportunities for moving into better paying employment (Julie Strawn, Mark Greenberg, and Steve Savner 2001). An Institute for Women's Policy Research study found that employed lone mothers were less likely to access employment-based health insurance after welfare reform (Jones-DeWeever, Peterson, and Song 2003). From 1996 to 2000, the percentage of employed welfare recipients with access to health insurance through their employment fell from 20.7 percent to 13.6 percent (Jones-DeWeever, Peterson, and Song 2003: 21).

Demographics of lone mothers

In addition to institutional differences in the US and German versions of a welfare state, the two countries have important demographic differences in their populations of lone mothers. These demographics have led to different outcomes from a political perspective.

The first major demographic difference between the US and Germany is in fertility rates, and specifically, fertility rates of women under the age of 20 and of unmarried women. Prior to unification, the FRG had one of the lowest birth rates in Europe (11.5 births per 1,000 inhabitants in 1980), while the GDR had a much higher birth rate (a peak of 14.6 births per 1,000 in 1980) (OECD 2002). After unification, however, birth rates in the East fell below birth rates in the former West Germany. By 1991, the fertility rate in the East was 6.8 births per 1,000 persons; it fell to 5.4 in 1995, and rose to 7.2 in 2000 (OECD 2002). One author claims that the number of births in the East fell by more than 50 percent from 1989 to 1992 (Katharina Pohl 1993).[10] Birth rates in the West also fell after unification, although less markedly than in the East, dipping from 11.3 births per 1,000 inhabitants in 1991, to 10.3 in 1995, and to 9.8 in 2000. Birth rates in the US were much higher. In 1970, the birth rate was 18.4 births per 1,000 inhabitants. By 1980, this figure had fallen slightly to 15.9. It increased to 16.7 in 1990 and fell again in 2000, to 14.7 (US Department of Health and Human Services 2003). The number of out-of-wedlock births in the US has increased at a higher rate than in unified Germany. The number of births to unmarried mothers as a percentage of live births in the United States increased from 18.4 percent in 1980 to 28 percent in 1990, reaching a peak of 32.6 percent in 1994. The rate of out-of-wedlock births fell to 31.7 percent of all live births in 1996 (Francis Fukuyama 2003).

In 2001, about one-sixth (16 percent) of all families in the unified Germany were headed by lone parents. The frequency of lone parenthood was higher in the East (21 percent) than in the West (15 percent) (Statistisches Bundesamt 2001: 24). As mentioned, this is in part the result of social policies that encouraged cohabitation rather than marriage in the former GDR. In the US, lone parents head 27 percent of all families (US Census Bureau 2002). Of particular concern is the much higher rate of teenage births in the US as compared to the rate in all of Europe (and in most other industrialized countries). In 1991, the birth rate for teenagers aged 15–19 was 62.1 births per 1,000 teenagers, a number that fell to 48.5 by the year 2000 (Stephanie J. Ventura, T. J. Mathews, and Brady E. Hamilton 2002). This figure compares to 13.1 births per 1,000 teenagers in Germany (OECD 2002). According to a UNICEF report on teenage births in wealthy nations, girls from poor backgrounds are disproportionately represented among teenage mothers. In the United States, teenagers from low-income families comprise less than 40 percent of the teenage population but account for more than 80 percent of teenage births (UNICEF 2002). Such differences among lone mothers in Germany and the US – in age, education, and experience in the labor market prior to the birth of the first child, etc. – may account for the different political approaches that the two countries take to the social problems associated with such differences.[11]

Race

In addition to differences in fertility rates and the ages of mothers in the two countries, there are also major demographic differences that may be associated with different policy responses in the US and Germany. As previously discussed, US welfare policy has been particularly infused by race. Welfare recipients are stereotypically identified as poor African-American women, who despite higher labor force participation rates than white women, and a history of being denied AFDC, are assumed to be lazy and motivated to take advantage of the system. Given a backdrop of social norms around work and cultural notions about who deserves state aid, policies that are punitive and paltry and are in practice directed toward lone black mothers are also politically popular.

In contrast, the German citizenry lacks the same degree of racial diversity, and the existing diversity is the result of immigration. Poor Turkish immigrants, for example, who are legal residents of Germany, are treated in the same manner as poor Germans. That is, they can qualify for means-tested social assistance.[12] As a result, social assistance has not been as divisive along racial lines.

CONCLUSION

Various states of commodification have characterized the US, East Germany, West Germany, and unified Germany over time. Through case studies based on Esping-Andersen's classifications, this paper has examined changes in the degree of commodification of lone mothers' labor in Germany and in the US across decades and large political developments; it has also considered the extent to which such policies enforced or enabled labor force participation among lone mothers. Figure 2 depicts the various degrees of commodification of labor and the enforcement/enablement of

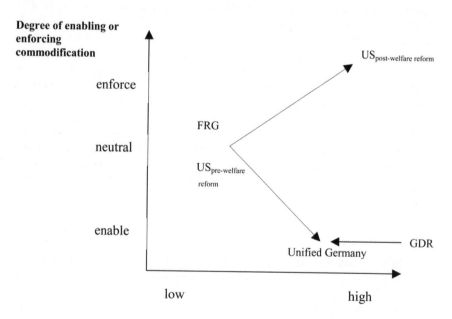

Figure 2 The Labor Force Participation Status of Lone Mothers in the US and Germany: Degrees of Commodification, Enforcement, and Enabling.

the commodification of lone mothers' labor in Germany and in the US, as well as changes in these statuses over time.

The German unification brought together two already-existing approaches: the enabling policies designed to achieve the commodification of lone mothers' labor in GDR and the voluntary commodification of lone mothers' labor observed in the FRG. However, the unified Germany favored the social norms and the family policy of the former FRG, with its bias toward the male-breadwinner model, in which women's primary role is as mother and caregiver. In consequence, while the GDR had enabled the commodification of lone mothers' labor (and therefore promoted a certain degree of economic independence), women in the unified Germany can choose between motherhood and career and, if they choose motherhood, may become dependent on a breadwinning male or on state subsidies. More often than not, however, these women choose labor force participation over a lifelong dependence on social assistance that offers no possibility of future decommodification of their labor.

In the US, policy reforms created a shift from nearly complete precommodication of lone mothers' labor to the enforcement of full commodification of such labor. At the same time, however, these reforms provided little or no possibility of future decommodification on retirement. Thus, the increase in labor force participation among lone mothers in Germany and the US occurred within completely different contexts. While labor force participation in Germany offered independence from welfare payments as well as future access to decommodification of labor, the workfare programs in the US required lone mothers receiving temporary welfare assistance to move off welfare rolls into precarious, low-wage employment, with limited opportunities to secure basic needs for their families.

In addition, there are clear differences between the two countries in both the institutional context in which lone mothers attempt to become economically independent and in the demographics of lone mothers and those on governmental assistance. The low-wage labor market in the US does not provide poor lone mothers with a decent opportunity to escape their poverty and attain future decommodification of their labor. Many lone mothers in the United States are younger than their German counterparts, and have therefore obtained less education and experience. These deficits further inhibit their ability to achieve economic independence. Finally, racial divides among lone mothers in the US have become politically charged. One possible outcome has been more punitive state policies that fail to enable lone mothers' commodification. The case studies considered here support the conclusion that voluntary commodification of labor, coupled with access to future decommodification of labor upon retirement, can provide women incentives to participate in the labor force that are equal to, or even greater than, the enforcement of labor market participation by workfare policies that provide no real protection from poverty.

NOTES

[1] Note that widows' rights were always defined in terms different from those of unmarried or divorced mothers.

[2] Note that poor married mothers in the US do not face the same social contempt as poor lone mothers. "If there is an expectation imposed on married mothers, it is rather that they should choose care-giving over wage-earning, if they can afford at all to make that choice" (Gwendolyn Mink 1998: 120).

[3] The term "federal" refers to federal US government policies, which individual states have to follow. "State" policies, in contrast, are local and refer only to specific states rather than to the US as a whole.

[4] Particularly punitive rules against lone mothers were enacted during the 1960s. For example, the state of Louisiana cut off benefits to AFDC families in which the mother gave birth to another child. In Newburgh, New York, benefits were cut for unwed mothers who had another child (Julie Strawn, Mark Greenberg, and Steve Savner 2001).

[5] Under the rubric of "work first," the best way to promote employment is to focus on immediate job placement (regardless of job quality) with education and job training deemed ineffective for unemployed parents before entering employment. It was believed that the best way to advance in the labor market was to build a work history or to participate in training activities while working (Strawn, Greenberg, and Savner 2001: 233).

[6] Note that there were no corresponding sanctions on the dependent child tax deduction (Albelda and Tilly 2001). See note 8 for an explanation of the deduction.

[7] The work requirements included either work for wages or volunteer work.

[8] The term "low-income" indicates an individual whose family's taxable income for the preceding year did not exceed 150 percent of the federal poverty level amount. The US Census Poverty Thresholds can be found at http://www.fta.dot.gov/library/policy/ns/2002/appc.html.

[9] There are still significant wage differences between the West and the East.

[10] This author attributes the drop in part to employment insecurities.

[11] The direction of causality might also move in the other direction; the differences in age, education, and experience in the labor market may themselves be the result of social policies.

[12] The only exception is if such residents do not have unlimited permission to stay in Germany; then they can be sent back to their country of origin.

REFERENCES

Adler, Marina A. 1997. "Social Change and Decline in Marriage and Fertility in Eastern Germany." *Journal of Marriage and the Family* 59(1): 37–49.

Albelda, Randy and Chris Tilly. 2001. "Moving Beyond 'Get a Job': What Real Welfare Reform Would Look Like," in Mary C. King (ed.) *Squaring Up: Policy Strategies to Raise Women's Income in the United States*, pp. 15–45. Ann Arbor, MI: University of Michigan Press.

Bäcker, Gerhard, Reinhard Bispinck, Klaus Hofemann, and Gerhard Naegele. 2000. *Sozialpolitik und Soziale Lage in Deutschland. Gesundheit und Gesundheitssystem, Familie, Alter, Soziale Dienste.* Bd. 2. Westdt. Verl.: Opladen, Leske & Budrich.

Bavier, Richard. 2000. "A Look at Welfare Reform in the Survey of Income and Program Participation." Unpublished paper.

Bernstein, Jared and Mark Greenberg. 2001. "Reforming Welfare Reform." *The American Prospect* 12(1): 10–16.

Bloom, Dan and Charles Michalopoulos. 2001. *How Welfare and Work Policies Affect Employment and Income: A Synthesis of Research.* New York: Manpower Demonstration Research Corporation.

Braun, Michael, Jacqueline Scott, and Duane A. Alwin. 1994. "Economic Necessity or Self-Actualization? Attitudes toward Women's Labour-Force Participation in East and West Germany." *European Sociological Review* 10(1): 29–47.

Buch, Holger and Peter Rühmann. 1998. "Atypical Work as a Form of Low-Wage Employment in the German Labour Market," in Stephen Bazen, Mary Gregory, and Wiemer Salverda (eds.) *Low Wage Employment in Europe*, pp. 111–27. Cheltenham, UK: Edward Elgar.

Cancian, Maria, Robert Haveman, Daniel R. Meyer, and Barbara Wolf. 2000. *Before and After TANF: The Economic Well-Being of Women Leaving Welfare.* Special Report 77. Madison, WI: Institute for Research on Poverty, University of Wisconsin-Madison.

Christopher, Karen. 2004. "Welfare as We [Don't] Know It." *Feminist Economics* 10(2), this issue.

Coe, Norma B., Gregory Acs, and Keith Watson. 1998. *Does Work Pay? A Summary of the Work Incentives Under TANF.* Series A, No. A–28. Washington, DC: Urban Institute.

Deutsches Institut für Wirtschaftsforschung (DIW). 1990. "Vereintes Deutschland – Geteilte Frauengesellschaft?" in *DIW-Wochenbericht* 41/1990. Berlin: DIW.

Dex, Shirley, Paul Robson and Frank Wilkinson. 1999. "The Characteristics of the Low Paid: A Cross National Comparison." *Work, Employment and Society* 13(3): 503–24.

Dingeldey, Irene. 2001. "European Tax Systems and their Impact on Family Employment Patterns." *Journal of Social Policy* 30(4): 653–72.

—— and Silke Reuter. 2003. "Beschäftigungseffekte der Neuen Verflechtung Zwischen Familien- und Arbeitsmarktpolitik." *Wirtschafts und Sozialwissenschaftliches Institut – Mitteilungen* 56(11): 659–65.

Duggan, Lynn. 1995. "Restacking the Deck: Family Policy and Women's Fall-Back Position in Germany Before and After Unification." *Feminist Economics* 1(1): 175–94.

Edsall, Thomas B. and Mary E. Edsall. 1991. *Chain Reaction: The Impact of Race, Rights and Taxes on American Politics.* New York: W. W. Norton.

Engstler, Heribert and Sonja Menning. 2003. *Die Familie im Spiegel in Der Amtlichen Statistik.* Berlin: Deutsches Zentrum für Altersfragen.

Esping-Andersen, Gøsta. 1990. *The Three Worlds of Welfare Capitalism.* Cambridge, UK: Polity Press.

Eurostat. 2002. "Kinder und Erwerbstätigkeit von Frauen – Unterschiedliche Muster in den Mitgliedstaaten." *Pressemitteilungen* 60: 1–4.

Fukuyama, Francis. 2003. "Births to Single Mothers as a Percentage of Live Births." Available http://www.sais-jhu.edu/fukuyama/figures/fig2–5.htm (August 7, 2003).

Gilens, Martin. 1999. *Why Americans Hate Welfare: Race, Media, and the Politics of Antipoverty Policy.* Chicago: University of Chicago Press.

Gordon, Linda. 2002. "Who Deserves Help? Who Must Provide?" in Randy Albelda and Ann Withorn (eds.) *Lost Ground: Welfare Reform, Poverty, and Beyond,* pp. 9–25. Cambridge, MA: South End Press.

Greenberg, Mark and Michael Laracy. 2000. "Welfare Reform: Next Steps Offer New Opportunities." Neighborhood Funders Group Policy Paper No. 4. Center for Law and Social Policy, Washington, DC.

Greenberg, Mark, Jodie Levin-Epstein, Rutledge Hutson, Theodora Ooms, Rachel Schumacher, Vicki Turetsky, and David Engstrom. 2000. *Welfare Reauthorization: An Early Guide to the Issues.* Washington, DC: Center for Law and Social Policy.

Gueron, Judith M. and Edward Pauly. 1991. *From Welfare to Work.* New York: Russell Sage Foundation.

Gysi, Jutta and Wulfram Speigner. 1983. Changes in the Life Patterns of Families in the German Democratic Republic. Berlin (East): Institut für Soziologie und Sozialpolitik an der Akademie der Wissenschaft der Deutschen Demokratischen Republik.

Hartmann, Heidi, Katherine Allen, and Christine Owens. 1999. *Equal Pay for Working Families.* Washington, DC: AFL-CIO and Institute for Women's Policy Research.

Haskins, Ron. 2001. "Effects of Welfare Reform at Four Years," in P. Lindsay Chase-Lansdale and Greg Duncan (eds.) *For Better and for Worse: State Welfare Reform and the Well-Being of Low-Income Families and Children,* pp. 264–89. New York: Russell Sage Foundation.

——, Isabel Sawhill, and Kent Weaver. 2001. "Welfare Reform: An Overview of Effects to Date." *Welfare Reform & Beyond, Policy Brief No. 1.* Washington, DC: Brookings Institution Press.

Helco, Hugh. 2001. "The Politics of Welfare Reform," in Rebecca Blank and Ron Haskins (eds.) *The New World of Welfare,* pp. 169–200. Washington, DC: Brookings Institution Press.

Hohn, Charlotte. 1992. "Population-Relevant Policies Before and After Unification of Germany," in P. Krishnan, Chi-Hsien Tuan, and Kuttan Mahadevan (eds.) *Readings in Population Research,* pp. 1–24. Delhi: Vedams.

Holst, Elke and Jürgen Schupp. 1990. "Frauen in Familie und Beruf." *DIW-Wochenbericht* 29/1990. Berlin: DIW.

Hradil, Stefan. 2001. *Soziale Ungleichheit in Deutschland,* ausg. 8. Westdt. Verl.: Opladen, Leske & Budrich.

Jones-DeWeever, Avis, Janice Peterson, and Xue Song. 2003. *Before and After Welfare Reform: The Work and Well-Being of Low-Income Single Parent Families.* Available http://www.iwpr.org/pdf/D454.pdf (December 2003).

Klett-Davies, Martina. 1997. "Single Mothers in Germany: Supported Mothers Who Work," in Simon Duncan and Rosalind Edwards (eds.) *Single Mothers in an International Context: Mothers or Workers?* London: UCL Press.

Lewis, Jane and Ilona Ostner. 1994. *Gender and the Evolution of European Social Policy.* Arbeitspapier nr. 4/94 des ZeS (Zentrum für Sozialpolitik). Bremen: Universität Bremen.

Loprest, Patricia. 1999. *Families Who Left Welfare: Who Are They and How Are They Doing?* Washington, DC: Urban Institute.

Mead, Lawrence M. 2001. "The Politics of Conservative Welfare Reform," in Rebecca Blank and Ron Haskins (eds.) *The New World of Welfare*, pp. 201–22. Washington, DC: Brookings Institution Press.

Mink, Gwendolyn. 1998. *Welfare's End.* Ithaca, NY: Cornell University Press.

Negrey, Cynthia, Stacie Golin, Sunhwa Lee, Holly Mead, and Barbara Gault. 2001. *Working First But Working Poor: The Need for Education and Training Following Welfare Reform.* Washington, DC: Institute for Women's Policy Research.

Niepel, Gabriele. 1994. *Alleinerziehende. Abschied von einem Klischee.* Westdt. Verl.: Opladen, Leske & Budrich.

Obertreis, Gesine. 1986. *Familienpolitik in der DDR 1946–1980.* Westdt. Verl.: Opladen, Leske & Budrich.

Organisation for Economic Co-operation and Development (OECD). 2002. *Society at a Glance: OECD Social Indicators.* Paris: OECD. Accessed on the web at http://www.oecdwash.org/PDFILES/society_glance.pdf (August 7, 2003).

Ostner, Ilona. 1997. "Lone Mothers in Germany Before and After Unification," in Jane Lewis (ed.) *Lone Mothers in European Welfare Regimes*, pp. 90–7. London: Jessica Kingsley.

Pavetti, Ladonna. 2000. "Welfare Policy in Transition: Redefining the Social Contract for Poor Citizen Families with Children." *Focus* 21(2): 44–50.

——. and Dan Bloom. 2001. "State Sanctions and Time Limits," in Rebecca Blank and Ron Haskins (eds.) *The New World of Welfare*, pp. 245–69. Washington, DC: Brookings Institution Press.

Pohl, Katharina. 1993. "Nichtehelichenquote in Deutschland: Tendenz Steigend." *Bundesinstitut für Bevolkerungsforschung (BIB) Mitteilungen* 3(93): 8–11.

Quadagno, Jill. 1994. *The Color of Welfare: How Racism Undermined the War on Poverty.* New York: Oxford University Press.

Razum, Oliver, Albrecht Jahn, and Rachel Snow. 1999. "Maternal Mortality in the Former East Germany Before and After Reunification: Changes in Risk by Marital Status." *British Medical Journal* 319(7217): 1104–5.

Sainsbury, Diane. 1994. "Women's and Men's Social Rights: Gendering Dimensions of Welfare States," in Diane Sainsbury (ed.) *Gendering Welfare States*, pp. 151–69. London: Sage.

——. 1996. *Gender, Equality and the Welfare States.* Cambridge, UK: Cambridge University Press.

Schäfer, Claus. 2000. "Niedrige Löhne – Bessere Welten?" *WSI-Mitteilungen* 53(8): 543–51.

Spalter-Roth, Roberta, Heidi Hartmann, and Linda Andrews. 1992. *Combining Work and Welfare: An Alternative Anti-Poverty Strategy.* Washington, DC: Institute for Women's Policy Research.

Statistisches Bundesamt. 1994. *Mikrozensus, 1994.* Available http://www.destatis.de.

——. 1998. *Mikrozensus, 1998.* Available http://www.destatis.de.

——. 2001. *Leben und Arbeiten in Deutschland: Ergebnisse des Mikrozensus 2001.* Available http://www.destatis.de/presse/deutsch/pk/2002/mikrozensus_2001.pdf (January 2004).

Strawn, Julie, Mark Greenberg, and Steve Savner. 2001. "Improving Employment Outcomes under TANF," in Rebecca Blank and Ron Haskins (eds.) *The New World of Welfare*, pp. 223–44. Washington, DC: Brookings Institution Press.

Teles, Steven M. 1996. *Whose Welfare? AFDC and Elite Politics.* St. Lawrence: University Press of Kansas.

Trappe, Heike. 1995. *Emanzipation oder Zwang? Frauen in der DDR Zwischen Beruf, Familie und Sozialpolitik.* Berlin: Akademie Verlag.

Turner, Jason A. and Thomas Main. 2001. "Work Experience Under Welfare Reform," in Rebecca Blank and Ron Haskins (eds.) *The New World of Welfare,* pp. 291–310. Washington, DC: Brookings Institution Press.

UNICEF. 2002. "UNICEF League Table of Teenage Births in Rich Nations." Available http://www.midirs.org/ (August 8, 2003).

US Bureau of Labor Statistics. 1988. *Labor Force Statistics Derived from the Current Population Survey.* Bulletin 2307. Washington, DC: US Government Printing Office.

US Census Bureau. 2002. "Employment Status of Women by Marital Status and Presence and Age of Children: 1970–2001," in *Statistical Abstract of the United States,* Table 570. Available http://www.census.gov/prod/2003pubs/02statab/labor.pdf (December 2003).

US Department of Health and Human Services. 2003. *National Center for Health Statistics.* Available http://www.cdc.gov/nchs/births.htm (August 8, 2003).

US House of Representatives, Committee on Ways and Means. 2000. *2000 Green Book: Background Material and Data on Programs within the Jurisdiction of the Committee on Ways and Means.* Washington, DC: US Government Printing Office.

Ventura, Stephanie J., T. J. Mathews, and Brady E. Hamilton. 2002. "Teenage Births in the United States: State Trends, 1991–2000, an Update." *National Vital Statistics Reports* 50(9).

Voges, Wolfgang and Ilona Ostner. 1995. "Wie Arm sind Alleinerziehende Frauen?" in Karl-Jürgen Bieback and Helga Milz (eds.) *Neue Armut.* Frankfurt: Campus Verlag.

Walther, Uwe-Jens. 1992. *Wohnsituation Alleinerziehender.* Heft 43. Bonn: Bundesforschungsanstalt für Landeskunde und Raumordnung.

WELFARE AS WE [DON'T] KNOW IT: A REVIEW AND FEMINIST CRITIQUE OF WELFARE REFORM RESEARCH IN THE UNITED STATES

Karen Christopher

INTRODUCTION

In the latter years of the twentieth century, welfare states across Western, affluent nations revamped their social assistance packages for lone mothers. Many of these states effectively ended their decades-long practices of allowing lone mothers to care for children at home by implementing policies that required or strongly encouraged employment for lone mothers receiving social assistance. In the United States, the 1996 Personal Responsibility and Work Opportunity Reconciliation Act (PRWORA), commonly referred to as "welfare reform,"[1] overhauled social assistance for poor families with children (most of which are headed by a lone mother). Under PRWORA, Temporary Assistance for Needy Families

(TANF), a system of block grants to individual states, replaced the federal-level Aid to Families with Dependent Children (AFDC).

Hundreds of empirical studies have assessed how current and former US welfare recipients fared after the implementation of PRWORA. However, because state-level TANF rules vary considerably, most of these studies have been carried out at the local or state level. Unfortunately, much of this research cannot be generalized to the larger US population. National-level research is less common, but essential to ascertain macro-level effects of welfare program changes. Moreover, compared to local or state level studies, national-level research can better inform federal policy responses and, by design, can reliably include a wide range of racial, ethnic, and immigrant groups. This paper emphasizes empirical research that uses nationally representative datasets as well as empirical studies that aggregate individuals across several states or cities.

After a brief overview of TANF's provisions, this paper reviews several national-level studies on four main subjects of interest – caseload reduction, labor force participation, income/poverty/hardships, and family formation (following Rebecca Blank 2002). The review finds that caseloads did indeed drop, and that the economic well-being of many lone mothers improved after PRWORA's passage. But many lone mothers' ongoing experience of poverty and material hardships – particularly during the midst of an economic boom – caution against drawing rosy conclusions from such evidence. A more rounded assessment of the impact of welfare reform requires a feminist perspective. The main thrust of this paper is to identify the characteristics of research in this area, to demonstrate its advantages over mainstream research, and to speculate about why there is comparatively little feminist research on welfare reform to date. It concludes by addressing ways to promote feminist research on this pressing topic.

This paper focuses on the experience of lone mothers under welfare reform, adopting a similar definition of lone motherhood to the one used for TANF eligibility – unmarried mothers with children living at home. While lone mothers may be cohabiting with or have other relationships with partners, among the population of interest considered here, partners' incomes are generally not sufficient to keep lone mothers from needing cash assistance. For decades, widows have not been eligible for AFDC/TANF. While married couples, single fathers, and grandfathers are eligible to receive TANF, they make up only a small percentage of adult TANF recipients. For example, in 2000, only 4 percent of TANF families included two or more adult recipients and 90 percent of all adult TANF recipients were female. The vast majority of those receiving TANF are single-parent households headed by women (US Department of Health and Human Services 2001). Therefore, this paper treats low-income lone mothers as the group most affected by welfare reform.[2]

A BRIEF OVERVIEW OF TANF

A major goal of PWRORA was to reduce use of government cash assistance by poor families, especially lone-mother families. Specifically, TANF imposes a five-year lifetime limit on receipt of cash assistance for individuals and families, save a hardship exemption granted for 20 percent of the caseload in each state. The legislation allows states to declare noncitizen immigrants ineligible for federal programs such as Food Stamps and Medicaid, as well as TANF and other state programs. Welfare reform also requires that almost all TANF recipients engage in a work activity (which varies by state) within two years of receiving assistance. Individuals who do not comply with work requirements face sanctions, which vary markedly by state. At the state level, work requirements for TANF recipients increase over time, so that by 2002, 50 percent of recipients have to work for pay. If these goals are not attained, states face economic penalties.

TANF gives states leeway in creating policies to encourage marriage and reduce nonmarital births. For example, many states have adopted "family caps" that prohibit increases in benefit levels if TANF recipients have additional children, and many states have strengthened provisions to disclose the paternity of children receiving welfare to establish child support. States with the steepest declines in nonmarital births receive bonuses from the federal government (Alan Weil and Kenneth Finegold 2002: xviii). Reauthorization of TANF, required in 2002, has been stalled in the US Congress, although boosting funding for marriage-promotion measures has figured prominently in the debates.

WELFARE REFORM AND CASELOAD REDUCTION

After almost two decades of little change in the numbers of families using welfare (ranging from 3.1 to 3.8 million between 1973 and 1989), welfare caseloads increased to 5 million in the recession years of the early 1990s (US Department of Health and Human Services 2003a). By 2001, however, caseloads fell to 2 million families. After the passage of welfare reform, the percentage of the total US population receiving TANF decreased roughly by half, from 4.8 percent in 1996 to 2.1 percent in 2001 (US Department of Health and Human Services 2003b). While the new TANF rules – particularly work requirements, sanctions, and time limits – undoubtedly pushed some women off welfare, other factors pulled them into the labor market (Sanford Schram and Joe Soss 2002). The booming economy in the late 1990s fostered unparalleled job growth, and increases in the Earned Income Tax Credit (EITC)[3] and minimum wage made employment more attractive for low-wage workers. Caseload increases in many states during the 2001 recession and during the period of high unemployment rates in 2002 provide further evidence for the effect of the economy on caseloads

145

(Douglas Besharov 2002; Elise Richer, Hedieh Rahmanou, and Mark Greenberg 2003). Administrative practices at welfare offices also reduced caseloads. For example, compared to earlier years, fewer women joined TANF rolls in the late 1990s due in part to diversion policies that "deflect claimants towards job searches or private assistance rather than adding them to the rolls" (Schram and Soss 2002: 69). All of these factors led to a steep rise in single mothers' employment over the late 1990s (Blank 2002; Schram and Soss 2002).

Because multiple factors affect caseloads, it is difficult to parcel out the distinct effect of new TANF rules on falling caseloads. Still, compared to the former AFDC program, TANF seems to have been very successful in moving lone mothers and their families off cash assistance. But while many politicians and pundits have used falling TANF caseloads as indicators of the success of PRWORA, caseload data reveal nothing about the well-being of lone mothers who have left welfare. For this kind of information, we must turn to research on the economic status of former welfare recipients.

LABOR FORCE PARTICIPATION

Because most research on lone mothers' post-TANF employment analyzes welfare leavers, this research is emphasized below. Unless otherwise noted, hereafter the term "welfare leavers" refers to women who left TANF and had not returned to welfare by the time they were surveyed.[4]

During the late 1990s, most welfare leavers found jobs. About 60 percent of former welfare recipients who left welfare between 1995 and 1997 (and had not returned by 1997) were employed when surveyed in 1997 (Pamela Loprest 1999a); about 64 percent of the welfare recipients who left between 1997 and 1999 (and had not returned by 1999) were employed when surveyed in 1999 (Pamela Loprest 2002). In a review of over thirty studies of welfare leavers, Ron Haskins (2001) concludes that 57–64 percent of welfare leavers reported working at the time they were surveyed. About 20 percent of welfare leavers report that they were *not* employed throughout a ten-month period prior to being surveyed (Haskins 2001).[5] Most employed welfare leavers worked for pay at least thirty hours a week (Sharon Parrott 1998; Haskins 2001), but over half of former recipients were not employed a full year (Elise Richer, Steve Savner, and Mark Greenberg 2001), and fewer than one-fifth of welfare leavers interviewed in 1997 and 1999 reported working at their current job for more than two years (Pamela Loprest 2001). Overall, close to two-thirds of former welfare recipients worked for pay in the late 1990s – most at thirty hours per week or more – and did not return to welfare in the short term. But, most welfare leavers did not hold jobs for long periods of time.

Moreover, a substantial minority of women who left welfare in the late 1990s returned to welfare within a two-year period. Of those who left welfare between 1995 and 1997, about 30 percent had returned to welfare by the time they were interviewed in 1997; of those who left between 1997 and 1999, 22 percent had returned to welfare by the time they were interviewed in 1999 (Loprest 1999a, 2002). A small but notable proportion of former recipients, about 20 percent in 1997 and 12 percent in 1999, reported no employment of their own or of a spouse and no receipt of social assistance or disability benefits (Loprest 1999a, 2002). So in the late 1990s, between a quarter and one-third of former welfare recipients returned to welfare within two years, and between one and two out of ten reported little to no income from either the labor market or social assistance programs.

There is little research documenting the type of jobs in which welfare leavers work. Of employed former recipients surveyed in 1997, almost 40 percent worked in service occupations, and about 20 percent worked in clerical/administrative support occupations (Pamela Loprest 1999b). About 15 percent worked in operative/transportation or craft/repair occupations, and only 15 percent of welfare leavers worked in better-paid managerial, professional, or technical occupations (Loprest 1999b). Recent research finds that "roughly two-fifths to one-half of leavers work in the service industries, with about another quarter in retail trade" (Richer, Savner, and Greenberg 2001: 7). Over two-thirds of employed leavers surveyed in 1997 worked for private companies; substantially fewer worked for the government, nonprofits, or were self-employed (Loprest 1999b). With respect to race and ethnicity, black welfare leavers were significantly less likely than white leavers to work in professional, technical, or managerial jobs, and Latina welfare leavers were the most likely to work in service jobs (Kenneth Finegold and Sarah Staveteig 2002). In general, welfare leavers have worked in jobs that offer few opportunities for advancement (Demetra Smith Nightingale 2002).

Welfare leavers often hold jobs that provide neither health insurance nor other benefits. Research compiled from several states finds that in the late 1990s, only about 25 percent of welfare leavers received employer-sponsored health insurance, and about one-third to one-half worked in jobs with paid sick leave or paid vacation (Richer, Savner, and Greenberg 2001). Nationwide, only about a third of welfare leavers worked in jobs that provided health insurance (Gregory Acs and Pamela Loprest 2001).[6]

Because leaver studies typically do not compare welfare leavers to any other groups, they give limited information on how TANF affects low-income lone mothers (Moffitt and Ver Ploeg 2001; Blank 2002).[7] However, comparisons between AFDC leavers and TANF leavers can tell us more about the distinct effects of PRWORA. For example, if welfare leavers under AFDC and TANF had similar economic profiles, this would suggest that work requirements, time limits, and other provisions of PRWORA have not notably improved the economic status of former recipients.

A comparison of AFDC and TANF leavers reveals few differences in employment outcomes. Like TANF leavers, most AFDC leavers – over 75 percent during their first four years after exiting AFDC – worked for pay in the 1970s and 1980s (Thomas Vartanian and Justine McNamara 2000).[8] About 40 percent of AFDC leavers between 1983 and 1988 returned to AFDC within two years of leaving (Kathleen Harris 1996). Like TANF leavers, many AFDC leavers, especially those who cycled back onto welfare, worked in service-sector jobs (Kathleen Harris 1993; Maria Cancian and Daniel Meyer 2000).

One notable difference between TANF and AFDC leavers is that the TANF leavers are more likely to work at least thirty-five hours per week, while only about one-third of AFDC leavers in the 1970s and 1980s worked this much, even up to four years after leaving AFDC (Harris 1993). It is important to note, of course, that from the 1970s to the late 1990s, *all* women increased employment rates and hours worked per week, and most experienced wage gains (Irene Browne 1999).

Overall, research provides good and bad news on the economic status of welfare leavers. While many leavers worked for pay, most held jobs for short periods of time, few had jobs providing benefits, and a considerable minority returned to welfare within two years. And while TANF rules were in part responsible for increased employment among welfare leavers, the booming economy in the late 1990s as well as other incentives to work also increased lone mothers' employment rates. Even given the improved economic status of women and booming economy in the late 1990s, welfare leavers under TANF still did *not* fare markedly better than those under AFDC. This casts doubt on the assertion that mandatory employment and other provisions of the 1996 welfare reform exceptionally improved the economic status of welfare leavers.[9]

INCOME, POVERTY, AND HARDSHIPS

Income

The relatively low wages of welfare recipients are not surprising given their concentration in service and retail jobs. The median hourly wage of former welfare recipients was about $6.60 in 1997 and $7.15 in 1999, somewhat higher than the federal minimum wage of $5.15 (Loprest 1999a, 2002). Finegold and Staveteig (2002: 207) report that in the same year, "the mean hourly wage among welfare leavers was $7.31 for whites, $6.88 for blacks, and $6.71 for Hispanics." Thus, wages among black and Hispanic welfare leavers were closer to the minimum wage than those of white welfare leavers. In 1999, former recipients who worked for pay earned about $1,000 per month (Robert Moffitt 2002).[10]

For the first time in decades, from 1994 to 1999 real-dollar wages grew markedly for all workers – including a wage increase of about 4 percent among female high school dropouts (Rebecca Blank 2001). Given these trends, we should also expect former recipients' earnings to rise over the late 1990s.

Research on welfare leavers' total incomes – including earnings, government assistance, and other family income – over time finds that many leavers increased their incomes after leaving welfare, though it often took one to two years after leaving for them to experience net gains in income.[11] Haskins (2001: 126) concludes that, "leaving welfare for work can substantially increase mothers' income if they work anywhere close to full time and year-round and if they receive the Food Stamps and EITC to which they are entitled." However, Wendell Primus's (2001) longitudinal analysis finds that only about one-half of welfare leavers had higher incomes after leaving welfare. Both Haskins (2001: 131) and Primus agree that a "small to moderate-sized group" of welfare leavers fared worse after leaving the rolls.

Research on lone mothers' total incomes often considers trends among all low-income lone mothers, not just welfare leavers. Studies on all lone mothers are beneficial due to their more inclusive samples that encompass those on welfare, those who have left welfare, and those who might go on welfare.

During the late 1990s, low-income lone mothers' disposable incomes generally increased, but not by much. Lone mothers' earnings and EITC payments grew, but they lost cash benefits and often failed to receive the Food Stamps and health insurance for which they remained eligible (Haskins 2001). Among lone mothers, the top 80 percent of earners' average disposable incomes grew over the late 1990s (figures from Wendell Primus, cited in Blank 2002). However, when using more refined disposable income measures – including earnings, Food Stamps, EITC payments, and any other government assistance, but deducting federal tax payments and childcare expenses – the incomes of the poorest quintile of lone mothers dropped by 8 percent between 1996 and 1998 (Sheila Zedlewski 2002).[12] Yet all other lone mothers experienced increases in this measure of disposable income from 1996 to 1998 (Zedlewski 2002). Avis Jones-DeWeever, Janice Peterson, and Xue Song (2003: 11) find that among low-income single-parent families, total inflation-adjusted family monthly income grew only slightly from $1,106 just before TANF implementation to $1,221 in the late 1990s, at the height of the US economic expansion.[13] In sum, family income inched up for low-income lone-mother families – an expected result during a period of economic expansion. However, as explored later, for many families, family costs increased significantly with employment.

Poverty

In the late 1990s, close to half of welfare leavers continued to be in poverty after leaving TANF. Poverty can be measured in various ways, though much of the welfare reform research does not use the US poverty line because of its well-known flaws.[14] Poverty measures that use post-tax, or disposable income, are better indicators than the US poverty line of the resources families have available to them. When measuring poverty with post-tax family income – including earnings of all family members, estimates of EITC payments and Food Stamps, and any cash benefits families received – 48 percent of women who left welfare between 1995 and 1997 were living in poverty when interviewed in 1997; 41 percent of women who left welfare between 1997 and 1999 were living in poverty when interviewed in 1999 (Loprest 2001). Using the same measure of poverty, about 25 percent of former recipients who worked full-time also lived in poverty in 1999, assuming they worked all year (Loprest 2002).

With a more precise measure of disposable income poverty that deducts any out-of-pocket childcare expenses reported by single mothers, Zedlewski (2002) shows that the poverty rates of all lone mothers declined from 41 percent in 1996 to 34 percent in 1998. However, lone-mother families experienced an increase in extreme poverty, or the percentage of families living under 50 percent of the poverty line (about $6,500 for a family of three in 1998). Using a poverty measure that deducts childcare expenses, extreme poverty among single mothers increased from about 6 percent to about 8 percent from 1996 to 1998. Another measure of poverty, the "poverty gap," which refers to the total amount of money required to bring all poor people up to the US poverty line, increased among working lone-mother families from about "$5 billion in 1995 to $6.3 billion in 1999" (Kathryn Porter and Allen Dupree 2001: 4). The "poverty gap" measures the severity of poverty, and thus implies that poverty among employed lone mothers grew deeper in the late 1990s.

Thus, poverty was common among welfare leavers in the late 1990s; close to half of all former recipients lived in poverty, though full-time, year-round work substantially reduced poverty rates. A minority of lone mothers – the poorest – experienced increasing difficulty over the late 1990s.

Hardships

Following a typology of material hardships used by Heather Boushey (2001), in this section I present the food, housing, healthcare, and childcare hardships experienced by welfare leavers, and briefly address the prevalence of domestic violence among welfare leavers.

Food hardships have been commonplace among TANF leavers and their families. About one-third of leavers in 1997 and in 1999 said they had to scale down the sizes of meals or skip meals when they ran out of food, and about half reported that they ran out of food or money for food in the past year (Loprest 2001). Aggregating state studies of employed leavers, Richer, Savner, and Greenberg (2001) find that in most of these studies, at least one-fifth reported food insecurity marked by hunger.[15] While the percentages of former recipients that report food hardship vary across different measures and studies, it is clear that at least a considerable minority of former welfare families experienced food hardship in the late 1990s.[16]

Housing hardships were also common among former recipients. About 40 percent of welfare leavers in 1997 and 1999 reported having trouble paying rent, mortgage, or utility bills in the past year (Boushey 2001; Loprest 2001; Finegold and Staveteig 2002). A small minority of these welfare leavers, about 8 percent, moved in with others because they could not cover their housing costs (Loprest 2001). Whites were more likely than other racial/ethnic groups to experience housing hardships.

Healthcare hardships were also prevalent among former recipients. Among employed welfare leavers, one-fifth to one-third could not afford healthcare they needed and did not receive care (Boushey 2001).[17] Substantial minorities of these employed leavers, 46 percent of part-time working leavers and 23 percent of full-time working leavers, did not have access to heath insurance in the late 1990s (Boushey 2001). Of all former welfare leavers, only about one-third of them and about half of their children had Medicaid in 1999 (Loprest 2002). Latino adults and children were the most likely to be uninsured (Finegold and Staveteig 2001).

A lack of sufficient childcare places welfare leavers and their children under considerable strain. Childcare takes up a substantial portion of low-income families' budgets; over 20 percent of poor families' budgets are devoted to childcare (Gina Adams and Monica Rohacek 2002). Thus, the lack of childcare is a material hardship.

Many low-income lone mothers have not received the childcare subsidies for which they are eligible. Despite substantial increases in funding for childcare in the late 1990s, in the year 2000, states provided childcare assistance to only 14 percent of all eligible children (Jennifer Mezey, Mark Greenberg, and Rachel Schumacher 2002). Most low-income families relied on relatives or other informal care arrangements for childcare (Julia Henly and Sandra Lyons 2000).[18] A study of former and current recipients in four large cities finds that sizable minorities had to quit a job or were not looking for a job due to inadequate childcare (Denise F. Polit, Rebecca Widom, Kathryn Edin, Stan Bowie, Andrew S. London, Ellen K. Scott, and Abel Valenzuela 2001). In sum, after welfare reform, most lone mothers were not receiving the childcare subsidies for which they were eligible, and many had unmet childcare needs.

Domestic violence is an especially damaging form of hardship among women, particularly among those with few resources to leave abusive relationships. The prevalence of domestic violence among low-income lone mothers is hard to assess, as national-level surveys of welfare recipients rarely cover topics of violence and abuse. In their review of research on welfare and domestic violence, Richard Tolman and Jody Raphael (2000) find that across studies, sizable minorities of welfare recipients experienced domestic violence, and they were battered more often than other low-income women. Other research that considered how work requirements have affected domestic violence found that the partners of some welfare recipients and leavers used violence to sabotage the work efforts of recipients (Lisa Brush 2000).

In sum, poverty is common among former welfare recipients, as are a host of material hardships. Given this prevalence of hardship – in spite of the booming economy of the late 1990s – one is hard-pressed to claim that the 1996 welfare reform has considerably improved most former recipients' lives.

Still, if TANF leavers were less likely to live in poverty and experienced fewer hardships than AFDC leavers, this would suggest that TANF is more successful in its amelioration of lone mothers' economic hardships than its predecessor. However, lone mothers who left TANF have generally fared no better on these measures than those who left AFDC. Among former recipients who worked after they left AFDC in the 1970s and 1980s, the median wage was $6.97 in 1994 dollars (about $7.80 in 1999 dollars), higher than the median wage for TANF leavers in 1999 (Vartanian and McNamara 2000). Under AFDC, of young welfare leavers (ages 16–32) who left welfare in the 1980s or early 1990s, about 50 percent lived in poverty two years after leaving welfare (Daniel Meyer and Maria Cancian 1998).

While little research examines material hardships among AFDC leavers, Kathryn Edin and Laura Lein's (1997) research on low-wage lone mothers, many of whom were former welfare recipients, shows that significant minorities of these women faced food, housing, and health hardships. Like TANF leavers, a significant minority of low-income working women in the 1980s lacked health insurance (Edin and Lein 1997). In general, sizable minorities of both groups of leavers faced material hardships of various sorts. This fact suggests that PRWORA has not substantially improved many welfare leavers' well-being.

FAMILY FORMATION

PRWORA was designed to alter family formation among low-income mothers, by reducing nonmarital childbearing and promoting two-parent families. Supporters of PRWORA believed that work requirements and time limits would discourage TANF receipt and encourage economic independence from the state via employment and/or marriage. In addition, supporters believed that family caps, more stringent child support enforcement, and increased benefits to two-parent families should decrease nonmarital childbearing (Robert Lerman 2002). Given the well-publicized negative economic, social, and psychological outcomes for those growing up in lone-parent households (see Charles Murray 2001 for a review), it is often suggested that declines in lone parenthood will lessen various kinds of hardship in families.

However, research on the effects of welfare policy on family formation finds that the relationship between the two is not at all straightforward. First of all, marital and fertility decisions are affected by a host of other macro-level factors: economic conditions that make men and women more or less "marriageable," social and cultural norms regarding childbearing and marriage, and tax and divorce law, to name a few. Further, research on the impacts of AFDC and TANF on family formation is decidedly mixed. Blank's (2002) review of ten national-level studies on the effects of TANF implementation, welfare waivers,[19] and family caps on marriage and fertility shows significant effects in some studies; for example, two studies found that family caps decreased nonmarital childbearing. But none of these significant relationships held up across several studies, and other studies reviewed found no relationship between welfare policy (including family caps) and family formation. Another study reports mixed trends in marriage rates and nonmarital births in the late 1990s, concluding that welfare reform had a modest effect on family formation, at best (Murray 2001).[20] Overall, the relationship between welfare policy and family formation is far from clear.

FEMINIST CRITIQUE OF WELFARE REFORM RESEARCH

The above review finds that since the passage of TANF, caseloads dropped and the economic well-being of many welfare leavers and low-income lone mothers improved slightly. However, lone mothers' widespread experience of poverty and material hardships during a period of economic expansion is troubling. In addition, the review uncovered few differences between the economic status of TANF leavers and AFDC leavers, suggesting that TANF was generally no more successful than AFDC in improving leavers' economic well-being. Moreover, a feminist analysis of welfare reform research points to several issues receiving too little attention in the welfare reform literature to date.

What characterizes feminist research on lone mothers and welfare reform? Granting that there may be as many answers to this question as there are feminists, as a starting point, I present five fundamentals of feminist research that are relevant to research on lone mothers and welfare reform.

First, feminist research questions and problematics are drawn from women's lived experiences (Sandra Harding 1987; Dorothy Smith 1987a).

153

Contemporary feminist research increasingly acknowledges and respects the diversity of women's experiences due to race/ethnicity, social class background, nationality, and sexuality (Patricia Hill Collins 1990; Maxine Baca Zinn and Bonnie Thornton Dill 1996). Feminist research on welfare reform draws from the varied daily experiences of low-income lone mothers; thus it includes the voices of poor lone mothers – or is at least informed by the issues raised by these women.

Second, while drawn from women's daily experiences, feminist research also addresses the influences of social, economic, and political institutions on women's everyday lives (Dorothy Smith 1987b). Feminist research on welfare then recognizes that while the welfare state is a complex institution that varies over time and across states, US welfare policy has always been influenced by gendered and racist ideology, and has shaped gender and race relations in fundamental ways (Ann Orloff 1993; Jill Quadagno 1996; Kenneth Neubeck and Noel Cazenave 2001).

A third fundamental of feminist research is that feminism is a theory of action. Feminist research is not only about women, but also *for* women, informing social and political change on their behalf (Harding 1987). In proposing social changes, feminists draw from the voices of all those affected by social changes. Thus, feminist welfare reform research works from the perspectives of lone mothers, not only those of government officials or the organizations and advocates that work with poor lone mothers. In doing so, feminist welfare reform research is no longer one more "objective" subject to study, but rather a vehicle to present well-informed analysis that seeks to both understand and change the conditions and policies that keep (or push) poor mothers and their children in poverty.

Decades of scholarship of feminist sociologists and feminists have documented the importance of unpaid caregiving work and the unequal sexual division of labor (for an overview see Francesca Cancian and Stacey Oliker 2000). Lone mothers are the primary caretakers and earners for their families. A fourth fundamental of feminist welfare reform research, then, is to acknowledge and account for women's unpaid work, a topic often ignored by mainstream welfare reform research.

Lastly, feminist research highlights power differences between women and men and explores how welfare bolsters (or undermines) women's power vis-à-vis men. The advent of federal social assistance to lone mothers in the 1930s somewhat lessened white single mothers' reliance on individual men. However, as women gained legal and political rights and entered employment in large numbers, lone mothers were increasingly expected to work for pay to gain "independence" from the state (see Nancy Fraser and Linda Gordon 1994 for an historical analysis of the discourse of "dependency"). But, as described above, many jobs held by lone mothers offer low pay and few benefits, so this form of independence is illusory for them. They can turn to welfare for short periods of time, but in the postindustrial era, welfare receipt became increasingly framed as a behavioral disorder – "welfare dependency" – particularly when recipients were young African American mothers whose multiple statuses (in addition to their assumed non-employment) were constructed as antithetical to "independence" (Fraser and Gordon 1994). When lone mothers cannot form autonomous, solvent households without men, this clearly diminishes their power (Orloff 1993). Feminist research on welfare reform includes critical analyses of women's "dependency" on men, low-wage work, and welfare.

I now apply these elements of a feminist critique to the aforementioned categories of welfare reform research. In so doing, I describe feminist welfare reform research and its improvements over mainstream welfare reform research.

Caseload reduction

Feminist welfare reform research is not preoccupied with caseload reduction, as it reveals little about lone-mother families' economic well-being. Furthermore, research on welfare caseloads has not been conducted on behalf of low-income women, but rather for government bureaucrats and politicians, among others – many of whom cite falling caseloads as evidence for the success of welfare reform. In US political discourse, falling caseloads are celebrated in large part because lone mothers' "dependence" on welfare has been deemed problematic (Schram and Soss 2002; Holloway Sparks 2003). For feminists, caseload reduction data are nowhere near a sufficient basis on which to evaluate the success of TANF.

Instead of applauding exits from TANF, feminist research frames TANF as a legitimate survival strategy, examining the extent to which low-income lone mothers on and off welfare can secure income and services to sustain their families (Janice Peterson 2002: 13). For example, Edin and Lein (1997) examined the paltry social assistance benefit levels available to lone mothers and the various kinds of strategies – such as legitimate employment, under-the-table work, and swapping services with friends and relatives – they used to support their families. Feminist research has documented the survival strategies of cycling in between welfare and employment and the "packaging" of work and welfare (Roberta Spalter-Roth, Beverly Burr, Lois Shaw, and Heidi Hartmann 1995; Harris 1996). In general, feminists have long critiqued the US welfare policies for their inadequacy, paternalism, and poorly designed incentives (for an overview see Linda Gordon 1990). Likewise, the research on material hardship presented above extends feminist welfare research into the post-TANF era. In sum, research that focuses solely on caseload reduction ignores crucial feminist issues: how women and their families are surviving, and what strategies could help improve their well-being.

LABOR FORCE PARTICIPATION

Much of the mainstream research on welfare reform fails to recognize the larger social contexts of low-income lone mothers' employment, such as persistent gender and racial inequalities in labor markets. In addition, the emphasis on paid work in mainstream research too often excludes the unpaid work that all lone mothers perform. A feminist analysis of welfare reform acknowledges that mothers' unpaid work and paid work are interrelated, and that the experiences of work and welfare vary considerably according to mothers' race/ethnicity and immigrant status.

Feminist welfare reform research recognizes women's diverse employment experiences based on race, ethnicity, and immigrant status, including persistent labor market inequalities experienced by women of color such as concentration in the lowest-paying jobs, little upward mobility, and discrimination (see Browne 1999). A handful of studies described above considered employment and hardship experiences by recipients' race/ethnicity, which is an important first step. But we need further research to ask how and *why* the post-TANF experiences of women of color differ from those of white welfare recipients. For example, Susan Tinsley Gooden (2000) showed that black welfare recipients in the Virginia TANF program had significantly lower wages than whites, even controlling for educational attainment; this was in part because black women were more likely to work in the most poorly paid food service and nursing aide jobs. Research in two Virginia counties revealed that caseworkers encouraged educational programs and offered transportation assistance in getting to work to white recipients more often than black recipients (Susan Tinsley Gooden 1998). Similarly, Joe Soss, Sanford Schram, Thomas Vartanian, and Erin O'Brien (2003) found that the most punitive family caps, time limits, and sanction rules were adopted in states where women of color constitute a higher proportion of the welfare caseload. These studies are emblematic of feminist research, because they pay attention to the diversity in women's everyday experiences and simultaneously critique the gendered and racist institutions that shape these experiences.

With its emphasis on paid work and income and its practice of equating work with employment, mainstream welfare reform research is too narrow in scope. This literature often fails to ask how welfare reform has affected the other (unpaid) work that all lone mothers do – taking care of children and other family members, and managing the household. For example, we need research that addresses the *quality* of childcare lone mothers are able to provide given work requirements of TANF (Randy Albelda 2001).

With their critiques of social citizenship – the right to economic security and welfare – Western European feminists have long been attuned to how welfare states affect women's care work (for example, see Berte Siim 1994; Anne Showstack Sassoon 1994; Ruth Lister 1997). Some advocate "gender difference" feminism – positing that welfare states should support women's caregiving work, and that care work should be sufficient to guarantee full citizenship for all citizens, just as paid work has been for men (for example, see Trudi Knijn and Monique Kremer 1997). While North American feminists have researched related ideas, such as women's disproportionate responsibility for household labor, until recently, few backed a welfare state that would fully support women's right to care.[21] Historically, North American feminists have been more likely to subscribe to "gender sameness" feminism, emphasizing the importance of women's employment in attaining equality with men. Certainly some North American feminists emphasize women's disproportionate completion of caregiving work and its role in perpetuating gender inequality; indeed, recently there has been a spate of theorizing and research on care work. (For example, see Cancian and Oliker 2000; Madonna Harrington Meyer 2000; Nancy Folbre 2001; Francesca Cancian, Demie Kurz, Andrew London, Rebecca Reviere, and Mary Tuominen 2002.)

Yet only a handful of studies has addressed how welfare reform affects women's care work, such as the research of Stacey Oliker (2000), Boushey (2001), and those working under the Urban Change project, a four-city study funded by the Manpower Research Demonstration Corporation. The Urban Change project found that in the post-TANF era, many lone mothers reported difficulties managing the multiple demands of paid, caregiving, and household work (Ellen Scott, Andrew London, and Kathryn Edin 2000; Andrew London, Ellen Scott, and Vicki Hunter 2002), particularly when they had children with health problems (Polit et al. 2001). Other research finds that African American mothers' reliance on relatives for childcare declined significantly from the mid-1970s to the mid-1990s (Karin Brewster and Irene Padavic 2002); the authors attributed the decline in part to higher employment rates among black mothers. These studies draw from lone mothers' everyday experiences of welfare reform, exploring the interconnectedness of women's paid and unpaid work and their effects on lone mothers' well-being.

Feminism informs many important new research questions regarding lone mothers' caregiving work. With its focus on paid work and employment income, most welfare reform research has ignored the "poverty of time" (Randy Albelda and Chris Tilly 1997) experienced by many lone mothers. Completing household labor is often more time-intensive for low-income lone mothers, who often must take the time to shop for bargains, leave the house to do laundry, and rely on public transportation (Albelda and Tilly 1997). Moving from welfare to paid work means that lone mothers have less time to complete these tasks, as well as less time to secure resources from social networks, odd jobs, or community agencies (Edin and Lein 1997). One study addressing these issues found that lone mothers expressed reservations about their ability to combine paid work, care work, and household work, and an oft-cited fear was losing "quality time" with their children (Ellen Scott, Kathryn Edin, Andrew London, and Joan Mazelis 2001). We need further feminist research on how time-poor lone mothers manage employment, housework, and parenting, as work requirements under welfare reform require lone mothers to perform all of these tasks.

In sum, we need more feminist welfare reform research that investigates the diversity in lone mothers' labor force participation experiences after welfare reform. Research needs to increasingly address not only how family responsibilities affect employment, but also how employment affects families, such as lone mothers' ability to engage in caregiving work.[22] Furthermore, feminist research recognizes the interconnectedness of these two issues: welfare reform requires participation in labor markets rife with gender and racial inequalities, and the jobs lone mothers obtain are often incompatible with their caregiving responsibilities. In addition, feminists stress that pushing lone mothers into low-wage jobs is not a solution, and in turn offers concrete strategies to improve women's earnings.

INCOME, POVERTY, AND HARDSHIPS

The above welfare reform literature on women's incomes, poverty rates, and material hardships includes many feminist research projects. In particular, much of the research on material hardships presented above pays close attention to the lived experiences of lone mothers, and considers what strategies could help women better meet their needs. However, the mainstream literature on these topics has at least two drawbacks. First, impacts-centered research is often limited by its focus on the impacts of welfare reform on individual lone mothers – their employment, incomes, poverty status, or experiences of material hardship. While undoubtedly useful in many respects, these analyses often overlook the more macro-level effects of welfare reform on poor women as a group – particularly poor women of color. Lisa Brush (2003) critiques the impacts-centered welfare reform research for its inattention to the structural effects of welfare reform on class, gender, and race relations; she contends that welfare reform will weaken workers vis-à-vis employers and strengthen white supremacy and male privilege. A focus on individual outcomes too often draws attention away from institutional inequalities; for example, one is hard-pressed to find research on welfare leavers' employment that examines the specific jobs welfare leavers hold, much less the gender and racial makeup of these jobs and whether or not these jobs are unionized. We need more research on how welfare reform affects power differentials between women and men, workers and management, and whites and people of color.

In overlooking the ways in which lone mothers survive, mainstream welfare reform research rarely addresses the new *costs* associated with working, such as childcare, transportation, and clothing. Edin and Lein (1997) find that welfare recipients engaged in a cost-benefit analysis to decide whether they should receive welfare or try to secure employment. Many lone mothers chose to receive welfare when the costs of employment outweighed the benefits.

Very little welfare reform research deducts the *costs* of employment from former or current recipients' incomes. Important exceptions are studies utilizing the "Self Sufficiency Standard" (Diana Pearce 2002: 168), a measure of the wage needed to provide families with the "cost of all major expenses including housing, child care, health care, transportation, taxes, and tax credits, as well as food." This standard includes any cash or near-cash income as family income, varies according to where families live, and is adjusted not only by family size, but also by the ages of children. Analyzing findings of welfare leaver studies using the Self Sufficiency Standard, Pearce (2002) found that in most of the localities included in her sample, a full-time job paid well below the Standard. Aside from this standard and Zedlewski's (2002) measures that deduct childcare costs from welfare recipients' incomes, other measures of family income overestimate lone mothers' economic resources by neglecting the steep costs of childcare and other costs of employment. We need more research that provides a realistic picture of economic hardship among lone mothers in the post-TANF era.

Family formation

Feminists have challenged TANF's goals of strengthening marriage and decreasing nonmarital fertility on several grounds. First, these goals are paternalistic, denying that lone mothers are best able to make their own marital and fertility decisions (Gwendolyn Mink 2002). Second, feminists have long recognized marriage as a patriarchal institution – in which violence against women and other less severe inequalities are not uncommon – and as heterosexist (Janet Gornick 2002). Third, citing marriage as the panacea to poverty bolsters women's economic dependence on men and fails to address the marked inequalities in women's paid and unpaid labor described above. Lastly, feminists critique the gendered and racist character of the US welfare state and of political discourse in general, both of which have long stigmatized lone mothers and deemed them unworthy for public assistance (see Collins 1990; Fraser and Gordon 1994; Gwendolyn Mink 1998; Sparks 2003). For example, the "dependency discourse" created by government officials and promoted by the media, cited lone mothers' welfare receipt and assumed lack of employment as causes of "unrestrained sexuality, drug problems, violence, crime, civic irresponsibility, and even poverty itself" (Schram and Soss 2002: 64). While recognizing that children growing up in lone-mother families tend to fare worse on social and economic indicators than those growing up in low conflict, two-parent families, feminists are critical of "dependency discourses" that blame lone motherhood for an array of social problems that are affected by many other phenomena. Further, promoting dependence on individual men or the low-wage labor market are not appropriate solutions to lone mothers' "dependency" on government assistance.

Given these feminist critiques of TANF family formation policies, it should be noted that feminist welfare reform research is not preoccupied with marriage and fertility rates per se, but rather lone mothers' experiences of marriage and fertility and how these experiences speak to family formation policies. For example, the Fragile Families Research Brief (2003) finds that only about one-third of unmarried parents faced no serious barriers to marriage (such as unemployment, depression, drug/alcohol problems, or past experience with domestic violence). While many unmarried parents professed hope that their relationships would lead to marriage, many also believed that steady employment – often untenable for those interviewed – was necessary for a strong marriage (Sara McLanahan, Irwin Garfinkel, Nancy Reichman, Julien Teitler, Marcia Carlson, and Christina Norland Audigier 2003). Kathryn Edin (2000) finds that low-income lone mothers were often reluctant to marry because rather than contributing resources, their partners added financial strain to their households; in addition, many lone mothers said they could not trust their partners, and that they enjoyed the freedom of being unmarried. Given these numerous barriers to stable marriages, it seems that family formation policies on their own are not likely to markedly improve lone mothers' well-being. These studies are feminist in their investigation into lone mothers' lived experience of bearing children and contemplating marriage.[23] We need further feminist research on marriage and fertility that examines the perspectives of lone mothers themselves, and that works outside of the "dependency discourse" that a priori condemns low-income lone mothers on welfare.

CONCLUSION

Despite the contributions feminist welfare research can and has made, we are left with the questions of why most mainstream welfare reform research has not been particularly feminist (or even informed by feminist welfare research) and how to engender more feminist research on welfare reform and lone mothers' poverty.

Several parties – politicians, the media, poverty researchers, and feminists themselves – have been blamed for the relative lack of feminist welfare reform research. Certainly the nonfeminist agenda shared by the architects of welfare reform – that of reducing caseloads and increasing employment and marriage among lone mothers – was important in directing research towards these areas. But one would expect more from researchers, particularly those who are feminist. Here, I offer three social scientists' insights into why mainstream welfare reform research is rarely feminist.

Alice O'Connor (2001), in her incisive historical analysis of poverty research in the United States, argues that several factors help explain the nature of mainstream welfare research. The required "neutrality" in quantitative social science research, the agendas of funding agencies, and the conservative political regime in the 1980s and early 1990s all centered attention on the individual behaviors of the poor rather than the political economy of poverty. Within this framework, even liberal poverty researchers distinguished the working poor, who were affected by structural inequalities like deindustrialization, from the "welfare poor," women assumed to be out of the labor force and dependent on the government. This latter group was targeted by welfare reform, based on the assumptions of conservatives and many liberals that "dependency" was the crux of the welfare problem and that it could be resolved by changing welfare to promote work and individual "self-sufficiency" (O'Connor 2001: 284). Thus, many poverty researchers have readily accepted this framework and churned out studies on declining caseloads, employment, and family formation. In so doing, they target the behavior of the "welfare poor" rather than critique the US political economy from a feminist perspective.

Schram and Soss (2002) lay out a similar but more structural analysis. The dependency discourse framed welfare receipt and recipients' assumed lack of employment as insidious social problems. This discourse thus rendered caseload and employment data sufficient grounds on which to evaluate the success of welfare reform. The "dependency discourse" was bolstered by media support and by its reliance on popular stereotypes of poor women of color as lazy and undeserving of support (Schram and Soss 2002; Sparks 2003). This focus blames poor people for their poverty, diverting political attention from a host of race, gender, and class inequities. Other issues, such as the effects of welfare reform on poverty, hardship, or on gender or racial inequality more generally, do not fall under the purview of the "dependency discourse" so receive less attention in mainstream research and reporting on welfare reform.

Lastly, Mink's (1998) analysis suggests that in addition to these popular discourses, feminists themselves are partly to blame for the relative lack of feminist research on welfare reform. Because feminists have celebrated women's independence via labor force participation, some mainstream (largely white, middle-class) feminists were not opposed to work require-ments or to other aspects of welfare reform. Given this blindness to the differential employment experiences of poor women and women of color, one should not be surprised that these issues have been absent from much welfare reform research.

O'Connor (2001) stresses the need for analyses of poverty researchers themselves and their roles in poverty debates. For example, greater respect for feminist research that may violate some of the steadfast rules of "objective" social science research, such as maintaining considerable distance between researchers and informants, could lead to more in-depth, experience-based research on poverty and welfare reform. Poverty knowledge needs to be generated from independent funding sources so that it can set the agenda for its own research rather than follow that of funding agencies (O'Connor 2001). Above all, O'Connor stresses the need for more poverty analyses that go beyond studies of individual behavior to examine "institutions, social and economic practices, work conditions, and especially the policy decisions that shape the economy and distribute economic opportunities" (p. 292). But changes in poverty research per se will not be sufficient to engender feminist research if the dependency discourse continues to prevail.

The dependency discourse is difficult to combat, given its resonance not only in political discourse, but also in popular media (Martin Gilens 1999) and in the mainstream population, to which anyone who teaches welfare to undergraduates can attest. We need further research that challenges the dependency discourse and offers alternative frameworks. For example, activist groups like the Kensington Welfare Rights Union (KWRU) have publicized the voices and experiences of poor people affected by welfare reform and other social policies.[24] KWRU calls for a state that guarantees economic human rights for all, including "food, housing, health care, education and a job at a living wage" (KWRU 2003). This group turns the dependency discourse on its head, claiming that the real problem with welfare is not that it fosters "dependency" on the government, but that the US state (and low-wage labor market) has eroded rather than ensured basic economic rights for low-income families. It is especially important that critiques of the dependency discourse challenge the racist stereotypes that fuel this discourse. For example, changes in media depictions of welfare recipients – in which recipients of color have been portrayed in a far more negative light than white recipients – are important in the formation of alternative discourses (Gilens 1999). These strategies provide critiques of the dependency discourse and build alternative frameworks for understanding welfare and poverty.

While some feminists have not been critical of welfare reform, many others have, such as those who challenge the dependency discourse and its underlying assumption that caregiving work is not real work. For example, acknowledging that care work is devalued in the workplace, unpaid at home, and often exacerbates women's economic disadvantage, the Women's Committee of 100 (2002) calls for a guaranteed caregivers' income (as well as a shorter work week and living wages, which make employment more tenable and beneficial for caregivers). This approach also contradicts the assumption that employment always confers "independence" by acknowledging the caregiving and household work on which many men are "dependent." This framework recognizes that lone mothers – and at some time or another, all adults – depend on others for their well-being and stresses *interdependence*. Organizations like the Women's Committee of 100 are important in challenging the "dependency discourse" and offering new frameworks from which feminist research questions can emerge.

In addition to challenges to discourses regarding lone mothers' "dependence" on welfare, we need more feminist research to challenge the existing beliefs about lone motherhood itself. Given the feminist critiques and research on TANF family formation policies discussed above, we need research that, while acknowledging its economic risks, treats lone motherhood as a legitimate choice rather than a social pathology. Like O'Connor's call for poverty research that looks beyond individual outcomes, we need more structural research on lone motherhood: research on the social, economic, and political conditions that bolster lone mothers' disadvantage, instead of on the individual-level outcomes attributed to lone motherhood. Indeed, the latter research studies often imply that higher marriage rates would be sufficient to ameliorate widespread social inequalities, while feminists stress that an amelioration of persistent institutional inequalities is necessary to reduce inequalities by race, class, and gender. Ideally, feminist areas of inquiry will also become more prevalent in mainstream welfare reform research, deepening our knowledge of the effects of welfare reform on lone mothers' lives and suggesting fruitful avenues for social and political change on their behalf.

ACKNOWLEDGMENTS

The author thanks several people for their constructive feedback: Randy Albelda, Susan Himmelweit, Jane Humphries, Avery Kolers, Cindy Negrey, Ellen Scott, Sarah Staveteig, Nancy Theriot, and two anonymous reviewers. She takes full responsibility for errors that remain.

NOTES

[1] I use the term "welfare reform" because it is so commonly used to refer to PRWORA. However, because "reform" carries the connotation of a positive change, this term is contested by feminists and others who see the legislation as more punitive toward poor families than the previous inadequate provisions.

[2] In 2000, about one-third of TANF families consisted of "child-only" cases – i.e., only a child in the household was receiving TANF cash assistance (US Department of Health and Human Services 2001: Table I-2). However, of these, one-half live with a parent – usually a mother. Parents are excluded from TANF for a range of reasons, including receiving another form of assistance, not being a US citizen, or being sanctioned for noncompliance of TANF rules (US Department of Health and Human Services 2001: Table II-3).

[3] Individuals must be employed in order to receive the EITC, so this program provides an employment incentive.

[4] See Blank (2002) or Robert Moffitt and Michele Ver Ploeg (2001) for in-depth discussions of "leaver studies" and their drawbacks. In particular, leaver studies "cannot give a full picture of the effects of policy changes because they focus only on those receiving welfare at a given time, not the entire population that might be affected" (Moffitt and Ver Ploeg 2001: 28).

[5] Former recipients who left welfare because they were sanctioned – or failed to follow the new rules under welfare reform – had substantially lower employment rates than women who left welfare voluntarily (Mary Corcoran, Sandra Danziger, Ariel Kalil, and Kristin Seefeldt 2000).

[6] These statistics are similar to those describing all of the poor in 2001, only about 38 percent of whom had private health insurance (about 47 percent of the poor had health insurance provided by the government) (US Census Bureau 2001).

[7] An exception is a recent study of low-income single-parent families conducted by the Institute for Women's Policy Research (Avis Jones-DeWeever, Janice Peterson, and Xue Song 2003). They find that a slight increase in labor force participation before and after welfare reform, but virtually no changes in the types of jobs low-income parents take.

[8] The Vartanian and McNamara (2000) study looks at leavers who initially left welfare in the 1970s and 1980s, some of whom returned to welfare during this time.

[9] See also Sharon Hays (2003) for in-depth accounts of the economic hardships in the lives of lone mothers many would deem "success stories" of TANF.

[10] Other research suggests that while most leavers earned about $2,500 in their first three months after leaving welfare, they experienced a 10–15 percent increase in quarterly earnings after the first year of leaving (Richer, Savner, and Greenberg 2001).

[11] One complicating factor is that the total family income of welfare leavers is more influenced by other family members' income than by their own. Of former recipients, Moffitt (2002: 3) writes:

> About half experience an increase in income immediately after leaving, with the other half experiencing a decline. After a year or two off the rolls, earnings gains slightly exceed the losses in TANF benefits. ... However, the major change in income comes from increased income from other family members. ... Such income is a larger component of total household income than either the earnings of the leaver herself or TANF and food stamp income.

[12] The poorest quintile of earners included those with disposable incomes of less than $7,850 in 1998 (Zedlewski 2002). Other research using these disposable income measures confirms that the poorest lone mothers' average disposable incomes fell between 1995 and 1997 (Wendell Primus, Lynette Rawlings, Kathy Larin, and Kathryn Porter 1999).

[13] This research compared two waves from the longitudinal SIPP (Survey of Income Participation Program) data from the US Census Bureau. The dates of the two waves were: December 1995–June 1996 and August 1999–February 2000. Low-income includes families whose income over the four-month period they were surveyed

averaged less than 200 percent of the poverty line ($13,290 for a family of three in 1999).

[14] The US poverty line uses pre-tax income, which overestimates the disposable income. Second, it does not include the value of noncash benefits such as Food Stamps as income, which underestimates the resources of families. Third, it does not take into account common expenditures of families that can also severely curtail family income, such as childcare or healthcare expenses. It also does not vary geographically or by urban/rural status. See Trudi Renwick and Barbara Bergmann (1993) for an alternative poverty line that takes into account some of these issues.

[15] Similarly, the Urban Change project, that examines welfare reform in four large US cities, found that 16 percent of stably employed low-income women (most of whom were former welfare recipients) surveyed experienced moderate or severe hunger (Denise F. Polit, Rebecca Widom, Kathryn Edin, Stan Bowie, Andrew S. London, Ellen K. Scott, and Abel Valenzuela 2001).

[16] One of the causes of food instability is the loss of Food Stamp benefits. Most welfare leavers remain eligible for Food Stamps, but only about four out of ten of former recipients whose families are eligible receive them (Sheila Zedlewski and Sarah Brauner 1999). Recent declines in Food Stamp participation have been the starkest among Latino families (Finegold and Staveteig 2002), and disproportionately common in families in which the children are citizens, but parents are not (Robert Greenstein and Jocelyn Guyer 2001). The loss of Food Stamps occurs because former recipients may not be able to perform administrative tasks such as appearing in person to apply for benefits or returning repeatedly to update information (Zedlewski and Brauner 1999; Greenstein and Guyer 2001).

[17] This is in part because some former recipients did not know they remained eligible for Medicaid after leaving TANF (Greenstein and Guyer 2001; Alan Weil and John Holahan 2002). However, in recent years the State Child Health Insurance Programs (SCHIP) have improved public awareness of health benefits available to low-income children.

[18] Very few nationally representative datasets ask about recipients' *preferences* for childcare, so it is difficult to know whether those who did not receive childcare subsidies actually wanted them. But a review of thirteen experimental welfare-to-work programs found that when given greater opportunity to have children in formal childcare programs (rather than informal care by relatives or friends), former recipients often chose formal care (Lisa Gennetian, Anna Gassman-Pines, Aletha Huston, Danielle Crosby, Young Eun Chang, and Edward Lowe 2001). Others suggest that while many welfare leavers receive childcare subsidies when they need them, other low-income lone mothers are not eligible because their incomes are too high, or because they do not know about childcare subsidies due to inadequate outreach efforts (Adams and Rohacek 2002).

[19] Welfare waivers were state-level policies through which states could be exempt from federal AFDC rules; many waivers began enforcing work requirements that became required under TANF.

[20] This is not surprising considering past research on the effects of welfare on family formation: Robert Moffitt's research reveals either inconsequential effects of welfare on family formation (1992) or small effects of welfare on fertility (1998) that are sensitive to the methodology one uses.

[21] For an analysis of this issue see Mink (1998).

[22] While most of it does not address mothers' caregiving per se, there is a substantial literature on the effect of welfare reform on children's behavioral outcomes and well-being. In their review of several local studies on the effects of TANF on children's achievement and behavior, Greg Duncan and Lindsay Chase-Landsdale

(2001: 403) conclude that "there is little evidence that elementary-school-aged children are harmed by the welfare reform packages." However, see the Letter to Members of Congress written by the National Center for Children in Poverty (www.nccp.org) for a summary of negative effects of welfare reform on children and adolescents.

[23] Though some feminists would disagree with the authors of the Fragile Families Study that policy-makers should "target the 'magic moment' when the likelihood of family formation is highest" in order to strengthen fragile families (McLanahan *et al.* 2003: 13).

[24] See Mimi Abramovitz (2000) for an in-depth discussion of other welfare rights organizations both pre- and post-TANF.

REFERENCES

Abramovitz, Mimi. 2000. *Under Attack, Fighting Back: Women and Welfare in the United States.* New York: Monthly Review Press.

Acs, Gregory and Pamela Loprest. 2001. *Final Synthesis Report of the Findings from ASPE's "Leavers" Grants.* Washington, DC: US Department of Health and Human Services.

Adams, Gina and Monica Rohacek. 2002. "Child Care and Welfare Reform," in Alan Weil and Kenneth Finegold (eds.) *Welfare Reform: The Next Act,* pp. 121–42. Washington, DC: Urban Institute Press.

Albelda, Randy. 2001. "Welfare-to-Work, Farewell to Families? US Welfare Reform and Work/Family Debates." *Feminist Economics* 7(1): 119–5.

—— and Chris Tilly. 1997. *Glass Ceilings and Bottomless Pits: Women's Work, Women's Poverty.* Boston, MA: South End Press.

Baca Zinn, Maxine and Bonnie Thornton Dill. 1996. "Theorizing Difference from Multiracial Feminism." *Feminist Studies* 22(2): 321–31.

Besharov, Douglas J. 2002. "Welfare Rolls: On the Rise Again." *Washington Post,* July 16. On-line. Available: http://www.aei.org/ra/rabesh020716.htm

Blank, Rebecca. 2001. "Welfare and the Economy." Policy Brief No. 7, The Brookings Institution. On-line. Available: http://www.brookings.org

——. 2002. "Evaluating Welfare Reform in the United States." *Journal of Economic Literature* XL (December): 1105–66.

Boushey, Heather. 2001. "Former Welfare Families Need More Help: Hardships Await Those Making Transition to Workforce." Economic Policy Institute Briefing Paper. On-line. Available http://epinet.org

Brewster, Karin L. and Irene Padavic. 2002. "No More Kin Care? Changes in Black Mothers' Reliance for Child Care, 1977–1994." *Gender and Society* 16(4): 546–63.

Browne, Irene. 1999. "Latinas and African Americans in the US Labor Market," in Irene Browne (ed.) *Latinas and African Americans at Work,* pp. 1–34. New York: Russell Sage.

Brush, Lisa D. 2000. "Battering, Traumatic Stress, and Welfare-to-Work Transition." *Violence Against Women* 6: 1039–65.

——. 2003. "Impacts of Welfare Reform." *Race, Gender, and Class* 10(3): 137–92.

—— and Daniel R. Meyer. 2000. "Work after Welfare: Women's Work Effort, Occupation, and Economic Well-Being." *Social Work Research* 24(2): 69–86.

—— and Stacey J. Oliker. 2000. *Caring and Gender.* Thousand Oaks, CA: Pine Forge.

——, Demie Kurz, Andrew S. London, Rebecca Reviere, and Mary Tuominen (eds.). 2002. *Child Care and Inequality: Rethinking Carework for Children and Youth.* New York: Routledge.

Collins, Patricia Hill. 1990. *Black Feminist Thought: Knowledge, Consciousness, and the Politics of Empowerment.* Boston, MA: Unwin Hyman.

Corcoran, Mary, Sandra K. Danziger, Ariel Kalil, and Kristin S. Seefeldt. 2000. "How Welfare Reform is Affecting Women's Work." *Annual Review of Sociology* 26: 241–69.

Duncan, Greg J. and P. Lindsay Chase-Landsdale. 2001. "Welfare Reform and Children's Well-Being," in Rebecca Blank and Ron Haskins (eds.) *The New World of Welfare*, pp. 391–420. Washington, DC: Brookings Institution Press.

Edin, Kathryn. 2000. "Few Good Men: Why Low-Income Single Mothers Don't Get Married." *American Prospect* 11 (January): 26–31.

—— and Laura Lein. 1997. *Making Ends Meet: How Single Mothers Survive Welfare and Low-Wage Work*. New York: Russell Sage.

Finegold, Kenneth and Sarah Staveteig. 2002. "Race, Ethnicity, and Welfare Reform," in Alan Weil and Kenneth Finegold (eds.) *Welfare Reform: The Next Act*, pp. 203–24. Washington, DC: Urban Institute Press.

Folbre, Nancy. 2001. *The Invisible Heart: Economics and Family Values*. New York: The New Press.

Fragile Families Research Brief. 2003. "Barriers to Marriage Among Fragile Families." May, No. 16. On-line. Available: http://crcw.princeton.edu/fragilefamilies/index.htm

Fraser, Nancy and Linda Gordon. 1994. "A Genealogy of Dependency: Tracing a Keyword of the US Welfare State." *Signs: Journal of Women in Culture and Society* 94(19:2): 309–36.

Gennetian, Lisa A., Anna Gassman-Pines, Aletha C. Huston, Danielle A. Crosby, Young Eun Chang, and Edward D. Lowe. 2001. "A Review of Child Care Policies in Experimental Welfare and Employment Programs." MDRC Next Generation Project, Working Paper No. 3. On-line. Available http://www.mdrc.org/NextGeneration/NGPublications.htm

Gilens, Martin. 1999. *Why Americans Hate Welfare: Race, Media, and the Politics of Antipoverty Policy*. Chicago: University of Chicago Press.

Gooden, Susan Tinsley. 1998. "All Things Not Being Equal: Differences in Caseworker Support toward Black and White Welfare Clients." *Harvard Journal of African American Public Policy* 4: 23–33.

——2000. "Race and Welfare: Examining Employment Outcomes of White and Black Welfare Recipients." *Journal of Poverty* 4(3): 21–41.

Gordon, Linda (ed.). 1990. *Women, the State, and Welfare*. Madison, WI: University of Wisconsin Press.

Gornick, Janet C. 2002. "Reconcilable Differences: What it Would Take for Marriage and Feminism to Say 'I Do'?" *The American Prospect* 13(7): 42–8.

Greenstein, Robert and Jocelyn Guyer. 2001. "Supporting Work through Medicaid and Food Stamps," in Rebecca M. Blank and Ron Haskins (eds.) *The New World of Welfare*, pp. 335–63. Washington, DC: Brookings Institution Press.

Harding, Sandra. 1987. "Is There A Feminist Method?" in Sandra Harding (ed.) *Feminism and Methodology*, pp. 1–14. Bloomington, IN: Indiana University Press.

Harris, Kathleen Mullan. 1993. "Work and Welfare among Single Parents in Poverty." *American Journal of Sociology* 99(2): 317–52.

——1996. "Life After Welfare: Women, Work, and Repeat Dependency." *American Sociological Review* 61(3): 407–26.

Haskins, Ron. 2001. "Effects of Welfare Reform on Family Income and Poverty," in Rebecca M. Blank and Ron Haskins (eds.) *The New World of Welfare*, pp. 103–30. Washington, DC: Brookings Institution Press.

Hays, Sharon. 2003. *Flat Broke With Children: Women in the Age of Welfare Reform*. Oxford: Oxford University Press.

Henly, Julia R. and Sandra Lyons. 2000. "The Negotiation of Child Care and Employment Demands Among Low-Income Parents." *Journal of Social Issues* 56(4): 683–706.

Jones-DeWeever, Avis, Janice Peterson, and Xue Song. 2003. *Before and After Welfare Reform: The Work and Well-Being of Low-Income Single Parent Families*. Washington, DC: Institute for Women's Policy Research. On-line. Available http://www.iwpr.org/pdf/D454.pdf

Knijn, Trudie and Monique Kremer. 1997. "Gender and the Caring Dimensions of Welfare States: Toward Inclusive Citizenship." *Social Politics* 4(3): 328–62.

KWRU (Kensington Welfare Rights Union). 2003. *Economic Human Rights*. On-line. Available www.kwru.org

Lerman, Robert. 2002. "Family Structure and Childbearing before and after Welfare Reform," in Alan Weil and Kenneth Finegold (eds.) *Welfare Reform: The Next Act*, pp. 33–52. Washington, DC: Urban Institute Press.

Lister, Ruth. 1997. *Citizenship: Feminist Perspectives*. New York: New York University Press.

London, Andrew S., Ellen K. Scott, and Vicki Hunter. 2002. "Children and Chronic Health Conditions: Welfare Reform and Health-Related Carework," in Francesca Cancian, Demie Kurz, Andrew S. London, Rebecca Reviere, and Mary C. Tuominen (eds.) *Child Care and Inequality: Rethinking Carework for Children and Youth*, pp. 99–112. New York: Routledge.

Loprest, Pamela. 1999a. "How Families that Left Welfare Are Doing: A National Picture." The Urban Institute New Federalism Project, Series B, No. B1. On-line. Available http://www.urban.org

——1999b. "Families Who Left Welfare: Who are They and How are They Doing?" The Urban Institute New Federalism Project, Discussion Paper 99-02. On-line. Available http://www.urban.org

——2001. "How are Families that Left Welfare Doing? A Comparison of Early and Recent Welfare Leavers." The Urban Institute New Federalism Project, Series B, No. B-36. On-line. Available http://www.urban.org

——2002. "Marking the Transition from Welfare to Work: Successes but Continuing Concerns," in Alan Weil and Kenneth Finegold (eds.) *Welfare Reform: The Next Act*, pp. 17–32. Washington, DC: Urban Institute Press.

McLanahan, Sara, Irwin Garfinkel, Nancy Reichman, Julien Teitler, Marcia Carlson, and Christina Norland Audigier. 2003. *The Fragile Families and Child Wellbeing Study: Baseline National Report*. On-line. Available http://crcw.princeton.edu/fragilefamilies/index/htm

Meyer, Daniel and Maria Cancian. 1998. "Economic Well-Being Following an Exit from Aid to Families with Dependent Children." *Journal of Marriage and the Family* 60: 479–92.

Meyer, Madonna Harrington. 2000. *Care Work: Gender, Labor, and the Welfare State*. New York: Routledge.

Mezey, Jennifer, Mark Greenberg, and Rachel Schumacher. 2002. "Increased Child Care Funding Needed to Help More Families." Center for Law and Social Policy. On-line. Available http://www.clasp.org

Mink, Gwendolyn. 1998. "The Lady and the Tramp (II): Feminist Welfare Politics, Poor Single Mothers, and the Challenge of Welfare Justice." *Feminist Studies* 24(1): 55–65.

——2002. "Violating Women: Rights Abuses in the Welfare Police State," in Randy Albelda and Ann Withorn (eds.) *Lost Ground: Welfare Reform, Poverty, and Beyond*, pp. 95–112. Cambridge, MA: South End Press.

Moffitt, Robert A. 1992. "Incentive Effects of the US Welfare System: A Review." *Journal of Economic Literature* 30 (March): 1–61.

——1998. "The Effects of Welfare on Marriage and Fertility," in Robert A. Moffitt (ed.) *Welfare, the Family, and Reproductive Behavior*, pp. 50–97. Washington, DC: National Research Council.

——2002. "From Welfare to Work: What the Evidence Shows." Welfare Reform and Beyond Brief No. 13, January, The Brookings Institution. On-line. Available http://www.brook.edu/dybdocroot/wrb/publications/pb/pb13.htm

—— and Michele Ver Ploeg (eds.). 2001. *Evaluating Welfare Reform in an Era of Transition*. Washington, DC: National Academy Press.

Murray, Charles. 2001. "Family Formation," in Rebecca M. Blank and Ron Haskins (eds.) *The New World of Welfare*, pp. 137–60. Washington, DC: Brookings Institution Press.

Neubeck, Kenneth and Noel Cazenave. 2001. *Welfare Racism: Playing the Race Card Against America's Poor*. New York: Routledge.

Nightingale, Demetra Smith. 2002. "Work Opportunities for People Leaving Welfare," in Alan Weil and Kenneth Finegold (eds.) *Welfare Reform: The Next Act*, pp. 103–20. Washington, DC: Urban Institute Press.

O'Connor, Alice. 2001. *Poverty Knowledge: Social Science, Social Policy, and the Poor in Twentieth-Century US History*. Princeton, NJ: Princeton University Press.

Oliker, Stacey J. 2000. "Examining Care at Welfare's End," in Madonna Harrington Meyer (ed.) *Care Work: Gender, Labor, and the Welfare State*, pp. 167–85. New York: Routledge.

Orloff, Ann Shola. 1993. "Gender and the Social Rights of Citizenship." *American Sociological Review* 58: 303–28.

Parrott, Sharon. 1998. "Welfare Recipients Who Find Jobs: What Do We Know About Their Employment and Earnings?" Center on Budget and Policy Priorities. On-line. Available http://www.cbpp.org

Pearce, Diana. 2002. "Measuring Welfare Reform Success by a Different Standard," in Gary Delgado (ed.) *From Poverty to Punishment: How Welfare Reform Punishes the Poor*, pp. 166–86. Oakland, CA: Applied Research Center.

Peterson, Janice. 2002. "Feminist Perspectives on TANF Reauthorization: An Introduction to Key Issues for the Future of Welfare Reform." Institute for Women's Policy Research Briefing Paper, February. On-line. Available http://www.iwpr.org/pdf/e511.html

Polit, Denise F., Rebecca Widom, Kathryn Edin, Stan Bowie, Andrew S. London, Ellen K. Scott, Abel Valenzuela. 2001. "Is Work Enough? The Experiences of Current and Former Welfare Mothers Who Work." Project on Devolution and Urban Change, Manpower Demonstration Research Corporation. On-line. Available http://www.mdrc.org

Porter, Kathryn H. and Allen Dupree. 2001. "Poverty Trends for Families Headed by Working Single Mothers: 1993 to 1999." Center on Budget and Policy Priorities. On-line. Available http://www.cbpp.org

Primus, Wendell. 2001. "Comment on 'Effects of Welfare Reform on Family Income and Poverty,'" in Rebecca M. Blank and Ron Haskins (eds.) *The New World of Welfare*, pp. 130–6. Washington, DC: Brookings Institution Press.

——, Lynette Rawlings, Kathy Larin, and Kathryn Porter. 1999. "The Initial Impacts of Welfare Reform on the Incomes of Single-Mother Families." Center on Budget and Policy Priorities. On-line. Available: http://cbpp.org

Quadagno, Jill. 1996. *The Color of Welfare: How Racism Undermined the War on Poverty*. New York: Oxford University Press.

Renwick, Trudi J. and Barbara R. Bergmann. 1993. "A Budget-Based Definition of Poverty, With an Application to Single-Parent Families." *Journal of Human Resources* 28(1): 1–24.

169

Richer, Elise, Hedieh Rahmanou, and Mark Greenberg. 2003. "Welfare Caseloads Increase in Most States in Fourth Quarter." Center for Law and Social Policy. On-line. Available http://www.clasp.org

Richer, Elise, Steve Savner, and Mark Greenberg. 2001. "Frequently Asked Questions About Working Leavers." Center for Law and Social Policy. On-line. Available http://www.clasp.org

Schram, Sanford F. and Joe Soss. 2002. "Success Stories: Welfare Reform, Policy Discourse and the Politics of Research," in Randy Albelda and Ann Withorn (eds.) *Lost Ground: Welfare Reform, Poverty, and Beyond*, pp. 57–78. Cambridge, MA: South End Press.

Scott, Ellen K., Andrew London, and Kathryn Edin. 2000. "Looking to the Future: Welfare-Reliant Women Talk About Their Job Aspirations in the Context of Welfare Reform." *Journal of Social Issues* 56(4): 727–46.

Scott, Ellen K., Kathryn Edin, Andrew London, and Joan Mazelis. 2001. "My Children Come First: Welfare-Reliant Women's Post-TANF Views of Work–Family Tradeoffs and Marriage," in Greg J. Duncan and P. Lindsay Chase-Lansdale (eds.) *For Better and For Worse: Welfare Reform and the Well-Being of Children and Families*. New York: Russell Sage Press.

Showstack Sassoon, Anne (ed.). 1994. *Women and the State: The Shifting Boundaries of Public and Private.* London: Hutchinson.

Siim, Berte. 1994. "Engendering Democracy: Social Citizenship and Political Participation for Women in Scandinavia." *Social Politics* 1(3): 286–305.

Smith, Dorothy E. 1987a. *The Everyday World as Problematic: A Feminist Sociology.* Boston, MA: Northeastern University Press.

——1987b. "Women's Perspective as a Radical Critique of Sociology," in Sandra Harding (ed.) *Feminism and Methodology*, pp. 84–96. Bloomington, IN: Indiana University Press.

Soss, Joe, Sanford F. Schram, Thomas P. Vartanian, and Erin O'Brien. 2003. "The Hard Line and the Color Line," in Sanford Schram, Joe Soss, and Richard Fording (eds.) *Race and the Politics of Welfare Reform*, pp. 225–53. Ann Arbor, MI: University of Michigan Press.

Spalter-Roth, Roberta, Beverly Burr, Lois Shaw, and Heidi Hartmann. 1995. *Welfare That Works.* Washington, DC: Institute for Women's Policy Research.

Sparks, Holloway. 2003. "Queens, Teens, and Model Mothers," in Sanford Schram, Joe Soss, and Richard Fording (eds.) *Race and the Politics of Welfare Reform*, pp. 171–95. Ann Arbor, MI: University of Michigan Press.

Tolman, Richard and Jody Raphael. 2000. "A Review of Research on Welfare and Domestic Violence." *Journal of Social Issues* 56(4): 655–82.

US Census Bureau. 2001. *Health Insurance in 2001.* On-line. Available http://www.census.gov/hhes/www/hlthin01.html

—— 2003. "American Community Change Profile 2000–2002," Table 3. On-line. Available http://www.census.gov/acs/www/Products/Profiles/Chg/2002/0102/Tabular/010/01000US3.htm (September 14, 2003).

US Department of Health and Human Services. 2001. "Characteristics and Financial Circumstances of TANF Recipients Oct. 1999–Sept. 2000." On-line. Available http://www.acf.dhhs.gov/programs/opre/characteristics/fy2000

—— and 2003a. "Recipients and Families 1936–1999." On-line. Available http://www.acf.dhhs.gov/news/stats/3697.htm (September 14, 2003).

—— and 2003b. "Temporary Assistance for Needy Families (TANF) Percent of Total US Population." On-line. Available http://www.acf.hhs.gov/news/stats/6097rf.htm (September 14, 2003).

Vartanian, Thomas P. and Justine M. McNamara. 2000. "Work and Economic Outcomes After Welfare." *Journal of Sociology and Social Welfare* 27(2): 41–76.

Weil, Alan and John F. Holahan. 2002. "Health Insurance, Welfare and Work," in Alan Weil and Kenneth Finegold (eds.) *Welfare Reform: The Next Act*, pp. 143–62. Washington, DC: Urban Institute Press.

Weil, Alan and Kenneth Finegold. 2002. "Introduction," in Alan Weil and Kenneth Finegold (eds.) *Welfare Reform: The Next Act*, pp. xi–xxxi. Washington, DC: Urban Institute Press.

Women's Committee of 100. 2002. "An Immodest Proposal." On-line. Available http://www.welfare2002.org/displays.html#top

Zedlewski, Sheila R. 2002. "Family Incomes: Rising, Falling, or Holding Steady?" in Alan Weil and Kenneth Finegold (eds.) *Welfare Reform: The Next Act*, pp. 53–78. Washington, DC: Urban Institute Press.

—— and Sarah Brauner. 1999. "Are the Steep Declines in Food Stamp Participation Linked to Falling Welfare Caseloads?" The Urban Institute New Federalism Project, Series B, No. B-3. On-line. Available http://urban.org

Mundane Heroines: Conflict, Ethnicity, Gender, and Female Headship in Eastern Sri Lanka

Kanchana N. Ruwanpura and Jane Humphries

INTRODUCTION

Until the end of the 1970s, Sri Lanka was a "model" of democracy and development. The adult franchise had been achieved in 1931, and there were regular elections until 1981 with governments changing through the electoral process. The performance of the economy was cited as exemplary. A strong and consistent welfare orientation on the part of successive governments resulted in a better distribution of income and social services and a good performance according to the Human Development Index (HDI). For a poor country, Sri Lanka's record in providing a relatively high quality of life is justly famed (Amartya Sen 1981, 1984; Jane Humphries 1993; Stephan Klasen 1993; UNDP 2000). Governments were also committed to the improvement of the status and well-being of women.

Outcomes here too were celebrated with the gender gap in physical well-being narrowing.

Sri Lanka remains a paragon of development economics. But there is an underside to this success story as far as the status of women is concerned, which, if neglected, may imperil advances both in Sri Lanka and in other countries where gender equality is sought. To reveal this underside, we will examine the progress of Sri Lanka from the standpoint of a doubly disadvantaged and neglected group, a group in jeopardy economically and geographically: female-headed households in the war-torn districts of eastern Sri Lanka.

For the last twenty years, the eastern region of Sri Lanka has been the site of civil war. Since 1983 more than 60,000 people have died in the ethnic conflict (Robert Rotberg 1999). The empirical evidence used to demonstrate Sri Lankan success has by and large excluded these war-torn districts, and resulted in too rosy a picture of Sri Lankan development. Many discussions of the welfare of women both in advanced industrial countries and in the developing world are misleading because they assume a "male breadwinner family" structure. Debates about welfare policies, for example, are too often premised on the ideal of a family headed by an adult male. Similarly, the current emphasis on bargaining between husbands and wives deflects attention from the high percentage of households with children but without adult males. A contribution of feminist economists in recent years has been to publicize the incidence of households headed by women not only in advanced industrial economies, but also in those same economies in the past, as well as in developing countries. In Sri Lanka, a fifth of households are female-headed, a much higher percentage than in Bangladesh or Pakistan.[1] This relatively high percentage may be caused by the political turmoil. But as early as 1981, when the conflict was barely under way, Sri Lanka's incidence of female headship was already unusual by the standards of the region. Moreover, recent evidence suggests that female headship has been increasing sharply even in "peaceful" parts of the country. It is important to try to trace the origins of female-headed households, since they bear on the type of policy that is most efficacious in assisting these households. We should not trust a claim that female headship is the product of war and turmoil, an aberration that will disappear when peace breaks out. This insistence continues the long line of "pathological" interpretations of female headship, which depict it as a social problem whose elimination is the correct policy goal.

Another important contribution of feminist economists in recent years has been to emphasize differences within the female experience. By rejecting falsely homogenizing accounts of women's lives, feminist economists have unlocked the multiplicity of ways in which gendered relations of dominance and subordination are maintained. A source of difference with perhaps increasing importance in the modern world is ethnicity. With its co-existing

Muslim, Sinhala, and Tamil groups,[2] eastern Sri Lanka provides a perfect context for the exploration of ethnicity as a source of variation in the origins of female headship and responses to being left alone to raise children, look after parents, and earn a living. The households included in this study share a common structure and face the same economic problems. They struggle for a better life in the same geographical area. Yet ethnic differences divide them. The combination of gender, ethnicity, and regional variables provides the basis for a study of gender and identity.

FEMALE-HEADED HOUSEHOLDS: CONCEPTUAL ISSUES

Sylvia Chant's (1997) review of female-headed households in developing countries identifies a large number of conceptual problems in defining both the household and headship (see also Mayra Buvinic, Nadia Youssef, and Barbara von Elm 1978: 7–12; Nadia Youssef and Carol Hetler 1981: 12–17, 26–31; 1984: 8–15). Households can be defined literally in terms of shared shelter and cooking arrangements. But such households then overlap with and relate to families, defined in terms of ties of blood and marriage, in untidy and confusing ways. The households that appear here almost invariably comprise members of the same family living under a single roof. It is their efforts that are summarized as a family survival strategy though often linked to and reinforced by assistance from relatives and friends residing elsewhere.

Headship, the notion of one person in the household being responsible for its other members, has been described as a patriarchal construct (Olivia Harris 1981). The identification of the husband/father as the "natural" source of authority enabled the state in Western Europe to reach and organize households for administrative and political purposes and was adventitiously exported around the world through colonialism (Nancy Folbre 1991). This hierarchical conceptualization masked a more complex reality in all societies, reducing the many dimensions of households to the characteristics of their male heads. Women within households became invisible, "their characteristics and contributions being largely ignored" (INSTRAW 1992: 236; cited in Chant 1997: 7).

Various strategies have been used to rescue women from this invisibility and illuminate their unappreciated responsibility for household survival and functioning. A focus on households without men forces women from the shadows. Indeed most national and international data collections concentrate on this formal *de jure* definition and report households, in which an adult woman, usually with children, resides without a male partner as "female-headed" (United Nations 1991). Still within this formal definition, distinct types of household abound. Feminist economists have struggled to establish a classification system. One useful typology suggested by Chant (1997) includes: lone-mother households, which themselves

175

include various types, depending on the marital status of the female head and her legal and actual relationship with the father(s) of her children; female-headed extended households; and female-singleton households.

But households that have no men present may be only the tip of the iceberg. An alternative strategy, which involves linking headship more explicitly to relative economic contributions, foregrounds the extent to which women are responsible for the maintenance of households or share such responsibility even when an adult male is present, thus revealing an otherwise submerged mass of "quasi-female-headed households" (Mayra Buvinic, Juan Pablo Valenzuela, Temistocles Molina, and Electra Gonzalez 1992; Mayra Buvinic and Geeta Rao Gupta 1997). Another increasingly important complication concerns households that are temporarily without male heads who may have migrated in search of work or be serving in the army, leaving their wives as *de facto* female heads (Nadia Youssef and Carol Hetler 1983). In theory and in empirical work, most attention has been on *de jure* lone mothers who constitute a relatively clear-cut category and usually predominate over other types of female heads. The struggle to develop a taxonomy that accommodates the many different types of female-headed households while simultaneously recognizing their common denominator, reflects an important general tension in feminist research between an insistence on the varied nature of women's experience alongside an identification of gender as a meaningful category of analysis.

While female-headed households themselves have been increasingly recognized as complex and varied, explanations for their existence, and indeed almost ubiquitous rise, have converged. These explanations involve both global forces, such as demographic patterns and the legacies of colonialism (Folbre 1991), as well as the pressures of economic development and urbanization, with local factors linked to regional variations (Chant 1997). More generally Simon Duncan and Rosalind Edwards (1994, 1997) have identified four main interpretations of lone motherhood that, despite being developed in the context of one particular advanced industrial country, the United Kingdom, have resonance with reactions and attitudes elsewhere. Lone motherhood is seen as (1) a social threat; (2) a social problem; (3) a "lifestyle" choice; and (4) an escape from patriarchy. Using this framework, how lone mothers in Sri Lanka see themselves and their struggles and are assisted or additionally disadvantaged by their wider kin and community is usefully related to the perception of lone motherhood as either social pathology or feminist reaction.

FEMALE-HEADED HOUSEHOLDS: GLOBAL AND REGIONAL INCIDENCE

The major problems involved in developing and standardizing universally applicable definitions of household types and/or household headship hinders comparative analysis of female headship. Even a serious scholar on the subject insists that her conclusions on "the macro-level dynamics of female headship" and inter- and intra-regional comparisons are "accordingly tentative" (Chant 1997: 69). Similarly Folbre, in her earlier (1991) survey, prioritized the need for detailed household surveys in order to uncover the extent of women's support for households and so gauge the frequency of female-maintained households.

Nonetheless, some conclusions are possible. Female-headed households in many countries of the developed and developing world appear to be on the rise. Various factors operating on a global scale have contributed. These include the globalization of economic production, the spread of neoliberal economic strategies under the aegis of the financial institutions of the advanced industrial economies, population growth, and the growing awareness of gender inequality promoted in part by the new interest and initiatives of international agencies (Youssef and Hetler 1984; Chant 1997). The increased attention afforded women's status and well-being, as well as policy initiatives to advance them, have relaxed divorce legislation and made it slightly easier for women to remain outside marriage worldwide (Chant 1997: 80–1).

These global forces are not so strong as to overpower local and regional conditions. The incidence and meaning of female headship varies widely between regions. In South Asia, rates of female headship are relatively low. In the early 1980s, for example, female-headed households were only 9.5 percent of households in Bangladesh and as few as 1.8 percent in Pakistan (Folbre 1991: Table 3.1). Sri Lanka in 1981 was an outlier for the region, with 17.4 percent of households headed by women.

Political turmoil undoubtedly contributed to the relatively high Sri Lankan rate of female headship. Nancy Folbre's 1991 survey of global influences noted the importance of armed conflict, with female headship tending to be higher in the aftermath of war and civil strife. But in 1981 the conflict was just beginning. Moreover, it appears that female headship has been increasing sharply in areas untouched by the ethnic conflict (Harsha Aturupane, Chandra Rodrigo, and Sasanka Perera 1997). By 1990, the Department of Statistics reported that women headed 20 percent of households, and this figure excluded the Northern and Eastern Provinces. What factors other than the political and civil unrest contributed to this incidence?

Another variable associated with female headship is the out-migration of men. Better opportunities both overseas and in other regions pull migrants while economic stagnation pushes them. Mothers are perhaps less willing, as well as less able, to move than are fathers, especially if that means leaving children behind. Thus, migration has become a male survival strategy, often synonymous with the desertion of women and children (Youssef and Hetler 1984, Diane Elson 1992). In Sri Lanka, the civil war exacerbated male out-migration from the Eastern Province, leaving families headed by women

177

stranded. Feminist development economists have recently emphasized women's property rights as an important underlying determinant of their status and well-being (Carmen Diana Deere 1990; Bina Agarwal 1997).

Command over rural resources is particularly important in determining women's ability to remain outside marriage (Deere 1990). The traditional legal code adhered to by the majority Sinhala community in Sri Lanka is relatively favorable to women (Yoga Rasanayagam 1993). Women in Sri Lanka have traditionally enjoyed rights to their own income, to keep their natal family name, and to represent themselves in a court of law without men's guardianship (World Bank 1995). On the other hand, Sri Lankan women's access to income-generating resources appears weak. They make up a smaller percentage of the labor force than of the population and experience higher unemployment rates (Vidyamali Samarasinghe 1993). Many work in the subsistence sector and so are not counted in the national statistics.

Within the national aggregates, distinct groups of Sri Lankan women display nonstandard characteristics often associated with ethnicity (Samarasinghe 1993). Consider Tamil plantation workers, who were originally brought to the island from impoverished areas of India by their British colonial rulers to work in the newly opened tea plantations. Now representing about 8 percent of the total population, this group is mainly Hindu and speak Tamil. Three-quarters of the Tamil population live in plantations in the central highlands. After the nationalization of the estates in 1975, more than 80 percent of Tamil plantation workers were employed by two semi-governmental organizations – which have been privatized since the 1990s. As a group, for historical and political reasons, they have been excluded from the state-sponsored welfare programs. Their immigrant status and "separateness" has left them generally disadvantaged in terms of housing, nutrition, and access to education (Kumari Jayawardena 1984).

Women of this group have fared particularly poorly. Despite higher access to wage employment in a sector that has been the main export earner, they have the lowest literacy rates and the highest maternal mortality (Samarasinghe 1993). The gender disparities that are disappearing in Sri Lanka remain firmly entrenched in this group. Their political and economic experience, combined with their cultural inheritance, has blocked any gains in status and well-being that they might have achieved as a result of their proletarianization. The isolation of the community and the generally low status of Tamil men, who react by reasserting male familial and community authority, have reinforced patriarchal Hindu cultural norms. The men of the community express no sympathy with women's double shift and insist that they go out to work (Rachel Kurian 1982). Yet the women's arduous employment as tea pluckers has had no effect on the intra-family distribution of even the most basic resources. Men, for example, retain their traditional preferential access to food. More generally, Kanchana N. Ruwanpura (2001) has shown that the civil conflict has promoted oppressive gender standards within both Sinhala and Tamil ethnic groups, and by emphasizing motherhood and sacrifice as the archetypal feminine path, have retarded women's struggle for equality (Ruwanpura 2001; see also Malathi de Alwis 1998a, 1998b).

Thus evidence suggests that female experience is fragmented by ethnicity and that ethnic differences can achieve new resilience and power in maintaining women's subjugation in postcolonial and conflictual situations. Yet ethnicity remains an under-explored category in feminist economics. Deconstruction of the female-headed household by ethnicity in Sri Lanka may help illuminate the sources of continued gender inequality, as well as provide a case study of the interaction of gender and ethnicity with implications for other studies in other times and places. Table 1 summarizes the factors promoting and inhibiting female headship differentiated according to the ethnic groups of eastern Sri Lanka.

Table 1 suggests that the routes into female headship might vary by ethnicity. Varying reasons for adopting the responsibilities of headship mean that the households are in different circumstances in terms of feasible survival strategies. Policies to help should be sensitive to this diversity, as effective assistance to widows with resident adolescent children, for example, may require different kinds of intervention than optimal aid to deserted women with dependent babies. At the same time ethnicity influences the feasible strategies available to the women and their households. The war and unrest has probably created particularly difficult conditions for Tamil female heads, especially if they were widowed or

Table 1 Factors influencing the formation of female-headed households in the Tamil, Muslim, and Sinhala communities of eastern Sri Lanka

Factors	Tamils	Muslims	Sinhala
Major precipitating factors			
Feminized sex ratio as a result of civil conflict	✓		
Rising gap between male and female life expectancy	✓	✓	✓
Male migration	✓	✓	✓
Upheaval leading to disguised desertion	✓		
Age gap between brides and grooms	✓	✓	✓
Sexual double standard	✓	✓	✓
Legal code (women traditionally enjoyed rights to own land, and to obtain and dispose of income)			✓
Major inhibiting factors			
Social ideas of marriage and motherhood	✓	✓	✓
Restricted gender roles for women	✓	✓	✓
Male–female earnings gap	✓		✓
Increased household extension during economic crises	✓	✓	
Restrictions on women's activities		✓	

Source: Adapted from Chant (1997: Fig. 5.1, p. 148).

abandoned as young women with dependent infants or if their wider kinship ties have been disrupted. Sinhala female heads might be expected to benefit from the women-friendly Sinhalese legal code and relaxed social attitudes as well as their majority status in the country as a whole. Muslim women may be hampered by the proscriptions on their activities, with especially severe consequences if these lead to their exclusion from income-earning opportunities.

THE ECONOMIC BACKGROUND

The economic base of eastern Sri Lanka is agricultural with irrigated rice cultivation being most important. With lagoons shaping the coastal belt, deep sea and lagoon fishing are other common occupations. However, there is also reliance on plantation crops, mercantile trade, and the informal economy. While these activities form the mainstay of the region, the level of economic development in each district varies.

Ampara, Batticaloa, and Trincomalee, the three districts that comprise the Eastern Province, all belong to the dry zone region of Sri Lanka and depend upon irrigation for paddy cultivation. However, accessibility to irrigation facilities varies, and the ongoing ethnic conflict has had a negative impact on the level and quality of irrigation programs in the region. There are no systematic data available on per capita income, or gross domestic production, or employment levels for eastern Sri Lanka. The intensity of the conflict at times during the past seventeen years permits only a sketchy outline of the level of economic development.

Ampara has been the least affected by the conflict, which is probably partially attributable to its geographic location in the southernmost part of the Eastern Province. Trincomalee, after many years of severe fighting, at the time when the fieldwork was undertaken, was enjoying a period of calm. This, however, did not hold true for Batticaloa, where only a mere 25 percent of the land mass was under state direction, since the remaining 75 percent was occupied by the Liberation Tamil Tigers for Eelam (LTTE), with continued conflict, battle, and skirmishes between the state forces and the LTTE taking place.[3] Consequently, Batticaloa has a low level of economic development with its infrastructure particularly battered. While a sense of economic "normalcy" has returned to Trincomalee, Ampara retains the strongest economy in the region. As a whole, the region is impoverished, with high levels of unemployment and low levels of formal economic activity.[4] Given the conflict-ridden state of affairs and the lack of detailed economic data, a comprehensive analysis is difficult. This limitation, however, should not devalue findings about the survival strategies and levels of economic well-being of female-headed households in the region. The lack of accurate official statistical economic information drives the need for a qualitative analysis of female headship.

METHODOLOGY

The fieldwork involved the administration of a customized questionnaire in Ampara, Batticaloa, and Trincomalee in 1998 and 1999. One of the authors, Kanchana Ruwanpura, administered 298 questionnaires, focusing on the origins, circumstances, and survival strategies of female-headed households.[5]

Ruwanpura identified and contacted households through local NGOs. The definition of female headship was broad. The women surveyed included both *de facto* and *de jure* female heads and they were identified according to both community perception and individual self-identification.[6] Given this sampling strategy, it is likely that our female heads are not representative of all female heads. They are probably more energetic and aware than most of their peers, a feature discussed further in the context of our findings. But note that while the sample as a whole is selected, there is no reason to believe that within the sample, energy and awareness are distributed differently by ethnicity, the characteristic that we are investigating. The aim was not to construct a sample from which inferences about the prevalence of female headship in the population could be made. Such work is desperately needed in most countries of the developing world. Censuses inevitably structure their data collection within patriarchal categories and so undercount married women workers and women's support for households. Only detailed household surveys can reveal the numbers of households maintained by women. But such a survey would have required a much greater commitment of resources than we could mount. Even within the category of female-headed households, broadly defined, there was no attempt to sample households randomly and the sizes of the samples, especially when subdivided by district or ethnicity, are sometimes too small to test hypotheses statistically. Where they are large enough to perform standard statistical tests, we do so with the caveat that, as with any nonrandom sample, any differences or similarities might be due to selection bias. Although we discussed poverty levels, they were not our focus. Instead the aim was to construct a sample from which inferences could be made about the paths into female headship and the survival strategies adopted. The questionnaires were designed to capture the economic situation of Muslim, Sinhala, and Tamil women heads of household. We also gathered information on demographic, kinship, social, educational, and religious variables. The regional variation was also investigated and findings reported by Ruwanpura (2001).

In contrast to the depreciation of subject-originating information normal in mainstream economics, feminist scholarship applauds the use of questionnaires to uncover evidence that would otherwise remain buried behind the implicit and unconscious assumptions of formal data collection (Martha MacDonald 1995: 175–91). Furthermore, feminist authors argue

181

that open-ended interviews can reveal relationships that would remain hidden even with gender-sensitive probing via questionnaires. Ruwanpura conducted 100 in-depth interviews simultaneously with the administration of the questionnaires. Some of the interviews convey an astonishing level of feminist awareness and understanding, reinforcing our suspicion that our sample may be self-selected. In addition, while finding cases had already relied on community recognition and self-identification as female heads, involvement in the study, and the interview in particular, undoubtedly deepened women's understanding of themselves as representatives of a specific kind of women's experience. The subjects of our study could not be entirely independent of or unresponsive to the process of being studied (Tony Lawson 1997, 1999).

But if the individuals are exceptional, the circumstances they face are not. The questionnaires and interviews provide both quantitative and qualitative accounts of the households and their circumstances. They allow us to link the statistical descriptions of the households' situations to the nuanced backgrounds conveyed in the conversations. Through these, our aim is to understand the structure and functioning of these households and their survival strategies, to try to look at the world from their point of view, and to explore how they became heads of households and survive as such. We can and do compare our evidence with other material for Sri Lanka and with findings from other studies of female-headed households. But the novel combination of standard quantitative indicators of material well-being and social deprivation with qualitative contextual information allows exposure of otherwise hidden dimensions of these households and how they fit into their communities. A particular interest is the nature and reliability of kinship support and its cost in terms of the conduct required if female heads are to retain respectability and be considered "deserving." More generally we were interested in deconstructing the idea of a "family strategy" to expose how a family's collective interest was understood and family decisions made. Thus we explored the extent to which the female heads were aware of conflicts between their own interests and those of the family collectively. Another issue is when and why mothers call on the help of children, sending them out to work to keep the family together. While the quantifiable evidence from the questionnaires provided a starting point, the interviews filled in the missing links and founded a deeper understanding. Ultimately the objective is to design policies that can be successfully targeted and maximally helpful to these mundane heroines.

HOUSEHOLD INCOMES

Analysis of poverty among households in Sri Lanka is often conducted in terms of household incomes rather than per capita incomes, because the government's poverty alleviation measures, such as the Samurdhi Program, use the former and not the latter as benchmarks (Aturupane, Rodrigo, and Perera 1997). In most surveys, household incomes are typically understated. Some argue that poor households have an incentive to understate income levels in order to appear eligible for benefits. Aturupane, Rodrigo, and Perera (1997), in their survey of households in low-income areas excluding the Eastern and Northern Provinces, found that average monthly income of female-headed households was Rs.2,528.35 per month for poor households and Rs.5,567.00 per month for nonpoor households. This compared unfavorably with average incomes for poor households with male heads of Rs.2,897.88 per month and nonpoor households with male heads of Rs.6,661.47 per month. Table 2 presents estimates from our sample of household incomes by ethnic group for the eastern districts.

As is to be expected for an area long embroiled in civil conflict, these female-headed households are poorer than poor female-headed households elsewhere in the country, but mean incomes are not dramatically different, reinforcing confidence in the information obtained from the questionnaires. The Sinhala households are the poorest and the Muslim households the least poor. Analysis of variance suggests that we can reject the null hypothesis that the average incomes of the ethnic populations are the same. The relative poverty of the Sinhala households highlights the danger in assuming that political oppression and economic deprivation are directly and transparently related.

Socio-economic indicators of poverty, such as housing quality, sources of drinking water, sanitation, and lighting also, not surprisingly, suggest lagging infrastructural development in the Eastern Province. For example Aturupane, Rodrigo, and Perera (1997) found that some three-quarters of poor households had access to private sanitary facilities, although a significant minority had access only to common facilities and about 15 percent had no toilet at all. In the east, however, a bare majority of female-headed households had access to private facilities, and almost 30 percent had neither private nor common toilet facilities. Within the sample, socio-economic deprivation followed household income in that Muslim households appeared to have the best quality housing and the greatest access to sanitation, piped water, and lighting. However, Tamils appeared more

Table 2 Mean household income by ethnic group

Ethnicity	Mean household income	Sample size	Standard deviation
Tamil	2,159.7	116	1,782.1
Muslim	2,592.8	113	2,145.8
Sinhala	1,869.0	69	988.4
Total	2,256.6	298	1,808.7

*Ethnic differences are statistically significant (F-stat. $= 3.78$; sig. $= 0.024$).

deprived than Sinhala families in terms of these facilities, testimony to their political and historical exclusion.

Most women heads of households engaged in some income-generating activities though the extent of inactivity and unemployment varied by ethnicity, as did the type of activity undertaken. As can be seen in Table 3, all Sinhala female heads had jobs, and only nine Muslim heads were in this position, 8 percent of the total. Wage labor and self-employment were the two most common ways of earning for all ethnic groups, but Tamil female heads also worked in a range of small-scale agricultural capacities. Muslim and Sinhala female heads were primarily either self-employed or wage laborers, with the former favoring self-employment and the latter wage labor. Chi-square tests on the association of ethnicity with occupational and employment status suggests that the differences are statistically significant.[7]

Differences in household incomes per capita follow the differences in household incomes by ethnic group with, again, the Sinhala households being poorest and the Muslim households the least poor. However, the larger mean size of Muslim households and their tendency to have more children reduces their per capita lead, while the Sinhala households contain more children than Tamil households despite having lower total incomes. Closer scrutiny reveals that Sinhala households are more likely to contain younger children. Thus while 68.1 percent of Sinhala households have no children under 6, 82.3 percent of Muslim households and 87.1 percent of Tamil households have no children under 6. Sinhala household heads are more likely to describe their own occupation and/or activities as being the main source of income in comparison with Tamil female heads. Surprisingly, Muslim women are the most likely of all to identify their own contributions as the mainstay. The different household compositions not only suggest how the constraints on family strategies may vary by ethnic group but also that the routes into female headship may have been different for women with different ethnic identities.

Table 3 Employment and occupational status of female heads by ethnic group

	Tamil	Muslim	Sinhala
Unemployed, not working	1.7% (2)	7.9% (9)	-
Wage labor	17.2% (20)	31.0% (35)	59.4% (41)
Service/clerical/Government worker	7.8% (9)	2.7% (3)	7.2% (5)
Domestic worker	6.9% (8)	13.3% (15)	-
Agricultural laborer (unpaid family worker)	3.4% (4)	3.5% (4)	10.1% (7)
Poultry-rearing/goat-rearing/cattle-herding	11.2% (13)	-	-
Home gardening	5.2% (6)	-	-
Self-employment	46.6% (54)	41.6% (47)	23.3% (16)
Total	100% (116)	100% (113)	100% (69)

* Ethnic differences are statistically significant ($\chi^2 = 87.00$; sig. = 0.000).

184

ROUTES INTO FEMALE HEADSHIP

How did the women in our sample become heads of their households and did the route vary for Muslims, Sinhalese, and Tamils? Table 4 summarizes the types of female-headed household by ethnic group. Widowhood was the prime cause of female household headship for all ethnic groups in eastern Sri Lanka, as it is for Asia as a whole (Janet Momsen 1991). Male migration out of the districts may also have contributed (Elson 1992; Buvinic, Youssef, and von Elm 1978: 76 – 9; Youssef and Hetler 1984: 42 – 5). Factors may be interrelated. Joan Mencher (1989) found in a study of the Muslim-dominated district of Malappuram in Kerala, India, that male migration to the Middle East was associated with increased numbers of divorced women in agricultural communities. Our data also reveal a surprising proportion of divorced Muslim women. Widowhood was an even more dominant source of female headship in the east than in other areas of Sri Lanka. Thus Aturupane, Rodrigo, and Perera (1997) found that 48 percent of poor and 59 percent of nonpoor female heads were widows. This is the grain of truth in the interpretation of female headship as an aberrant development associated with the pathology of civil conflict. But female headship is far from identical with and should not be reduced to war widowhood.

One surprise is the sizable minority of married women heads of households: testimony to feminist claims that women's economic and emotional centrality is often disguised behind conventional assumptions about familial authority and economic responsibility. These households would not have been enumerated as women-headed in many censuses or indeed in household surveys that did not probe behind physical composition. Over one-tenth of Tamil and one-fifth of Muslim and Sinhala female-headed households fall into this *de facto* category.

Aturupane, Rodrigo, and Perera (1997) also found a significant minority of female heads was married, 40 percent of poor households and 31 percent of nonpoor ones, although they did not separately identify deserted wives. In our sample the married category constitutes women whose husbands remain in the household but for physical or mental reasons are unable to shoulder the burden of headship. It is vital to include

Table 4 Types of female-headed household by ethnic group

Ethnicity	Married	Divorced	Deserted	Separated	Widowed	Total
Tamil	12.9% (15)	1.7% (2)	7.8% (9)	10.3% (12)	67.2% (78)	100.0% (116)
Muslim	20.4% (23)	5.3% (6)	6.2% (7)	7.1% (8)	61.0% (69)	100.0% (113)
Sinhala	21.7% (15)	2.9% (2)	13.0% (9)	10.2% (7)	52.2% (36)	100.0% (69)
Total	17.8% (53)	3.4% (10)	8.4% (25)	9.1% (27)	61.4% (183)	100.0% (298)

* Ethnic differences are not statistically significant ($\chi^2 = 9.69$; sig. = 0.287).

this group not only because of its numerical importance and tendency to be overlooked but also because of its particular problems. The presence of a dependent adult male in the household entails additional demands on resources while simultaneously making it more difficult for the *de facto* female head to tap into support from kin or the state. Strangely, Aturupane, Rodrigo, and Perera (1997: 11) read the importance of this group as testimony to the popularity of marriage! More likely it suggests the fragility of the male-breadwinner family system and the need to think about how resources can be channeled to families whose male head is sick, alcoholic, or unemployed (Rohini Weerasinghe 1987; Myrtle Perera 1991; Sepali Kottegoda 1996; Ruwanpura 2001). Further probing reveals additional variance in experience.

Table 5 looks behind the title of widow to the cause of the husband's death, which, as might be expected, had important implications for how widowhood was experienced and survived. Although the routes into female headship did not differ significantly in the statistical sense by ethnicity, the causes of widowhood did, with conflict-related deaths being highest for Tamils. Husbands who died in the civil conflict were younger than husbands who died of natural causes, as were their widows. Aturupane, Rodrigo, and Perera (1997) found that younger widows were poorer on average. A younger widow's earnings may be reduced by the need to devote time to childcare. If a husband dies young, the income accruing to his family through a pension is likely to be low. When we compare the incomes of households headed by widows and non-widows by ethnicity in Table 6, we see the importance of these factors.

Muslim widows were the least poor widows, although their mean income was actually slightly lower than that of Muslim nonwidows, a difference that was not statistically significant. Tamil and Sinhala widows do less well than Muslims, although they do better than nonwidows in the same ethnic group. The ethnic differences in household incomes of widows are not statistically significant, whereas those for nonwidows are. Perhaps the

Table 5 Reasons for partner's death by ethnic group

Ethnicity	Natural causes	Suicide	Killed (state-sponsored)	Killed (para-military)	Killed (non-conflict)	Missing	Total
Tamil	19.2%	6.4%	64.1%	7.7%		2.6%	100%
	(15)	(5)	(50)	(6)		(2)	(78)
Muslim	56.5%	1.4%		20.3%	1.5% (1)	20.3%	100%
	(39)	(1)		(14)		(14)	(69)
Sinhala	58.3%	11.1%		27.7%		2.8%	100%
	(21)	(4)		(10)		(1)	(36)
Total	(75)	(10)	(50)	(30)	(1)	(17)	(183)

* Ethnic differences are statistically significant ($\chi^2 = 110.456$; sig. $= 0.000$).

Table 6 Household incomes of widows and nonwidows by ethnic group (Rs. per month)

Ethnicity	Widows	Nonwidows
Tamil	2,286.22	1,900.00
Muslim	2,557.07	2,648.86
Sinhala	1,998.61	1,727.57

experience of widowhood provides some cross-cultural constants in economic treatment, whereas there is more cultural diversity in what befalls women who have had to assume headship of their households for other reasons. The status of "the widow" is more universally respected, her fate understood as not her fault, and there are uniform pressures on kin and community to provide support (Youssef and Hetler 1984; Jane Humphries 1998). These pressures may dissipate when their subjects are deserted women or divorcees, who might be held partially responsible for their own situations.

This should not distract from the absolute poverty of Sinhala and Tamil widows or indeed their poverty relative to Muslim widows. The different circumstances of households headed by widows show how misleading it can be to focus on routes into female headship in terms of superficial categories without probing the surface of general titles like "widow." The needs of a young widow with several dependent children whose husband has been killed in ethnic violence may be very different from the needs of a middle-aged widow with several children old enough to work whose husband died of natural causes after an industrious and provident life.

I got married when I was 16 years old and was widowed by the time I was 38 years old – with my oldest daughter aged 21 years and my youngest son a baby. When my husband was alive we lived a comfortable and respectable life, and this has changed through the years, especially since my husband passed away.

After my husband's death, we were supported by my younger brother and my two older sons – my second and third children, respectively. Their education was disrupted, as they had to take over the running of the business. So while we have gone through many rough patches, I always had several sources of income to support my family. And at present, the household income ranges at around Rs.8,000.00, which is sufficient for all of us to eat properly – though not enough for me to save towards my daughters' dowries. (Zainab, a 53-year-old *de jure* Muslim female head from Batticaloa, and mother of eight children)

I have several sources of income, and I consider my main occupation to be a tailor. Through this occupation and poultry farming I earn a monthly income of Rs.800.00. We also get a monthly income of Rs.200.00 from the saving deposit, which we obtained from the state after I was able to prove that my husband was abducted and killed. Additionally, I am undergoing a training session in carpentry organized by a Canadian-funded nongovernmental organization that provides a monthly stipend of Rs.800.00. So in total I receive an income of Rs.1,800.00 to spend on my two daughters and myself. The income I earn through the carpentry program is only for this year, since we are expected to use this training to seek employment.

It may seem that Rs.1,800.00 is sufficient for three people, [but] the reality is that because Jivanthi is mentally handicapped – which happened after she got recurrent epileptic fits after learning that her father was killed – I spend about Rs.1,000.00 on her medication. Even though in theory hospitals here are supposed to be freely accessible, the pressures put on by the current conflict mean that we don't get priority treatment. Therefore, I have to buy medicines for Jivanthi through the open market, and these are expensive. Consequently, we have only about Rs.800.00 to spend on food, education, and other related household expenses. And this means having to stretch my income in many ways and directions. (Mangalika, a 41-year-old *de jure* war widow. She is a Tamil female head from Batticaloa, and mother of two daughters)

Moreover, families in these different circumstances may have different nonstate sources of support, help from kin and from the community.

NONWIDOWS AND THEIR NEEDS

The relative poverty within the category of female heads of nonwidows in comparison with widows has been found in other studies (Humphries 1998). Aturupane, Rodrigo, and Perera (1997) found that 52 percent of poor female heads were nonwidows, whereas only 41 percent of nonpoor female heads fell into this category. The reversal of this relationship in the case of Muslims refers back to the routes into female headship by ethnic group. Relatively more Muslim nonwidows take up the responsibilities of headship upon divorce; they have had the opportunity to bargain around the divorce table to extract a settlement. In contrast, Sinhala and Tamil women are more likely to have been unceremoniously deserted.

Lurking behind these categories are notions of merit. Widows fall into the "deserving" category of female heads. Their status is not of their choosing. They are victims (see also Youssef and Hetler 1984: 42–5; Chant 1997;

Humphries 1998). In contrast, nonwidows are often viewed as "undeserving" female heads. They are construed as somehow culpable for their troubles. If they had been better wives, they would not have been deserted or their husbands would not have taken to drink. Married or separated women are in a particularly treacherous situation. Their economic need may be hidden behind the presence of an adult male or their assumption of headship constructed as emasculating and aggressive.

> The family that helps me most in the community regards my family and me sympathetically. This is not so with others, who help me but only in limited ways – usually by loaning money for short periods of time. People in the community think of me in two distinct ways. Some people look at me with respect because I look after my family well. Others not so, because I do not live with my husband. People think that I am being arrogant because now that I earn a living I do not want to take my husband back. But I feel that I do not need a husband who spends everything I earn, and pawns my jewelry too. (Kamalini, a *de facto* Tamil female head from Trincomalee, and mother of two young sons)

The in-depth interviews were invaluable in exposing the conditionality of help and the goodwill of kin and community. Respectability in the eyes of relatives and friends emerged as the key to assistance. Yet the quest to maintain respectability often involved not only sacrifices in terms of isolation and loneliness but also constraints on economic activities. Women often found themselves walking a tightrope between the self-help vital to the family exchequer and the maintenance of that genteel status needed to secure kin solidarity and support. While these issues emerged as endless problems to be navigated in the family survival strategy, they would not have been brought to the surface through the questionnaires alone. The open-ended discussions revealed how female heads are perceived and perceive themselves, perceptions that rebounded to constrain and influence economic options and outcomes.

The importance of nonwidows among female heads suggests that the civil unrest cannot be seen as the ultimate cause of the increasing number of such households. Their deep roots in the changing social and economic conditions must be understood. Even if the conditions of the war have been partially responsible for an upsurge in female headship, this does not mean that such households will disappear if peace breaks out. The social and economic adjustments are nonreversible. The additional number of widows created as a result of the conflict put pressures on traditional support networks, particularly on the smaller number of men (fathers, brothers, and sons) who remain to provide economic aid. This burden unravels the traditional codes of conduct, stretching networks of economic support beyond their limits. To meet the demands upon them, men migrate in search of better economic opportunities or move to the city to work. Repatriated income flows are important in sustaining households left behind, but often these too disappear over time.

> When the conflict began to escalate rapidly and economic conditions were becoming bad here in Trincomalee, we thought it was best that my husband go in search of wage labor to neighboring Polonnaruwa. It was not too far from our village and there were more opportunities there. This seemed like a good idea at the time, and for about seven to eight years it worked out fine. However, eventually this separation took its toll on our relationship, and now I am left to fend for the family – though fortunately, my older son's, now 20 years old, earnings go towards the household income too. (Gauthami, a 42-year-old *de facto* Sinhala female head from Trincomalee, and mother of three children)

The initial shock caused by the increase in widowhood has cumulative repercussions, as some surviving men default on kinship obligations that then become even more concentrated on those women relatives who continue to play a traditional role. The result undermines patriarchal systems of support and forces female heads to look for other means to sustain their families. The survival of female-headed households outside the traditional networks then has demonstration effects that precipitate additional defaults and maybe even additional marital instability. The war may have been an original factor in the increase in female headship but this type of household is now founded in other social and economic processes – as the experience of Gauthami reveals.

Nor is the increasing incidence of female-headed households a product of hard times, something that will disappear with economic recovery. In fact female headship in the eastern districts is partially caused by the prosperity elsewhere. The sample contained many women whose partners had migrated elsewhere to work because of the adverse effects of the unrest on the local economy and then deserted, thereby compounding the pressures on those men remaining.

> When I came to recognize that my husband had eventually abandoned me after leaving to work in Colombo, I initially had to rely on my brothers for support. This was because my children were young and I had no steady source of income. So, until I got my feet on the ground, my two brothers helped me – and this seemed like a normal option since my parents were dead by the time my husband left me for another woman. (Nayana, a 48-year-old *de facto* Sinhala female head from Ampara and mother of three children)

Recognition that female-headed households are not the products of war or even of hard times has important implications for a policy-oriented, longer-term analysis. It refutes the view that female headship is a temporary social aberration.

It may appear as if women head more and more households because the conflict has killed men in great numbers. This is true for many of the households, but should not mean that other forms of household formations should get ignored. Unfortunately, this is what keeps happening, because the focus of NGO activity is only on war widows.

I had to assume headship because my husband abandoned me after two years of marriage. There are several female-headed households in the area, where women assume headship because their spouses are alcoholics, unemployed, physically maimed or disabled, and/or separated. We have difficult times too in supporting our households, and it would be good for people to recognize that such households are here to stay. (Siththi, a 35-year-old *de facto* Muslim female head from Batticaloa and mother of one child, a daughter)

If female headship is here to stay, the strategy can no longer be to offer short-run subsidies. Policies need to have a longer time horizon and aim to make these households self-supporting.

CHILDREN IN FEMALE-HEADED HOUSEHOLDS

Children are known to be a vital resource in female-headed households whose survival often depends upon the residence of working-age children. Children's ages are crucial. Problems of poverty in these families are compounded by the presence of dependent children, while escape to more comfortable circumstances often involves retaining children until they earn adult wages.

Children play an important role in female-headed households. If I look around my village, children help their mothers in numerous ways. Younger children tend to help their mothers by doing the household chores, while teenage children do either household chores or engage in homework-based occupations – as a way of supplementing the household incomes. Older children, invariably, may bring the primary source of income to the household, supplement household income, or be one of the several sources of income-generation for female-headed households. The extent to which children support their mothers invariably depends on their economic circumstances – and how crucial

191

mothers and children think their income is vis-à-vis getting educated.
(A woman activist from Batticaloa district, working for a local NGO)

Figure 1 shows how households in the ethnic groups break down according
to the numbers and ages of resident children. For example, 101 Tamil
households, representing 87 percent of the total, contain no child under 6.
The proportions of households that contain children vary significantly by
ethnicity for children under 6, children aged 6 to 10, and young people
over 18 but not significantly for children aged 11 to 18.[8]

Sinhalese households are more likely to contain children under 6, which
relates back to the lower incidence of Sinhala widows. Sinhalese households
are also more likely to contain children aged between 6 and 10. Although
older and more independent, these children are unlikely to be contributing economically. Households in all three ethnic groups contain similar
relative numbers of children aged 11 to 18. But the Sinhala higher
frequency of young children is not matched by a higher frequency of young
adults over 18. Almost 60 percent of Sinhala households contain no
children from this most useful age group, as compared with 37 percent of

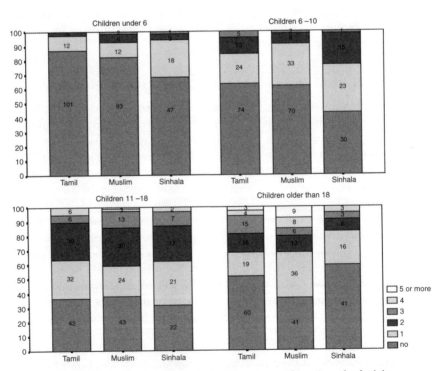

Figure 1 Households by age of children (in residence) and ethnicity.

192

Muslim households and 52 percent of Tamil households. The Sinhala households are doubly disadvantaged, burdened with dependent children but lacking those who are old enough to contribute economically. The less-oppressive poverty of Muslim households owes much to the number and ages of the children they contain.

While the numbers and ages of children in female-headed households in part relate back to the routes into female headship characteristic of the different groups, these findings suggest that ethnicity is also important in conditioning household composition. Muslim families are larger on average, but their ability to retain grown children is especially important in fending off poverty.

The economic reliance of female-headed households on children often results in their premature entry into the labor market. Early working often interrupts, if not terminates, schooling. The adverse effects on human capital formation of poverty and child labor in female-headed households are widely noted. Often when education and training have been disrupted by precocious employment, the gaps cannot be made good at a later date. Timely intervention becomes imperative (Sara Horrell, Jane Humphries, and Hans-Joachim Voth 1998). The adverse effects of poverty on children's nutrition and health, as well as the problems created for their education when children are sent out to work, create strong externality arguments for intervention to raise incomes in female-headed households. But the economic arguments do not convey the bitterness and heartbreak many women felt when forced to withdraw a child from school either to have them substitute as a childminder at home or to have them look for work themselves.

> For me educating children is important, because otherwise they would suffer like me. I feel that I had very little choice with Shivanthi. My husband had died and not even a year after this I met with a motorbike accident, which led to my hospitalization for a couple of months. During this time Shivanthi's education got disrupted because she took over the responsibilities of looking after her siblings and caring for me. And after I was discharged and came back home, I had to make the hard choice that I needed Shivanthi's help – both in the household and in cash-crop cultivation. Therefore, I had to discontinue her education – and to this day, I wish I could have had things differently because I do think educating children is important. (Durga, a 49-year-old *de jure* Tamil female head from Tricomalee and mother of four children)

These decisions often involve trading off one child's individual interests against those of another child and force mothers into invidious and painful comparisons. Mothers often think they have to represent "the collective

193

interest.'' Not surprisingly, women often agonize over decisions and their reliving of some soul-searching in the interviews shows the way interests were weighed and considered. Contrary to some feminist expectations, these choices do not appear to victimize girls. Boys and girls were both chosen as sacrifices according to family circumstances and local employment opportunities. There was no systematic gender preference.

After separating from Vijaya many times, I decided about ten years ago that this separation had to be final. From then I took over the role of earning an income by growing cash crops in a land leased by a *mudalali* (landowner) close-by to our house. Of my six children, the oldest was a daughter, followed by two sons – and these were the only children I thought who would be able to help me with my income-generating activities. I decided that I would disrupt the education of my two sons and get them to help me with the cash-crop schemes. This is because I thought they were better able to physically help me, which was what was necessary for growing cash crops. (Vasuki, a 44-year-old *de facto* Tamil female head from Batticaloa and mother of six children)

When my husband was killed, both my children were young – they were under 10 years old. So just after I was widowed, it was my sister who came to my help. She was educated and a clerical worker in the region, and therefore chose to financially help me. But by the time my oldest son was a teenager, he spoke with me and said that we should stop depending solely on *punchie* (younger-aged aunt) for financial help. He said that he had spoken with some fishermen in the neighborhood, and they had agreed to take him on their fishing trips. So from the time my son was about 13 to 14 years old, he started bringing home an income – and we have now come to depend on his financial help, with my daughter continuing to get her education. (Savithri, a 44-year-old *de jure* Sinhala female head from Trincomalee and mother of two children)

With the "opening-up" of the economy, my husband found that it was difficult to do business. So things became more and more difficult for us, and by 1983 or so he had to wind down his business. Fortunately, by this time our oldest daughter was just finishing her A-level education. She is quite an intelligent and enterprising young woman, so she is the one supporting our six children and us by taking up a variety of income-generating activities. The activities she is involved in range from teaching in Montessori in the mornings to working part-time in NGOs in the area to teaching sewing classes to young girls in the evening hours. So she is the person supporting our household – and more or less on her own. (Zeena, a 39-year-old *de facto* Muslim female head from Ampara and mother of seven children)

To design policies to help these families, we must probe behind these decisions and understand the reasoning. The unique information from the interviews shows how the different ethnic groups rationalized their choices in different ways. Muslim female heads often chose to withdraw boys from school and send them to work because it was culturally inconceivable to place girls in the labor market. But if working at home was available, then girls were chosen because this meant that the family did not then have to expend time chaperoning girls back and forth from school. Muslims and Tamils both were inclined to choose boys to work because the duration of their loyalty to their households of origin is limited by their allegiance on marriage to their wives and their wives' families.[9]

> Even though we depend on our older sons' income to support the household, I know that this support will stop after they get married, because this is usually the practice here. As my husband died, it was my unmarried brother who supported us – but once he married, his responsibility shifted towards his wife and her family. Similarly, my sons will stop helping us when they marry. In the meantime, they not only financially support our household expenses – but also make every effort to keep aside saving for their sisters' dowries. (Kathija, a 55-year-old *de jure* Muslim female head from Batticaloa and mother of eight children)

The issue of family strategies in terms of child labor is explored further along with its policy implications by Ruwanpura (2001).

SUPPORT NETWORKS: WIDER KIN AND COMMUNITY

Both the questionnaires and the interviews highlighted the importance to these households of wider support from the kin and community. But there were some surprises in the sources of support, the way in which women valued different kinds of support and, above all, the identification of a "price" paid for the support. Table 7 shows clear ethnic differences in terms of the frequency with which households received remittances from outside. Muslims and Tamils are very similar, with almost three-quarters of families in receipt of some outside financial support while Sinhalese families are much less likely to be helped in this way.

Although not all households in receipt of remittances provided estimates of their cash value, the evidence that is available suggests that not only are Sinhala female heads less likely to get help from outside but even when such help is forthcoming, its cash value is less. Thus both lower frequency of

Table 7 Frequency and value of income remittances from outside sources by ethnic group

	Tamils	Muslims	Sinhala	Total
Receiving remittances	72.4% (84)	74.1% (83)	46.4% (32)	67.1% (199)
Not receiving remittances	27.6% (32)	25.9% (29)	53.6% (37)	32.9% (98)
Average value of remittances received	1,478 (56)	2,217 (82)	1,441 (29)	1,728 (167)
Average value	713 (116)	1,609 (112)	605 (69)	1,582 (297)

*Ethnic differences are statistically significant, in proportions ($\chi^2 = 19.05$; sig. = 0.001); in values (from ANOVA, $F = 13.72$; sig. = 0.000).**The status of one Muslim household is unknown; sample sizes in parentheses.

receipts and lower unit values mean Sinhala households benefit less than other ethnic groups from outside financial aid.

These findings are backed up by additional information from the questionnaires and interviews. For example, Muslim and Tamil female heads are more likely to have relatives in foreign countries than are Sinhala. In fact, 40 percent of Tamil women had relatives overseas. Perhaps the disadvantages that Tamils have endured have forced more mobile members of families overseas. Again, the Muslim households appear to retain ties and to benefit from traditional sources of support more so than do other households in other ethnic groups. They have a lower incidence of relatives resident abroad, and slightly fewer Muslim households receive help than do Tamil households, but the pecuniary value of remittances was greater.

Another surprising finding involved the value female heads attached to nonfinancial assistance from kin and community. There is an interesting tie-in here with historical work, which has documented the value attached by women to nonfinancial help and the female networks through which such assistance was managed and channeled (Janet Finch 1989; Humphries 1998). The appreciation for such support was especially strong on the part of Sinhala female heads who, as we have seen, are much more likely than women from other ethnic groups to participate in wage work and simultaneously to have to cope with young children. Help with childcare is probably a priority for these women and indeed may be worth more than occasional and small-scale financial subsidies.

> Looking after children on occasions and more importantly giving children food and meals is common practice amongst us. These practices are done of matter-of-fact and this support we provide is something I do not really think about. Besides this, my sisters and I help each other in pounding rice – which is important, since it helps me earn more income. (Ashanthi, a 38-year-old *de facto* Tamil female head from Trincomalee and mother of four children)

On the other hand, childcare is of less value to many older Muslim female heads who have fewer young children and are unlikely to work outside the home. Here we see women together creating packages of assistance customized to help with particular needs and family strategies.

Similarly too we found neighbors and friends to be a surprisingly important source of assistance, particularly when its definition is broadened to include the nonfinancial help many women found invaluable.

> Women need to perform traditional rights and duties because they are more dependent upon norms of reciprocity within community structures because they are potentially a more vulnerable group. Moreover, as my husband was killed it was partially because all the women in the neighborhood would spend time with me that it eased my emotional pain and difficulties. And to this day, we help each other in numerous ways – including doing grocery shopping, looking after my daughter when I am not home, lending me money during emergencies, etc., etc. (Ahila, a 41-year-old *de jure* Tamil female head from Ampara and mother of one child)

These friends and neighbors are often better placed than more distant kin to offer the kind of support many female heads needed, such as childcare, help chaperoning children to school, help with cooking, and emotional support. The in-depth interviews caution against dismissing the value of friendship and conversation in the lives of these female heads. Like most humans, these female heads needed bread but *araliya* (frangipani) too!

> I am lighthearted since my exposure and interaction with other female heads. This happened with me seeking income-generating activities through a local NGO. Even though my own mother frowns at me for interacting with other female heads so frequently, I think us talking with each other and sharing our experiences help us to feel more emotionally stable and secure. We all realize that it is the conflict that thrust us to this role, and talking to each other about our husbands' disappearances or killings is in many ways therapeutic and is a way of cementing our relationships. (Thishanthi, a 40-year-old *de jure* Tamil female head from Batticaloa and mother of three children)

Female heads in our sample did receive help from male relatives and did benefit from traditional systems of support. Muslim women in particular appear to be able to call on such support. Moreover, male kin were the only possible sources of certain kinds of assistance, especially for women who were reluctant to appear in public and engage with people outside their immediate circle. Muslim women, for example, relied on male relatives to represent them and their families in interactions with state support agencies and other formal economic institutions. But this help is public and visible. It is easy to overestimate it. In the same way, it is easy to assume that the economic support from male relatives that would traditionally be forthcoming is still available. In the economic and social context of eastern Sri Lanka such help appears decreasingly reliable and often of reduced importance. The circumstances of the women in our sample were varied, but within all ethnic groups, financial support from male relatives outside the immediate family paled into insignificance in comparison with the women's own efforts and the contributions of children. Other factors also shade the importance we should attach to traditional sources and kinds of support. Nonpecuniary help, almost invariably provided by female relatives or friends and neighbors, appears to have been treasured. Moreover, a majority of women in all ethnic groups found female relatives to be more dependable than male relatives. That a large majority of Sinhalese expressed this view can be explained by the ethnic emphasis on the female lineage, but Muslim women expressed the same view although less emphatically.

> Men too support the family, especially when we have to travel and in-teract with working people in banks, offices, and so forth. But women are more likely to help each other during difficulties because of cultur-al norms that require us to support each other. I think cultural norms of reciprocity are shaped in such a way that implicitly recognizes that women can be the more vulnerable members of the community. (Nishani, a 25-year-old *de facto* Sinhala female head from Trincomalee and mother of two children)

> Of course, as women we come to assist each other during difficult times. I suppose one can say that this is important for our well-being. But from my point of view the financial support we get from uncles, brothers, and sons is much more important. If we didn't get this finan-cial support, how will we survive? (Fayaza, a 37-year-old *de jure* Muslim female head from Ampara and mother of four children)

Another feature of kin and community support that we would probably not have registered without the focused interviews is the costs that female heads of all ethnic groups associated with it. These are not the expectation of relatively immediate reciprocation assumed by some economistic interpretations. It is more that access to support is conditional on the good opinion of key figures in the extended family or in the community. Thus to be able to benefit from traditional support, women have to maintain their "deservingness" in the eyes of male and female kin who often bring conservative values to bear in judging conduct. Female heads faced with the exigencies of earning a living may simply be unable to both behave in a way that is approved and seize the economic opportunities available to them.

> People are always on the watch about women whose husbands are not with them. If anyone sees me talking with another man, then it leads to speculation and gossip. In this context, we have to think about every step we take, the kind of help we get and the work we do. Unfortunately, what people think does matter – because we always have to depend on the help we get from others in the community. (Sarala, a 45-year-old *de jure* Sinhala female head from Ampara and mother of three children)

> I make the final decisions, because I think my decisions are best. But I also ensure that my decisions are acceptable to the community as well. After all, I cannot ignore that I live in a village, where what people think matter – and the help they give me will be largely based on their opinions of me. (Damayanthi, a 32-year-old *de jure* Tamil female head from Trincomalee and mother of two children)

Nor is it only male kin whose judgments about conduct can open or close channels of support. Even the female-dominated local support systems might implicitly require certain conduct in order to include female heads as recipients of collective aid. While unrecognized in the literature, our evidence suggests that the need to retain respectability and merit in the eyes of kin and community often place female heads in a painful double bind. Once these hidden costs of support are acknowledged, it may be clearer why women may even choose not to avail them of such help.

> While I am aware of what people think and say about me, I do not allow these perceptions to influence me. I think my first concern is looking after the welfare of my children, and if I do this well then what people think should not matter. This is difficult for women, but I think I have to change when my circumstances are changing. People may have difficulty accepting these changes, but precisely because of this I try to keep depending on my neighbors at a bare minimum. (Rani, a 37-year-old *de facto* Tamil female head from Batticaloa and mother of two children)

CONCLUSION

Our study of female-headed households in the eastern districts of Sri Lanka debunks some myths. These households are not temporary products of war, whatever role the conflict may have played in precipitating the increase in female headship. Households headed by women are here to stay, created and recreated by the social and economic conditions. But if common experiences bind these women together, ethnic distinctions are evident in the ways in which they became the heads of their households and the strategies they embrace in order to cope. These differences should not be forgotten in seeking to understand the situation in which lone mothers find themselves and in trying to develop policies to assist them.

These households are unable to rely on traditional sources of support from extended kin. The social and economic conditions, the background of conflict, and the proportion of female heads in the population weigh against this. But times and views are changing. Women can no longer rely on traditional sources of support when they are widowed or deserted and so they struggle to cope in other ways and in so doing undermine the traditional networks even further. The women in our sample have been lone mothers and female heads at a terrible time, not only in a context of civil war but in a world of change where "traditional" help is crumbling, but nothing as yet has taken its place.

The economic case for assistance to households headed by women is strong. Our work suggests how such help might best be structured and delivered. First, help cannot be limited to occasional subsidies but must encourage female-headed households to help themselves and to do so without relying on the labor of school-age children. Second, remedial policies need to recognize the many and varied circumstances of the households, and not bundle them together as a social problem to be dealt with by a single social solution.

Female headship in eastern Sri Lanka is neither a passing social problem nor a social pathology with its roots in civil conflict; nor is it a lifestyle choice. None of the women in the sample can be thought of as opting to head their own households. To think in such terms is to trivialize the tragedies that have overtaken them. Many female heads, in the face of misery and deprivation, have struggled to make a life for themselves and their surviving family members. In so doing, they have acquired a pride in their achievements and a sense of their own worth. Their autonomy was often unsought, an unintended consequence of personal misfortune or collective disaster, but it has left them feeling empowered, perhaps ambivalently and anxiously empowered, but empowered nonetheless.

> Islamic culture is resistant to change, even when material realities are changing. Islam remains Islam keeping women secluded. Just because there is no husband how long can we be inside the house? Only if we earn can we eat.

> If Chandrika, a widow, can be the President of Sri Lanka, then all other women can aspire to similar heights. It is usually men that prevent women from realizing their abilities. I think of my present status as one

where I am *free* and I will do all I can to help and uplift other women like me, in the community!! (Hidaya, a 32-year-old *de facto* Muslim female head from Batticaloa and mother of one child)

ACKNOWLEDGMENTS

This paper is revised from an earlier working paper done for the International Labor Office's IFP/CRISIS program. We thank Janine Rodgers for her role in initiating the original version of this work, the role of the two reviewers, and equally Randy Albelda and Sue Himmelweit in their help to finalize this version. The lead author is particularly grateful for the generous funding provided by the American Association of University Women, Cambridge Political Economy Society Trust, and the International Federation of University Women, which supported her doctoral studies – on which this article is based.

NOTES

[1] From a feminist perspective, using "female headship" and "female-headed households" as an analytical category may be subject to criticism. In feminist discourse, "female" refers to a biological category rather than a social category. Feminist literature in development discourse, however, uses "female headship" and "female-headed households" as a social concept. We abide by the social convention of development discourse rather than feminist discourse here, even though this is an issue that needs to be debated in development studies.

[2] Ethnicity in Sri Lanka is not solely linked to either religion or language. Muslims and Tamils are identified as the Tamil-speaking community in Sri Lanka, but have distinct religious identities. Muslims practice Islam and Tamils largely identify with Hinduism. Language separates Sinhalese and Tamils, groups that also have distinct religious affiliations, with the Sinhalese being primarily Buddhist and Tamils mostly Hindus. However, some Sinhalese and Tamils are Christians. In addition, of course, there is an array of religious practices that "Sinhala-Buddhists" have adopted whose roots can be traced to the Hindu tradition, clouding distinct ethno-religious and ethno-linguistic identities even further. Differences stem from prevailing social and political circumstances. For an excellent collection of essays on the intrinsic instabilities of ethnic formation in Sri Lanka, see Pradeep Jeganathan and Qadri Ismail (1995). On Sinhala people, see David Scott (1995); on Tamil nationalism and women, see Sitralega Maunaguru (1995) and Qadri Ismail (2000), and on Muslim identity formation, see Qadri Ismail (1995) and Vijaya Samaraweera (1997).

[3] Like all situations of conflict, the case in Sri Lanka is no different in being in a continuous state of flux. This summary reflects impressionistic judgments of the circumstances prevailing in 1998–99 during fieldwork in the region. In late 2001, conditions in eastern Sri Lanka changed drastically with an escalation of violence noted in both Trincomalee and Ampara – as both BBC news reports and informal sources of information in Sri Lanka reported. By mid-2002 the ongoing peace talks have led to a cessation of hostilities with sporadic violence in the Eastern Province.

[4] There are no recent government statistics on economic conditions in the area. These statements are based on the lead-author's field-experience and knowledge of eastern Sri Lanka and on personal communication with people working, usually through NGOs, in the region. Here thanks are due to Simon Harris (OXFAM), Daniel Sinnathamby (CARE), and P. Senthurajah (SWOAD) for sharing their information and understandings of the region. Furthermore, Batticaloa was noted as one the poorest districts in Sri Lanka even prior to the rise of hostilities, with the conflict impoverishing the district further. Ampara, on the other hand, is noted for enjoying the highest level of agricultural productivity in Sri Lanka. Chithra Maunaguru (SURIYA) gave this information and we note it with gratitude.

[5] A copy of the questionnaire is available from the authors on request.

[6] Self-representation as a female head was sometimes qualified, and often hesitant, but responsibilities and autonomy acknowledged.

[7] Ten cells have a count less than five, which might be held to invalidate conventional statistical judgments. However, it is easy to combine categories: for example, throwing the small-scale agricultural activities together. The ethnic differences in employment type emerge across the compressed categories. This is true in all cross-tabulations where statistical significance is reported.

[8] For children under 6, $\chi^2 = 14.11$ and sig. $= 0.028$; for children 6–10, $\chi^2 = 16.03$ and sig. $= 0.014$; for children 11–18, $\chi^2 = 8.65$ and sig. $= 0.560$; and, for children over 18, $\chi^2 = 28.57$ and sig. $= 0.012$.

[9] Eastern Sri Lanka is characterized by matrilineal kin structures, which is well noted for both Muslim and Tamil communities (Dennis McGilvray 1982, 1989; Bina Agarwal 1990, 1996). Therefore, partially the reasoning provided by female heads on the potential limitations to the support of their sons is not surprising.

REFERENCES

Agarwal, Bina. 1990. "Gender and Land Rights in Sri Lanka." World Employment Program Research: Working Paper No. 49 – Rural Employment Policy Research Program Policy Series, ILO, Geneva.

——1996. *A Field of One's Own: Gender and Land Rights in South Asia.* New Delhi: Cambridge University Press (first edition, 1994).

——1997. "'Bargaining' and Gender Relations: Within and Beyond the Household." *Feminist Economics* 3(1): 1–51.

Aturupane, Harsha, Chandra Rodrigo, and Sasanka Perera. 1997. "Poverty among Female-Headed Households in Sri Lanka." Reported prepared for the World Bank, Washington, DC, and the Regional Development Division, Ministry of Plan Implementation, Ethnic Affairs and National Integration, Colombo, Sri Lanka.

Buvinic, Mayra and Geeta Rao Gupta. 1997. "Female-Headed Households and Female-Maintained Families: Are They Worth Targeting to Reduce Poverty in Developing Countries?" *Economic Development and Cultural Change* 45(2): 259–80.

Buvinic, Mayra, Nadia Youssef, and Barbara Von Elm. 1978. *Women-Headed Households: The Ignored Factor in Development Planning*. Washington, DC: International Center for Research on Women.

Buvinic, Mayra, Juan Pablo Valenzuela, Temistocles Molina, and Electra Gonzalez. 1992. "The Fortunes of Adolescent Mothers and their Children: The Transmission of Poverty in Santiago, Chile." *Population and Development Review* 18(2): 169–97.

Chant, Sylvia. 1997. *Women-Headed Households: Diversity and Dynamics in the Developing World*. London: Macmillan.

de Alwis, Malathi. 1998a. "Motherhood as a Space of Protest," in Patricia Jeffery and Amrita Basu (eds.) *Appropriating Gender: Women's Activism and Politicized Religion in South Asia*, pp. 185–201. London: Routledge.

——1998b. "Moral Mothers and Stalwart Sons," in Lois Ann Lorentzen and Jennifer Turpin (eds.) *The Women and War Reader*, pp. 254–71. New York: New York University Press.

Deere, Carmen Diana. 1990. *Household and Class Relations: Peasant and Landlords in Northern Peru*. Berkeley, CA: University of California Press.

Duncan, Simon and Rosalind Edwards. 1994. "Lone Mothers and Paid Work: State Policies, Social Discourses and Neighborhood Processes." Mimeo, London School of Economics and Politics: Gender Institute.

Duncan, Simon and Rosalind Edwards. 1997. "Lone Mothers and Paid Work: Rational Economic Man or Gendered Moral Rationalities?" *Feminist Economics* 3(2): 29–62.

Elson, Diane. 1992. "From Survival Strategies to Transformation Strategies: Women's Needs and Structural Adjustment," in Lourdes Beneria and Shelley Feldman (eds.) *Unequal Burden: Economic Crises, Persistent Poverty and Women's Work*, pp. 26–48. Boulder, CO: Westview Press.

Finch, Janet. 1989. *Family Obligations and Social Change*. Cambridge, UK: Polity Press.

Folbre, Nancy. 1991. "Women on their Own: Global Patterns of Female-Headship," in Rita S. Gallin and Ann Ferguson (eds.) *The Women and International Development Annual, Vol. 2*, pp. 69–126. Boulder, CO: Westview Press.

Harris, Olivia. 1981. "Households as Natural Units," in Kate Young, Carol Wolkowitz, and Roslyn McCullagh (eds.) *Of Marriage and the Market*, pp. 48–67. London: CSE Books.

Horrell, Sara, Jane Humphries, and Hans-Joachim Voth. 1998. "Stature and Relative Deprivation: Fatherless Children in Early Industrial Britain," *Continuity and Change* 13: 73–115.

Humphries, Jane. 1993. "Gender Inequality and Economic Development," in Dieter Bos (ed.) *Economics in a Changing World, Vol. 3: Public Policy and Economic Organization*, pp. 218–33. New York: St. Martin's Press.

——1998. "Female-Headed Households in Early Industrial Britain: The Vanguard of the Proletariat?" *Labor History Review* 63(1): 31–65.

Ismail, Qadri. 1995. "Unmooring Identity: The Antinomies of Elite Muslim Self-Representation in Modern Sri Lanka," in Pradeep Jeganathan and Qadri Ismail (eds.) *Unmaking the Nation: The Politics of Identity and History in Modern Sri Lanka*, pp. 55–105. Colombo, Sri Lanka: Social Scientist Association.

——2000. "Constituting Nation, Contesting Nationalism: The Southern Tamil (Woman) and Separatist Tamil Nationalism in Sri Lanka," in Partha Chatterjee and Pradeep Jeganathan (eds.) *Subaltern Studies XI: Community, Gender, Violence*, pp. 212–82. New Delhi: Permanent Black.

Jayawardena, Kumari. 1984. "The Plantation Sector in Sri Lanka: Recent Changes in the Welfare of Children and Women." *World Development* 12: 317–28.

Jeganathan, Pradeep and Qadri Ismail (eds.). 1995. *Unmaking the Nation: The Politics of Identity and History in Modern Sri Lanka*. Colombo, Sri Lanka: Social Scientist Association.

Klasen, Stephan. 1993. "Gender Inequality and Development Strategies: Lessons from the Past and Policy Issues for the Future." World Employment Program Research – International Employment Policies, Working Paper No. 41, ILO, Geneva.

Kottegoda, Sepali. 1996. "Female Headed Households in Situations of Armed Conflict." *Nivedini* 4(2): 10–19.

Kurian, Rachel. 1982. *Women Workers in the Sri Lanka Plantation Sector*. Geneva: ILO.

Lawson, Tony. 1997. *Economics and Reality*. London: Routledge.

——1999. "Feminism, Realism and Universalism." *Feminist Economics* 5(2): 25–59.

MacDonald, Martha. 1995. "The Empirical Challenges of Feminist Economics: The Example of Economic Restructuring," in Edith Kuiper and Jolande Sap, with Susan Feiner, Notburga Ott, and Zafiris Tzannotos (eds.) *Out of the Margin: Feminist Perspectives on Economics*, pp. 175–97. London: Routledge.

Maunaguru, Sitralega. 1995. "Gendering Tamil Nationalism: The Construction of 'Woman' in Projects of Protest and Control," in Pradeep Jeganathan and Qadri Ismail (eds.) *Unmaking the Nation: The Politics of Identity and History in Modern Sri Lanka*, pp. 158–75. Colombo, Sri Lanka: Social Scientist Association.

McGilvray, Dennis. 1982. "Mukkuvar Vannimai: Tamil Caste and Matriclan Ideology in Batticaloa, Sri Lanka," in Dennis McGilvray (ed.) *Caste Ideology and Interaction*, pp. 34–97. Cambridge, UK: Cambridge University Press.

——1989. "Households in Akkaraipattu: Dowry and Domestic Organization among Matrilineal Tamils and Moors of Sri Lanka," in J. N. Gray and D. J. Mearns (eds.) *Society from the Inside Out: Anthropological Perspectives on the South Asian Household*, pp. 192–235. London: Sage.

Mencher, Joan P. 1989. "Women Agricultural Laborers and Land Owners in Kerala and Tamil Nadu: Some Questions about Gender and Autonomy in the Household," in Maithreyi Krishnaraj and Karuna Chanana (eds.) *Gender and the Household Domain: Social and Cultural Dimensions*, pp. 117–41. New Delhi: Sage.

Momsen, Janet. 1991. *Women and Development in the Third World*. London: Routledge.

Perera, Myrtle. 1991. "Female-Headed Households – A Special Poverty Group," in CENWOR (ed.) *Women, Poverty and Family Survival*, pp. 27–64. Colombo, Sri Lanka: CENWOR.

Rasanayagam, Yoga. 1993. "Women as Agents and Beneficiaries of Rural Housing Programs in Sri Lanka," in Janet Momsen and Vivian Kinnaird (eds.) *Different Places, Different Voices: Gender and Development in Africa, Asia and Latin America*, pp. 146–58. London: Routledge.

Rotberg, Robert. 1999. "Sri Lanka's Civil War: From Mayhem toward Diplomatic Resolution," in Robert Rotberg (ed.) *Creating Peace in Sri Lanka: Civil War and Reconciliation*, pp. 1–16. Washington, DC: Brookings Institution Press.

Ruwanpura, Kanchana N. 2001. "Matrilineal Communities, Patriarchal Realities: Female-Headship in Eastern Sri Lanka – A Feminist Economic Reading." Unpublished PhD dissertation. Newnham College, University of Cambridge, UK.

——and Jane Humphries. 2003. "Female-Headship in Eastern Sri Lanka: A Comparative Study of Ethnic Communities in the Context of Conflict." IFP/CRISIS in association with the Bureau for Gender Equality. Working Paper No. 10, ILO, Geneva.

Samarasinghe, Vidyamali. 1993. "Access of Female Plantation Workers in Sri Lanka to Basic-Needs Provision," in Janet Momsen and Vivian Kinnaird (eds.) *Different Places, Different Voices: Gender and Development in Africa, Asia, and Latin America*, pp. 131–45. London: Routledge.

Samaraweera, Vijaya. 1997. "The Muslim Revivalist Movement, 1880–1915," in Michael Roberts (ed.) *Sri Lanka. Collective Identities Revisited: Vol. I*, pp. 293–321. Colombo, Sri Lanka: Marga Institute.

Scott, David. 1995. "Dehistoricising History," in Pradeep Jeganathan and Qadri Ismail (eds.) *Unmaking the Nation: The Politics of Identity and History in Modern Sri Lanka*, pp. 10–24. Colombo, Sri Lanka: Social Scientist Association.

Sen, Amartya. 1981. "Public Action and the Quality of Life in Developing Countries." *Oxford Bulletin of Economics and Statistics* 43(4): 287–319.

——1984. "Development: Which Way Now?" in Amartya Sen, *Resources, Values and Development*, pp. 485–508. Oxford: Blackwell. (First published in 1983 in *Economic Journal* 93: 745–62.)

United Nations. 1991. *The World's Women 1970–1990: Trends and Statistics*. New York: UN.

United Nations Development Program. 2000. *Human Development Report, 2001*. Oxford: Oxford University Press.

Weerasinghe, Rohini. 1987. *Female Headed Households in Two Villages, Sri Lanka*. Colombo, Sri Lanka: Women's Education Center.

World Bank. 1995. *Advancing Gender Equality: From Concept to Action*. Washington, DC: World Bank.

Youssef, Nadia and Carol B. Hetler. 1981. *Women-Headed Households and Rural Poverty: What Do We Know?* Washington, DC: International Center for Research on Women.

Youssef, Nadia and Carol B. Hetler. 1983. "Establishing the Economic Condition of Women-Headed Households in the Third World: A New Approach," in Mayra Buvinic, Margaret A. Lycette, and William Paul McGreevey (eds.) *Women and Poverty in the Third World*, pp. 216–43. Baltimore, MD: Johns Hopkins University Press.

Youssef, Nadia and Carol B. Hetler. 1984. "Rural Households Headed by Women: A Priority Concern for Development." World Employment Program Research: Working Paper No. 31 – Rural Employment Policy Research Program Policy Series, ILO, Geneva.

THE ROUTE MATTERS: POVERTY AND INEQUALITY AMONG LONE-MOTHER HOUSEHOLDS IN RUSSIA

Shireen Kanji

INTRODUCTION

The position of lone mothers and their children in modern Russia is of vital interest to feminists. Elsewhere, lone mothers have been urged to better their material circumstances by improving their education or participating more in paid labor. Such prescriptions cannot be applied to Russian and Soviet women who have been in the vanguard of female educational and labor force participation.

Nevertheless, lone mothers face structural constraints that have intensified since the collapse of the Soviet Union in 1991. Not only has the political structure of Russia been overturned, but also societal norms and attitudes to families are changing along a different, independent trajectory. Both have operated to the disadvantage of women with children.

Only three years after the collapse of the Soviet Union, Maxine Molyneux (1994) was arguing that women had begun to play a reduced role in public life. Increasingly, as the state has withdrawn its support for the rearing of children, caring roles have been privatized and reconsigned to individual women within their families. A decade of output contraction in the 1990s was accompanied by a dramatic decline in fertility,[1] indicating that the economic and political changes significantly affected childbearing decisions. This precipitous decline in fertility was superimposed on a more gradual downward trend as Soviet women controlled their fertility, despite limited contraceptive possibilities. Even now, with fertility levels among the lowest in the world and in spite of Russia's historical preoccupation with increasing its natality rates, the state has paid little attention to the problem of combining the care of children with the need to secure a living. Child poverty is acknowledged, but interpreted as the result of failure by individual parents. Fathers are seen as delinquent for failing in their breadwinning duties, or mothers are considered defective for opting out of unhappy marriages.

In the Soviet Union, although poverty was officially unrecognized, lone mothers comprised one of the groups the state identified as needing assistance because they, like war veterans, were considered "under-provisioned." The cult of motherhood meant that, unlike their counterparts in the West, Soviet lone mothers were held to be deserving because they had fulfilled their maternal duties to the state, which perceived that higher population numbers meant more prestige, and, at a practical level, more workers and soldiers.

Lone motherhood remains a central theme in the child poverty debate in Russia today. But this is not simply because children in lone-mother households experience higher rates of material poverty. As Bina Agarwal (1997) argues, "Gender relations like all social relations embody the material and the ideological." It is not by chance that in Russia and elsewhere, the foremost representation of lone mothers is that they and their children are poor and disadvantaged. It is part of a remarkably widespread family ideology that two parents are better than one. In Soviet Russia, the ideal was a two-parent, dual-worker family with children. The early Bolshevik vision of freedom in relationships was lost in the harsher Soviet reality of low-cost production, including human reproduction.

Using evidence from the *Russian Longitudinal Monitoring Survey* (RLMS), this paper questions the widespread use of the aggregate category of "lone-mother household" to identify the risk of child poverty. Types of lone-mother households are identified by reference to the mother's route of entry into lone motherhood, that is according to whether the lone mother is widowed, divorced, cohabiting but not married, separated but still married, or never married. The paper analyzes children's poverty rates both in terms of these types of lone-mother households and compared with the "ideal" two-parent household. The results show that, in general, the children of lone mothers experience higher poverty rates, but also that child poverty rates vary widely between types of lone-mother households and so depend on a family's specific history and circumstances.

Furthermore, sources of income and ways of deriving a livelihood also vary considerably between types of lone-mother households. These differences are reflected in a very high level of inequality in income across all lone-mother households. But there is also considerable inequality within each of the subdivisions. Indeed, decomposing the inequality in all lone-mother households using the generalized entropy index measure of inequality, GE (-1),[2] shows that most of this inequality is within and not between lone-mother types.

Against this backdrop of diversity, the analysis builds a picture of lone mothers facing extra burdens: they have higher labor force participation and work longer hours on average than mothers in two-parent households, and they survive on household incomes that are derived less from cash earnings than those of two-parent households. Cash earnings are the most enabling form of income in Russia today because they bring flexibility and allow choice in expenditure, in contrast to income from pensions and contributions from family and friends which may be in-kind or subject to payment arrears. The low level of means-tested child benefits means that the state makes little contribution to the budgets of most lone-mother households.

LONE MOTHERS IN RUSSIA

There have always been lone mothers in Russia and the Soviet Union. Their numbers increased greatly as a result of men's deaths and disappearances during the civil war, Stalinist purges, and World War II. In the Soviet Union, few lone mothers started out in that category. After a brief interlude in the 1920s, marriage was strongly encouraged (Ekaterina Alexandrova 1984), and usually swiftly followed extra-marital conception (Sergei Zakharov and Elena Ivanova 1996). Since the collapse of the Soviet Union, the composition of lone-mother households according to their origins has changed. Many more women bear children without marrying, although they may cohabit and so be alone only legally and not in fact. The proportion of live births to unmarried women rose from 13.5 percent in 1989 to 27.9 percent in 1999 (UNICEF 2002). However, the RLMS data presented in Table 1 suggest that divorce is currently the main route into lone motherhood, a finding that is consistent with high divorce rates: 4.3 divorces per 1,000 (using the mid-year population) in 2000 (Goskomstat 2002a).

Table 1 Children's households' composition

Child's family status	Percentage of all children	N
Two parents (2PHH)	68.8	1,701
Woman-maintained (WMH)	3.8	95
Lone-mother (LMH)	19.1	473
Never-married lone mother	3.6	89
Registered married lone mother	2.8	69
Co-habiting lone mother	3.8	94
Divorced lone mother	6.7	165
Widowed lone mother	2.3	56
Lone father	4.2	105
Father or mother and step-parent	3.6	88
Without parents	4.2	105
Total	100.0	2,472

Source: RLMS.

DATA

The data for this analysis are from round nine of the RLMS, a survey that was designed to provide a nationally representative sample of households in the Russian Federation.[3] Ten rounds of the RLMS have been completed.[4] Round nine of the RLMS took place in the year 2000, the second year of positive growth after seven years of output collapse and two years after the financial crisis. The 2000 survey gathered data from 4,006 households and 11,261 individuals, including 2,472 children under age 16.

The RLMS is the only nationally representative Russian dataset that allows analysis from the child's perspective and permits analysts to construct their own household typologies. The proportions of children living in different household types can thus be calculated, rather than the relative distribution of different household types in which children are present.

BUILDING A TYPOLOGY OF LONE MOTHERS

This analysis examines the differences in children's material welfare within lone-mother households by subdividing lone-mother households by the mother's current marital status, which serves as an indicator of the mother's route of entry into lone motherhood. Table 1 shows the division of children in this typology of households. By far the highest proportion of children living in lone-mother households (35 percent) resides with divorced lone mothers.

Although lone-mother households may be categorized as though there are clear boundaries between them, in reality, the demarcation between types of households is blurred. Anomalies in the identification and counting of lone-mother households are common. For example, a woman who cohabits with a man who is not her child's father is considered a lone mother by the Russian state, as is the practice in the United States (Kurt Bauman 1999). But women who later marry men who are not the fathers of their children are not necessarily considered lone mothers.

Two-parent households that are exclusively or primarily maintained by women represent another possible anomaly. For example, households in which the woman's earnings contribute the major part of the household's income, set in this analysis at 70 percent of total household income, are identified in the tables as "woman-maintained households" for comparative purposes. Such households would not usually be defined as lone mother households. However, the distinction between these "woman-maintained" households and more conventionally defined lone-mother households is contestable. In particular, women maintaining households face many of the same constraints and limitations in labor markets that lone mothers face, and in both cases the disadvantages the woman confronts as a result of being the main earner have negative effects on the economic well-being of their families.

Leaving "woman-maintained" households out of the picture results in underestimation of the number of children living in lone-mother or "quasi-lone-mother" households. For example, in the Russian data, the proportion of children living in woman-maintained households (3.8 percent) is as high as the proportion of children who live in lone-mother households in which the woman is cohabiting with a man (3.8 percent) and higher than the proportion in never-married lone-mother households (3.6 percent).

The fluidity of people's living arrangements also undermines efforts to define lone motherhood as a distinct form of household. Increasingly, it may be better conceptualized as a stage in some women's lives. This is particularly the case in Russia, where the average ages of first marriage and of having a first child are fairly young and divorce rates are high.

To acknowledge that there are many different types of lone-mother or quasi-lone-mother households is in line with the thinking of those anthropologists who argue in favor of conceptualizing a plurality of households as nodal points in flows of resources. Such flows occur both within the household and also between individuals, between the household and wider family networks, and between the state and society (see Jane Guyer and Pauline Peters 1987; Henrietta Moore 1992).

Wider family networks have played a particularly important role in helping Russian families cope with adversity. Household structure is not simply determined by partnerships or the marital status of parents. The boundaries of families can be redrawn to include wider kin, if their inclusion is mutually beneficial and facilitates collective survival (Deniz Kandiyoti 1999). In the case of lone-mother households, other kin can provide benefits in the forms of additional earnings, pension income, or potential childcare services. It is not surprising that 27 percent of children from lone-mother households live with one or two grandparents, compared to only 17 percent of children in two-parent households.[5] The proportion of lone mothers living with their parents is highly correlated with their route into lone motherhood, which is also correlated with the lone mother's age: the RLMS shows that 64 percent of never-married lone mothers lived with one or both of their parents, compared with only 9 percent of widows. Further, the tendency to expand the boundaries of family and include wider kin in living arrangements, while always important in Russia, may be increasing in response to economic uncertainty and hard times. Thus, Michael Lokshin, Kathleen Mullen Harris, and Barry Popkin's (2000) analysis of the RLMS found that while in 1992, 55.5 percent of lone-mother households were living as nuclear families, that is families comprising only parents or a parent and children, only 43.8 percent had this living arrangement in 1996.

POVERTY

The incidence of children living in household poverty is measured by comparing household expenditure[6] with the cost of the consumption basket defined in the official Russian minimum subsistence level, the *prozhitochnyi minimum.*[7] Prior to 2000, the food share in the subsistence minimum was fixed at 70 percent.

The equivalence scale adjustments this analysis uses are those adopted in official Russian poverty calculations. The economies-of-scale adjustments are those developed by Barry Popkin, Alexander Baturin, Marina Mozhina, and Thomas Mroz (1996). Actual prices in the specific sites of the survey are used, rather than the prices of the Russian State Statistical Committee (Goskomstat), which are used in official calculations of the poverty lines.[8] The effect of using survey prices is to report lower levels of poverty than would be the case using official *oblast* (administrative district) level prices.

Household poverty rates for children living in all types of lone-mother households are compared with those for children living in households with two parents and with those for children residing in woman-maintained households. This analysis assumes equal sharing of household resources, as is the practice in standard poverty analyses. Such analyses are extremely influential, particularly through the work of international agencies, although a considerable body of research criticizes the conceptualization of the household as working by an equal sharing or unitary model (Nancy Folbre 1986; Lawrence Haddad, John Hoddinott and Harold Alderman 1997; Gillian Hart 1997; Elissa Braunstein and Nancy Folbre 2001). In addition, Richard Rose and Ian McAllister (1996) have questioned whether money should be used as the measure of welfare in Russia because of the degree of demonetization. Despite these important criticisms, equal

Table 2 Children living in poor households

Children living in household type	Headcount poverty FGT(0)	Poverty gap FGT (1) (average normalized poverty gap)
All	26.6	0.09
All two-parent households	23.8	0.08
Of which:		
Woman-maintained	34.8	0.14
All lone mothers	35.2	0.14
Of which:		
Never married	41.4	0.20
In a registered marriage	28.1	0.11
Cohabiting	37.2	0.15
Divorced	35.5	0.12
Widowed	28.3	0.09
Lone father	37.5	0.12

Source: RLMS.

sharing of resources is assumed and money-based welfare measures used to demonstrate that the differences amongst lone-mother households are clear, even using standard poverty analyses.

Table 2 presents child poverty by type of household using two indices of the FGT[9] class formulated by James Foster, Joel Greer, and Erik Thorbecke (1984). The child poverty rate, FGT(0), is the proportion of children living in households with expenditures below the poverty line. The poverty rate provides a useful indication of the overall scale of child poverty in different household types, but it does not provide any measure of the severity of poverty, that is the poverty shortfall. An alternative measure is the poverty gap, FGT(1), which accounts for the depth of poverty. The poverty gap summarizes the mean proportionate shortfall from the poverty line for the entire child population.

Table 2 shows strikingly that the child poverty rate overall is very high in Russia at 26.6 percent. Even in two-parent households, the child poverty rate is 23.8 percent, a level that is remarkably high when compared with, for example, that of the United States. Poverty rates are even higher for children in lone-mother households. Moreover, there is not only a difference in the child poverty rates between two-parent households and lone-mother households, but there are also differences in poverty rates between types of lone-mother households. Poverty rates for children who live with a mother who has never been married are the highest at 41.4 percent and the depth of poverty, as measured by the poverty gap, is substantially higher for these families than for all other groups. Children whose mothers cohabit with a man who is not their father or stepfather also experience much higher poverty rates than those with a widowed mother or with a mother still in a registered marriage, although no longer co-resident with the husband. This remains true even when the income, if there is one, of the cohabitant is included.

213

Table 3 Contribution of different sources of income to total household income-mean by household type. Coefficient of variation (standard deviation divided by the mean) reported in parentheses

Household type	Cash earnings	Pensions	Child benefit	Alimony	Contributions from family and friends	Other*
All	41.1 (0.9)	26.8 (1.3)	1.3 (5.3)	0.5 (9.2)	7.6 (2.5)	22.7 (1.2)
With children	54.9 (0.7)	9.6 (2.2)	2.9 (3.5)	1.1 (0.2)	8.9 (2.2)	22.6 (6.9)
Two parents with children	60.0 (0.6)	5.9 (30.8)	2.5 (4.1)	0	7.9 (2.2)	23.7 (2.4)
All lone mothers	46.7 (0.7)	15.8 (1.5)	3.5 (2.9)	3.7 (3.4)	11.7 (2.1)	18.6 (2.3)
Never married	43.9 (0.8)	21.8 (1.3)	6.5 (2.5)	1.0 (3.7)	10.4 (2.3)	16.4 (1.5)
Registered married	51.9 (0.7)	11.0 (1.7)	1.5 (2.2)	5.9 (3.1)	9.7 (1.9)	20.0 (1.3)
Living together not registered	44.5 (1.2)	12.3 (1.7)	1.7 (1.6)	2.4 (3.6)	7.4 (5.6)	31.7 (2.5)
Divorced and not remarried	46.6 (0.8)	12.5 (1.82)	3.3 (3.2)	6.2 (2.5)	16.4 (1.8)	15.0 (1.7)
Widow	41.7 (0.8)	27.1 (1.0)	4.5 (2.0)	0.5 (6.7)	2.8 (2.8)	23.4 (1.3)
Woman maintained	71.6 (0.4)	22.0 (2.2)	1.5 (3.1)	0.4 (6.3)	1.0 (4.9)	3.5 (11.0)

Source: RLMS.

*Other includes, for example, earned noncash income, home produce, student stipends, unemployment benefits, apartment benefits.

Table 3 shows the mean contribution of the money equivalent of different types of income to total household income compared across household types. It provides a livelihoods context for differences in poverty rates.

Overall, children whose mothers are widowed experience a much lower incidence of poverty than children in other types of lone-mother households. The explanation could be that, as Table 3 shows, these households draw their main support from pension income (the mean proportion of total income is 27.1 percent) and crucially are also able to supplement incomes with their savings. In Russia there remain many types of pensions, including those for invalids, military veterans, and retirees. Hence the contribution of pensions to income for all household types is larger than would be the case in many other countries. Woman-maintained households and never-married lone-mother households derive a substantial proportion of household income from pensions (22 percent and 21.8 percent, respectively). In both cases, this is because of the prevalence of extended families among these categories of lone-mother households. A high proportion of woman-maintained households (21 percent) include a resident grandparent, giving some indication of how lone mothers manage childcare while devoting their time to getting cash income.

Registered married[10] lone-mother households have lower child poverty rates than those of divorced lone mothers. This disparity is not the result of differences in alimony, which provides approximately the same proportion of total household income for those who are still registered married (5.9

percent) as for those who are divorced (6.2 percent). Divorced lone-mother households benefit from much higher contributions from family and friends (16.4 percent) than do still-married lone-mother households (9.7 percent). This difference probably relates to the low proportion of divorced lone mothers living in extended family arrangements. Instead of helping by sharing housing, family members send money. Widowed lone mothers and women who maintain their households economically receive a very low proportion (2.8 percent and 1.0 percent) of total household income from family and friends.

Child benefits make very little contribution to these households, which is hardly surprising as the means-tested benefit to lone mothers amounted to only 10 percent of the child-subsistence minimum in 2000, or the cash equivalent of US$5 per month (Goskomstat 2002b). Child benefit is most important to households headed by never-married women, but even here it comprises only 6.5 percent of total income.

Perhaps the most striking finding from Table 3 is the many, varying sources of income that lone mothers mobilize. Lone mothers with different backgrounds appear to derive their livelihoods in different ways. Moreover, in addition to the differences in the composition of income in Table 3, the generally large values of the coefficient of variation (the standard deviations in relation to the mean proportions) point to huge diversity in income sourcing within household types. Only the share of cash earnings in total household income shows uniformity within household types, with much lower values for the coefficient of variation. This suggests that comparisons of the share of cash income across the different household types of Table 3 can be more meaningfully generalized than comparisons between the other items of income that have higher values of the coefficient of variation and thus more variation within the subgroups. Two-parent households clearly derive a much higher proportion of their income from cash earnings than lone-mother households. The high proportion of income derived from cash earnings in woman-maintained households is a result of the definition employed in this paper: woman-maintained households are those in which a woman's cash earnings contribute 70 percent or more of total household income.

Reported earnings still make up only 41.1 percent of total household income for all households, including those without children. Such earnings comprise 54.9 percent of total income for all households with children; 60 percent for households with two parents; and 46.7 percent of total income for all lone-mother households. The relatively low contributions that reported earnings make to total household incomes reflects the fact that in Russia, household members pursue their livelihoods in very diverse ways and with considerable complexity in time allocation.

Working in the private sector brings the highest rewards in terms of wages, but also requires the longest hours. The share of household income derived from work in the private sector is directly correlated with well-being, as measured by expenditure as a proportion of the poverty line. Lone mothers are disadvantaged in obtaining private-sector jobs because of their need for work flexibility and the long hours such jobs require. In the workplace they may face a subtle form of discrimination or be overburdened with work. Irina Tartakovskaya (2000) has suggested that lone mothers may be pressed to work exceptionally long hours. The prejudice against lone mothers as social failures tarnishes their bargaining position in the workplace and vis-à-vis potential employers, exposing them to exploitation.

In addition to financing expenditures out of current income, lone mothers also resort to running down their savings. But this possibility is not open to all lone mothers. Divorced lone mothers are able to finance a significant amount of their expenditures through savings, whereas other lone mothers, in particular those who have never married, have few savings to draw upon.

INEQUALITY WITHIN LONE-MOTHER HOUSEHOLDS

The wide variation in child poverty rates implies that children in contemporary Russia experience very diverse material circumstances. Along with consistently high rates of poverty, there has been a huge increase in inequality in the 1990s. While there was inequality in living standards in Soviet Russia, it is generally considered to have been much less than in the post-Soviet period; earnings inequality was certainly much lower. The Gini coefficient of earnings was 0.277 in 1986 in the USSR (Anthony Atkinson and John Micklewright 1992), but rose dramatically thereafter, climbing to 0.483 by 1996 (UNICEF 2002). Inequality in wealth is probably much higher.

In this analysis, inequality across the range of household types (see Table 4) is investigated by two decomposable measures: the coefficient of variation of the ratio of household expenditure to needs (*exppov*) and the generalized entropy index for *exppov*. Household needs are defined as the household's poverty line. The coefficient of variation of *exppov* is the standard deviation of *exppov* divided by its mean. In its favor are that its value is independent of the expenditure scale and does not depend on the number of people in the population. While it provides a good measure of the dispersion of the distribution, it is affected in the same way by transfers at all parts of the distribution and is therefore considered more useful for capturing transfers at the higher end of the distribution than those at the lower end. The generalized entropy index is also independent of the expenditure scale and does not depend on numbers in the population. In addition, it can be parameterized to reflect different perceptions of inequality with lower values indicating a higher degree of inequality aversion. In this analysis, the parameter c is chosen to be -1, GE (-1), to

Table 4 Inequality in different household types

Household type	Coefficient of variation *exppov*	Generalized entropy index (-1) *exppov*
All households with children	1.33	0.56
Two Parent	1.47	0.55
Woman-maintained	0.97	0.60
All lone-mother households	1.29	0.65
Never-married lone mothers	0.91	0.70
Registered married	1.23	0.62
Co-habiting	0.77	0.48
Divorced and not remarried	1.43	0.72
Widows	0.73	0.36

Source: RLMS.

give a high weight at the lower end of the distribution indicating relatively high sensitivity to inequality in the lower tail of the distribution.[11] The formula for the generalized entropy index is given by:

$$I_c = \frac{1}{n} \frac{1}{c(c-1)} \sum_i \left[\left(\frac{y_i}{\mu} \right)^c - 1 \right] \quad c \neq 0, 1,$$

where n is the number of individuals in the sample, y_i is household income i, and $\mu = (1/n) \sum y_i$, the arithmetic mean income. The inequality aversion parameter is c.

The square of the coefficient of variation corresponds to a value of $c=2$ in the generalized entropy formula, which reflects the higher weight given to rich groups in the measure and highlights the difference in implicit social welfare preferences between GE(-1) and the coefficient of variation. Consequently, the ranking of inequality between household types in Table 4 differs between the two measures of inequality.

The higher aversion to inequality of GE(-1) than the coefficient of variation may be considered more appropriate in Russia, where relative advantage and disadvantage are likely to play much greater roles in defining individual welfare and potential exclusion in the future than was the case in Soviet society, especially for children.

The values of GE(-1) range from zero to infinity, with zero representing an equal distribution and higher values representing higher levels of inequality. Higher values of the coefficient of variation also represent higher levels of inequality. A further advantage of the coefficient of variation and the generalized entropy measure is that the values for each index can be compared across each of the main groups and subgroups (see Table 4). The generalized entropy index GE(-1) shows greater inequality for lone-mother households than for two-parent households, although a different ranking obtains with reference to the coefficient of variation.

217

There are high levels of inequality for all the subgroups of Table 4, indicating diversity of living standards within all types of households. But inequality is more pronounced for some groups than others. Thus inequality, as measured by GE(− 1), is highest within divorced lone-mother households at 0.72, compared to inequality within widowed lone-mother households, which at 0.36 is the lowest. Lower inequality within widowed lone-mother households and also within cohabiting lone-mother households suggests that the material circumstances are more uniform within these groups than within others; while the high degree of inequality within divorced lone-mother households reflects widely varying material circumstances. Lone mothers are clearly not a homogeneous group. Their heterogeneity is explored further in the inequality decompositions of Table 5.

An extremely useful aspect of the coefficient of variation and the generalized entropy index is that they can be additively decomposed into the constituent parts of within- and between-group inequalities. The decomposition equation for the generalized entropy measure is:

$$I_c = \sum_k v_k(\lambda_k)^c I_c^k + \frac{1}{c(c-1)} \sum_k v_k[(\lambda_k)^c - 1] \quad c \neq 0, 1,$$

where $v_k = n_k/n$ is the proportion of the population in household type subgroup k and $\lambda_k = \mu_k/\mu$ is its mean income relative to that of the whole population.

The first term in the equation (the "within-group component") is a simple weighted average of the inequality values within each subgroup. The second term is the "between-group component," which is the sum of the inequality existing between subgroups of a population. In a decomposition by household type, this term represents the "pure type" effect of differences between households and corresponds to the value of the index if the incomes of all households are replaced by the mean income of the subgroup to which they belong. Such a procedure eliminates all within-household-type income variations. Table 4 reports the total inequality GE(− 1) in the lone-mother group of 0.65, which is the sum of the between-group inequality of 0.02 and the within-group inequality of 0.63 as

Table 5 Between- and within-group inequality of welfare

Measuring inequality	Generalized entropy index (− 1) exppov
Within all lone-mother and two-parent households	0.55
Between all lone-mother and two-parent households	0.002
Within all types of lone-mother households	0.63
Between types of lone-mother households	0.02

Source: RLMS.

reported in Table 5. Thus, in the decomposition of inequality for all lone mothers, the contribution of the mean differences by type of lone mother is 0.02, or 3 percent of the 0.65 aggregate inequality reported for this category of household in Table 4. Even recognizing the seeming diversity of lone-mother households by lone-mother type (as defined in this paper), between-lone-mother-group differences explain very little of the inequality in lone-mother households as a whole, which is primarily the product of inequality within the subgroups. Differences between lone-mother and two-parent households explain even less of the aggregate inequality in households with children. Almost all of the inequality is within the two subgroups; that is, within lone-mother households and within two-parent households.

High levels of inequality among children living in lone-mother households are further illustrated by the finding that 7.5 percent of children in lone-mother households are in the top decile of the whole population welfare distribution, while 16 percent are in the bottom decile.

This situation, in which lone mothers reside at both the top and the bottom of the material welfare spectrum, is reminiscent of the position of lone mothers throughout the twentieth century in Russia. Rich women campaigned for divorce in order to be released from unhappy marriages, while poor women needed to remain married so as to survive materially. If poor women were unsuccessful, they became lone mothers and faced the enormous structural constraints that came from seeking to survive outside marriage.

These constraints persist today and affect all women, not only poor women and not only lone mothers, although the outcomes of women's struggles with these constraints are conditioned by their wealth and family status. However, in Russia today it seems legitimate to raise the fundamental issue of equity only when it results in poverty for women and their children, or in low birth rates. As a result, materially better-off lone mothers are screened out of consideration, their experiences deemed irrelevant to policy decisions. In the next section I argue that lone mothers share a number of limitations on their opportunities and, indeed, share them with women who live in other kinds of households. The elimination of such structural constraints will enable better access to decent jobs for all women, including those raising children alone.

COMMON PROBLEMS

Employment participation

Labor force participation rates in modern Russia remain high, although high participation rates co-exist with a high incidence of low-quality, low-paid jobs (Simon Clarke 1999). According to RLMS data, across all categories, 75 percent of working-age men and 67 percent of working-age women reported having a job. Lone mothers are especially active. Seventy-one percent of working-age women in lone-mother households reported they had a job, compared with 67 percent of working-age women in two-parent households. Interestingly, while 76 percent of working-age men in two-parent households reported having a job, only 61 percent of working-age men who live in lone-mother households reported employment. So, working-age men in two-parent households tend to be economically more active than working-age men who reside in lone-mother households.

Hours worked

One of the key differences between employed men and women is in the number of hours worked for wages. Table 6 shows that, on average, men work longer hours than women, especially men in households with children. Fatherhood is correlated with longer working hours for men. Overall, women in households with children work slightly fewer hours than women as a group. But this is not true for women in lone-mother households; their working hours are as long as other women's.

Table 6 shows that women in lone-mother households work longer hours than women in two-parent households, a finding that is indicative of the additional economic pressures they face. Moreover, Table 7 shows that this difference in hours worked between women in lone-mother households and in two-parent households is statistically significant.

Women in lone-mother households work the same hours as other women who maintain their households economically, implying a similar set of constraints or needs (Table 6). Men who are the main earners in the

Table 6 Hours worked per month for those with a job. Standard Deviation reported in parentheses.

	Hours worked in primary employment	Hours worked in secondary employment	Total hours worked
All men	180.7 (65.0)	3.3 (20.3)	184.0 (65.8)
All women	158.4 (56.1)	3.2 (20.2)	157.9 (57.7)
Men in 2PHH	186.2 (66.3)	3.5 (20.7)	189.7 (66.9)
Women in 2PHH	154.7 (57.7)	3.2 (20.2)	157.9 (57.7)
Women in LMHH	158.4 (56.1)	4.0 (22.3)	162.5 (57.4)
Women in WMH	159.9 (55.9)	5.1 (23.5)	165.0 (55.4)

Source: RLMS.
Note: 2PHH is two-parent households; LMHH is lone-mother households; WMH is women-maintained households.

Table 7 Significance of the differences in working hours for women in lone-mother household (LMHH) and two-parent households (2PHH)

Difference in working hours for women in 2PHH and LMHH	*t-statistic for difference*
Primary employment	− 2.17*
Secondary employment	− 1.77*
Total hours worked	− 2.87**

Note: **$p < 0.01$; *$p < 0.05$.
Source: RLMS.

household work significantly longer hours than all men, but not significantly longer hours than other men with children.

Interestingly, women in lone-mother households, if they work in secondary employment, work longer hours in their second jobs than do men at their second jobs. If women in woman-maintained households have second jobs, they work the longest hours of all workers in secondary employment. Simon Clarke (2002) has observed that the nature of jobs in secondary employment "tends to be episodic or unstable rather than providing a regular activity and steady source of income." The apparent willingness of women in lone-mother households to seize any and all labor-market opportunities to augment their incomes testifies to their need for additional resources.

The wage gap

Even after decades of high labor-force participation in the Soviet Union, women's representation in managerial and higher grades remains noticeably poor. In the Russian economy today, women occupy very few of the top positions. None of the so-called Russian oligarchs is a woman. Addressing male–female wage inequalities is not on the political or social agenda when low wages are endemic. The gender–wage gap, or the ratio of female-to-male wages, was estimated at 0.75 in 1995 (Elena Glinskaya and Thomas Mroz 2000). Lower pay for women originates in part from occupational segregation. But their recent analysis of the RLMS suggests that in addition there may be differential pay rates for the same jobs for men and women. At any rate, lone mothers along with all other women face pay discrimination in addition to their other disadvantages in the labor market.

CONCLUSION

Lone mothers and their households are often presented as a homogeneous group, sharing similar disadvantages and existing as a group distinct from other women and from two-parent households. The crude conflation of all lone-mother households, despite their varying histories and experiences, facilitates the social construction of lone motherhood as a social problem. Within the context of contemporary Russia, this paper decomposes the aggregate category of lone-mother households into various subgroups according to the route taken into lone motherhood. The sources of income for lone mothers, and the poverty rates of their children, are shown to differ widely according to how the women entered lone motherhood. The circumstances and income sources of divorced lone-mother households, for example, turn out to be very different from those of never-married lone mothers, while those of widowed lone mothers are different again. Moreover, the differences this analysis exposes between types of lone-mother households are overshadowed by an even greater diversity within the types of lone-mother households it identifies. Not all lone-mother households are poor and deprived, and those that are, are not poor and deprived in identical ways. Moreover, not all lone-mother households of a specific type, such as divorced lone-mother households, are poor and deprived, and, once again, those that are, are not poor and deprived in identical ways.

While recognizing differences and diversity, the paper identifies the common problems that lone mothers face in contemporary Russia. These include struggling to combine long hours at primary and secondary jobs with caring for children and finding and maintaining flexible sources of income. For example, lone mothers cannot work as many hours as men in two-parent households, and therefore they have reduced access to more lucrative private-sector employment. Moreover, occupational segregation and persistent wage discrimination in Russia further handicap lone mothers and other women who maintain households. The persistence of sex discrimination highlights the common denominator that gender provides.

The disadvantages that lone mothers and other women maintaining households face in accessing good jobs with equal pay are also faced by most other Russian women. However, tackling women's structural disadvantages is not even on the policy agenda, since the quality of most jobs is so poor. Combating women's disadvantage in labor markets would mean paying women wages equal to men's, enacting radical programs to return women to public life and to senior positions in the workforce, and providing enhanced levels of quality childcare – a step that would benefit all women, and lone mothers in particular.

Lone mothers have received some attention in Russia, in the context of policies intended to tackle child poverty. The result has been paltry means-tested child benefits for lone mothers, which conform to the overall low level of means-tested child benefits. The state seems to have little interest in a fairer or more sustainable division of the costs of rearing children. While pressures for additional state support for children growing up in lone-mother and other households at risk of poverty should be maintained, campaigns for labor market equality should also be pursued. Greater equality in access to jobs and fair pay would benefit not only lone mothers but also other women in Russia. Assistance in these ways would prevent the depiction of poor lone mothers as a social problem, while enabling all women to exploit labor market opportunities and choose their domestic arrangements more freely. These developments would have positive implications for Russian society as a whole.

ACKNOWLEDGEMENTS

I am grateful to all the editors of the special edition, the anonymous referees, Thomas Aldridge, and Ceema Namazie.

NOTES

[1] The total fertility rate, that is, the theoretical average number of children born to a woman in her lifetime, fell from 1.90 in 1990 to 1.17 in 1999 (Goskomstat 2002a).

[2] Heuristically, the generalized entropy index $GE(-1)$ provides a measure of the degree of disorder in a distribution; that is, how far a distribution is from a state in which each observation has an equal share (for a fuller description see Frank Cowell 1995). If there were complete inequality, with one household receiving all the income, the value of the index would tend toward infinity; with equal incomes in the distribution the value of the index would be zero. Higher levels of $GE(-1)$ represent higher levels of inequality. Essentially, in this analysis, $GE(-1)$ is the weighted geometric average of the relative values of our welfare measure, *exppov*, where the weights are the fraction of aggregate welfare received by each unit. The choice of -1 in the generalized entropy class represents a relatively high sensitivity to changes in the lower tail of the distribution.

[3] In the rapidly changing population of early post-Soviet Russia, it is unlikely that any survey was truly representative. However, the sample design of the RLMS improved considerably from its early rounds, when it covered only about twenty primary sampling units (PSUs); since 1994 it has been based on sixty-five PSUs. In common with all household surveys, it can be criticized for excluding households and individuals at both ends of the distribution. As a household survey it necessarily excludes the homeless and those living in institutions. These shortcomings also apply to Goskomstat's *Family Budget Survey* (FBS) (see Jane Falkingham and Shireen Kanji 2000). Although the FBS covers nearly 50,000 households, the sampling frame has been criticized (Alistair McAuley 1979; Stephen Shenfield 1983; Anthony Atkinson and John Micklewright 1992).

[4] Since 1993 the survey has been conducted by the University of North Carolina in conjunction with the Institute of Sociology of the Russian Academy of Sciences.

[5] Author's calculations from the RLMS.

[6] Expenditure comprised all food and nonfood items, in addition to savings, loans made, assistance received, alimony payments, and the total value of household production consumed or given away.

[7] This is an absolute measure, based in the main on a fixed range of goods that represent minimum nutritional requirements (the food basket) and also nonfood items and services for three groups of the population: those able to work, pensioners, and children (Jane Falkingham, Shireen Kanji, and Samantha Yates 2003).

[8] The official Russian poverty line is drawn up by administrative district (*oblast*) to allow for the wide divergence of prices and dietary patterns across Russia. However, prices vary considerably within *oblasts* and therefore the approach here, to record the actual prices in the location, better reflects the actual purchasing power of money in the survey sites.

[9] Poverty and inequality are computed using a Stata program written by Stephen Jenkins.

[10] In Russia, "registered married" is the equivalent of a formal state marriage, whereas "citizens' marriage" refers to a cohabiting union.

[11] For the relevant technical details see Francois Bourguignon (1979) and Dilip Mookherjee and Anthony Shorrocks (1982).

REFERENCES

Agarwal, Bina. 1997. "'Bargaining' and Gender Relations: Within and Beyond the Household." *Feminist Economics* 3(1): 1 – 51.

Alexandrova, Ekaterina. 1984. "Why Soviet Women Want to Get Married," in Tatyana Mamanova (ed.). *Women and Russia*, pp. 31 – 50. Oxford: Blackwell.

Atkinson, Anthony B. and John Micklewright. 1992. *Economic Transformation in Eastern Europe and the Distribution of Income*. Cambridge, UK: Cambridge University Press.

Bauman, Kurt. 1999. "Shifting Family Definitions: The Effect of Cohabitation and Other Nonfamily Household Relationships on Measures of Poverty." *Demography* 36(3): 315 – 25.

Bourguignon, Francois. 1979. "Decomposable Inequality Measures." *Econometrica* 47(4): 901 – 20.

Braunstein, Elissa and Nancy Folbre. 2001. "To Honor and Obey: Efficiency, Inequality and Patriarchal Property Rights." *Feminist Economics* 7(1): 25 – 44.

Clarke, Simon. 1999. *New Forms of Employment and Household Survival Strategies in Russia*. Coventry, UK: Centre for Comparative Labour Studies, University of Warwick.

——. 2002. *Making Ends Meet in Contemporary Russia*. Cheltenham, UK: Edward Elgar.

Cowell, Frank. 1995. *Measuring Inequality*. Hemel Hempstead, UK: Harvester Wheatsheaf.

Falkingham, Jane and Shireen Kanji. 2000. "Measuring Poverty in Russia: A Critical Review." Report prepared for the Department for International Development.

Falkingham, Jane, Shireen Kanji, and Samantha Yates. 2003. "Poverty in Nizhegorodskaya Oblast." Report prepared for the Department for International Development.

Folbre, Nancy. 1986. "Hearts and Spades: Paradigms of Household Economics." *World Development* 14: 245 – 55.

Foster, James E., Joel Greer, and Erik Thorbecke. 1984. "A Class of Decomposable Poverty Indices." *Econometrica* 52: 761 – 6.

Glinskaya, Elena and Thomas A. Mroz. 2000. "The Gender Gap in Wages in Russia from 1992 to 1995." *Journal of Population Economics* 13(2): 353 – 86.

Goskomstat. 2002a. *The Demographic Yearbook of Russia, 2002.* Moscow: Information and Publishing Centre, Statistics of Russia.

——. 2002b. *Sotsial'noe polozhenie I uroven' zhizni naseleniya Rossii, 2002 [Social Situation and Living Standards of the Russian Population, 2002].* Moscow: Statistika Rossii.

Guyer, Jane, and Pauline Peters. 1987. "Introduction," in "Conceptualising the Household: Issues of Theory and Policy in Africa." Special issue of *Development and Change* 18(2): 197–214.

Haddad, Lawrence, John Hoddinott, and Harold Alderman. 1997. "Introduction: The Scope of Intrahousehold Resource Allocation Issues," in Lawrence Haddad, John Hoddinott, and Harold Alderman (eds.) *Intrahousehold Resource Allocation in Developing Countries: Models, Methods, and Policy.* Baltimore, MD: Johns Hopkins University Press.

Hart, Gillian. 1997. "From 'Rotten Wives to Good Mothers': Household Models and the Limits of Economism." *Institute of Development Studies Bulletin* 28(3): 14–25.

Kandiyoti, Deniz. 1999. "Poverty in Transition: An Ethnographic Critique of Household Surveys in Post-Soviet Central Asia." *Development and Change* 30(3): 499–523.

Lokshin, Michael, Kathleen Mullen Harris, and Barry Popkin. 2000. "Single Mothers in Russia: Household Strategies for Coping with Poverty." *World Development* 28(12): 2183–98.

McAuley, Alistair. 1979. *Economic Welfare in the Soviet Union.* Madison, WI: University of Wisconsin Press.

Molyneux, Maxine. 1994. "Women's Rights and the International Context: Some Reflections on the Post-Communist States." *Development and Change* 30(3): 499–524.

Mookherjee, Dilip and Anthony Shorrocks. 1982. "A Decomposition Analysis of the Trend in UK Income Inequality." *Economic Journal* 92(368): 886–902.

Moore, Henrietta L. 1992. "Households and Gender Relations: The Modelling of the Economy," in Sutti Ortiz and Susan Lees (eds.) *Understanding Economic Process,* pp. 131–47. Lanham, MD: University Press of America.

Popkin, Barry, Alexander K. Baturin, Marina Mozhina, and Thomas Mroz. 1996. "The Russian Federation Subsistence Income Level: The Development of Regional Food Baskets and Other Methodological Improvements." 1996 Report to the Russian Federation and the World Bank.

Rose, Richard and Ian McAllister. 1996. "Is Money the Measure of Welfare in Russia?" *Review of Income and Wealth* 42(1): 75–90.

Shenfield, Stephen. 1983. "A Note on Data Quality in the Soviet Family Budget Survey." *Soviet Studies* 35(4): 561–8.

Tartakovskaya, Irina. 2000. "The Changing Representation of Gender Roles in the Soviet and Post-Soviet Press," in Sarah Ashwin (ed.) *Gender, State, and Society in Soviet and Post-Soviet Russia,* pp. 118–36. London: Routledge.

UNICEF. 2002. *TransMONEE Data Base.* Florence: UNICEF Innocenti Research Center.

Zakharov, Sergei and Elena Ivanova. 1996. "Fertility Decline and Recent Changes in Russia: On the Threshold of Second Demographic Transition," in Julie DaVanzo (ed.) *Russia's Demographic "Crisis,"* pp. 36–82. Santa Monica, CA: Rand.

All the Lesbian Mothers are Coupled, All the Single Mothers are Straight, and All of Us are Tired: Reflections on Being a Single Lesbian Mom

June Lapidus

INTRODUCTION

Item: During Family Week (a week of activities and discussions for lesbian and gay parents and their children) in Provincetown, Massachusetts, the stores up and down a thriving Commercial Street sported "I love my two moms" T-shirts, coffee mugs, and baby bibs. Amid blocks crammed with stores catering to the lesbian and gay tourists, I could not find one "I love my lesbian mom" item for sale.

Item: A local gay and lesbian community center in the city in which I live contacted a local gay and lesbian family group asking for a lesbian couple and their kids who could be featured as part of a promotional campaign to show the range of people in our community. The request was specifically for a couple. I asked about the reason for the specificity of the choice and was informed that it was simply not possible to represent our community in all its diversity within the constraints of budget and space. The political implications of the decision were not acknowledged.

These experiences teach us something – politically, personally, and theoretically – about the state of our movements and the state of our theories. Specifically they provide another vantage point from which to sharpen our analysis of the family as an institution. While in our lives families take many forms, there is a Western ideology of the family as natural, nurturing, and private. When I refer to the family, I mean this ideology.

*   *   *

"Lone mothering" is an odd phrase. I am a single lesbian mother but I certainly do not mother alone. A web of relationships surround my son and me: the friends who have taken him to breakfast every Saturday since he was born; my best friend with whom I struggle around issues of discipline and the theories and practice of raising children; the woman who came into our lives as my lover when my son was 3 and remains in our lives, though she and I are no longer lovers; the friends who sat in the hospital waiting room providing Thai food to my labor coaches; the teachers at my son's school who continue to think with me about his needs; the 14-year-old boy down the street who baby-sits; and the woman who provided love and nurturance in her home so that I could both work and parent. We are part of an extended biological family of grandparents, aunts, uncles, cousins, and nieces and nephews. We are also simultaneously members of many communities, some as mother and son, and some individually. Yet the phrase "lone mothering" conjures up a deprivation model, a second-best alternative when the two-parent nuclear family model is not available.

The growth of commitment ceremonies and the inclusion of gay and lesbian couples in the *New York Times* wedding pages indicate that the social definition of family has expanded. In the US, gay and lesbian parents are featured on talk shows, magazine covers, and even billboards that advertise cars. (The *Oprah Winfrey Show* saved me a lot of explaining when I told my parents they were getting another grandchild.) Yet the range of family formations depicted among gay and lesbian parents remains narrow. I was taken aback the first time I heard one member of a lesbian couple describe herself as a stay-at-home mom. That experience is no longer unusual, although it still gives me pause. Don't get me wrong. I fully understand that parenting is a more than full-time, undervalued, and unrecognized job. It is the vocabulary, the ease with which the statement rolls off the tongue. Are we passively accepting the heterosexual nuclear family as a model to be emulated? What are the class and racial/ethnic privileges that allow for this choice, and what are the implications for lesbian, gay, and feminist politics?

Single lesbian parenting provides a unique vantage point from which to view societal assumptions about the family and about parenting. Single lesbian moms are at the intersection of lesbians raising children, often in couples, and heterosexual single women raising children. We attempt to straddle these two worlds but are often invisible in both.

HOW IS THIS FAMILY DIFFERENT FROM ALL OTHER FAMILIES?

I am a single lesbian parent. Does it matter that instead of not having a male partner I do not have a female partner? While the distinction is central to my identity, it is secondary to my son. He is quite explicit that he wants a larger family, even if it's, "you know, the two-mom kind." My son's perception that the single/partnered dichotomy trumps the lesbian/heterosexual distinction is widely held, at least according to my cursory look at the literature of lesbian parents.

In *Single Mothers By Choice: A Guidebook for Single Women Who Are Considering or Have Chosen Motherhood* (Jane Mattes 1997), the sole index entry under lesbian, gay, or homosexual is: lesbian couples, adoption by. In the section on dating, Mattes assures readers that single mothers by choice find dating to be more enjoyable: "Having already had a baby, they now can relax about that and take their time having fun and getting to know the *man* they are dating" (emphasis added). In the 370 pages that make up *The Lesbian and Gay Parenting Handbook: Creating and Raising Our Families* (April Martin 1993), exactly five are devoted to single lesbian parenting. All five assume that parenting alone is a last resort for those who find themselves in the unfortunate position of being still-single as the alarms ring on their biological clocks.

The single-parenting-as-last-resort theme also appears in *On Our Own: Unmarried Motherhood in America*. In this excellent book, Melissa Ludtke (1999) insightfully differentiates the experiences of relatively well-off women in their 30s and 40s from unwed teenage mothers. It was therefore even more disappointing that the words lesbian, gay, same-sex, and homosexual do not appear anywhere in her book. The impetus for Ludtke's research was her own experience of being divorced, childless, nearing 40, and desperate to be a parent. In her discussion of the importance of her parents' support, I wondered whether the support would have been the same had Ludtke been a lesbian rather than heterosexual and divorced. Ludtke's parents' acceptance and support were based in part on their understanding that she might not meet the right man "in time." I am afraid of a future in which unmarried women are only entitled to donor insemination if they want a male partner but are nearing the end of their childbearing years and have yet to meet Mr. Right.

Ludtke's path to acceptance of donor insemination as her route to parenthood was littered with grief for the lost married-with-children life she assumed she would have one day. As a lesbian, my decision to pursue donor insemination was somewhat separate from these considerations. Perhaps because I had never pictured the wedding/marriage thing for myself, my process was easier. By the time many lesbians pursue donor insemination we have already experienced the internal transformation that accompanies being "outside the mainstream." My decision to parent felt relatively independent of whether or not I was or expected to be in a relationship. I (naively) thought the only difference in my dating future would be ruling out women who did not like kids. I even thought I might have a market niche: lesbians who wanted to parent but had no desire to be pregnant. (As a femme, I considered this to be a potential selling point.)

There have been cracks in the institutional wall that is the ideology of The Family. Any time women or men raise children in a loving but unconventional way, the social space for a spectrum of potential family arrangements gets a little wider. Single parents of all sexual persuasions, lesbians and gay couples having children, nonbiological parents pushing for second-parent same-sex adoptions, and people outside of the conventional family formation asserting their right to be foster parents all widen the social space and make my life as a lesbian single mom easier. Still, the invisibility of lesbian single mothers is personally disappointing and, I believe, politically unwise.

CAN THIS FAMILY BE SAVED?

The socialist–feminist analysis in which I was schooled saw the family as a patriarchal institution. While heterosexual relationships were depicted as occurring between one man and one woman, the context was the relationship between all men and all women. Through a sexual division of labor in the home that left women with less leisure time than men, a gendered labor force which left women with less money, and a compulsory heterosexuality which left women with fewer choices, the family was a key institutional component of men's power over women. Lesbian and gay families, stripped of a biologically-based sexual division of labor, provide an opportunity to examine what remains of the family as an institution without its traditional gendered form.

All women who have children outside of heterosexual marriages threaten the relationship between marriage and reproduction. Lesbian motherhood goes beyond this and weakens the link between sex and reproduction. The vigor of legislative challenges to the rights of lesbians and gay men to become foster or adoptive parents and/or to marry confirms just how threatening a realignment of norms of sexuality, partnering, and parenting can be.

In one such challenge in 1996, the US House of Representatives and US Senate passed, and President Clinton signed, the Defense of Marriage Act (DOMA). In introducing the bill into the Senate, Senator Don Nickles declared: "This ... legislation ... is about the defense of marriage as an institution and the backbone of the American family" (Don Nickles 1996). The bill passed in the US House of Representatives with a vote of 342 to 67. It explicitly defines marriage as occurring between one man and one woman (a definition not in the US Constitution) and makes an exception to the full faith and credit provisions in the Constitution that require states to recognize legal actions taken in other states. DOMA would allow states to opt not to accept marriage licenses granted by other states to same-sex couples.[1]

The passage of DOMA is part of a larger, frightening backlash against the push for full rights for lesbian and gay people. As I write this, the Pope and the President of the US are using their pulpits – bully and otherwise – to warn of the threat inherent in gay marriages, intensified by the November 2003 State Judicial Supreme court ruling in Massachusetts which found it unconstitutional in that state to deny gays and lesbians the same civil right that other adults have to marry. Yet I also fear that there may be unintended consequences in our rush to prove to our critics that we are just like everybody else. We need to be careful that the boundary between married heterosexual and married same-sex couples is not replaced with a new line of demarcation between two-parent families (good) and single-parent families (bad).

Public diatribes against single mothers, from unmarried teen moms to Murphy Brown, pervade the political landscape in the United States. (Murphy Brown was the fictional star of a long-running television series from 1988–98 in the US. A professional woman in her 40s, she decided to have and raise a child. Vice-presidential candidate Dan Quayle attacked the show, its creators, and its sponsors for showing single motherhood in a positive light.) The US government has even demonstrated its opposition to single-parent families where it counts: in the federal budget. The federal government in the US has recently allocated $300 million to promote marriage among poor women, though of course lesbians and gays are prohibited from marrying. Perhaps an exception will be made allowing single lesbian mothers on welfare to marry.

Conservative politicians are not alone in their opposition to single-parent families. In his warm, funny, and insightful book, *The Kid: What Happened After My Boyfriend and I Decided to Go Get Pregnant: An Adoption Story,* Dan Savage (2000) writes that deep down, "I'm really Dan Quayle. ... Working in a day care for a couple of years left me of the opinion that two-parent homes are better than one." Conservatives and liberals alike are fond of trotting out studies showing that children from two-parent families have better outcomes than children of single parents, even when differences in income and race are controlled for. But we do not know what would happen if there were support for multiple forms of childrearing; that is, what would happen if two-parent families were measured against a host of socially supported alternatives.

Dan Savage and his boyfriend would do well to heed the warnings of Lisa Saffron (1994) that the line between couples as parents and single parents is fluid. In a chapter titled "Singles and Couples" she writes:

> But this chapter is for all women, even those starting off in a co-parenting partnership. The reality is that couples do split up and people do die and become seriously ill. Any mother can become a single parent through circumstances outside her control. (1994: 75)

If Saffron is correct, and I believe she is, relying on pooled resources via marriages – gay or straight – to ensure children's well-being is inadequate.

A VILLAGE OR A TOWNHOUSE?

Valerie Lehr (1999) suggests that in addition to being a sex/gender system, the household system is also a crucial component of the public/private dichotomy. If same-sex families perform all the functions of nuclear families without challenging the ideology of the family as a "haven in a heartless world," perhaps the gendered definition of family can be stretched without tearing the social fabric. I believe that the private nature of the family may prove more resistant to change than its compulsory heterosexuality. Challenging the conception of the family as private ultimately questions the link between the well-being of children and the financial, educational, and emotional status of parent(s): single or coupled, gay or straight. The conservative political climate in the US makes it difficult to imagine mobilizing to end the distribution of income, rights, and privileges to people based on their family status. Nevertheless, we need to expand the public dialogue to ask whether the state should privilege long-term, monogamous relationships over other types of relationships such as friendship and community.

Perhaps we could start the dialogue by establishing a series of benchmarks for the conditions under which children and parents thrive. Iris Young (1996) challenges us to create "a just policy of pluralism [that] would ... positively differentiate among some kinds of families for the sake of providing them with the support that will make them flourish equally with others." Young's approach would encourage a richly textured set of relationships that would move us beyond the dichotomous choices of marriage/nonmarriage and two-parent families/single-parent families. Since the structures of traditional families are so closely tied to patriarchy and compulsory heterosexuality, genuine liberation for sexual minorities has a greater chance of success if the very models are challenged.

A just policy would have to include both a shorter workday and a generous, non-means-tested child allowance. It would be a step toward acknowledging that parenting takes both time and money, is a contribution to the general good, and that two-parent nuclear families are one but not the only way to provide them. Such a platform would create an opportunity for cross-class political alliances among mothers. A just pluralism would also recognize that while they share some features in common, families play different roles and take different forms across communities. Unfortunately, public policy in the US is moving in precisely the opposite direction, toward a unitary definition of what constitutes a family.

The families thus anointed are extended many benefits, one of which is the right to privacy. Many of the political actors in the US leading the so-called pro-family movement are supporters of minimal governmental intervention in people's lives. However, freedom from state intervention is only extended if they have sufficient resources not to require government assistance *and* they are heterosexual. Lesbians and gay men have been deprived custody and, in some cases, even access to their children.

Poor women seeking government assistance lose all rights to privacy and control over parenting decisions (Gwendolyn Mink 2002). The current policy that governs payments to single mothers in the US is called TANF (Temporary Assistance to Needy Families). Enacted in 1996, the law has among its provisions a reward for states that succeed in increasing family formation. Applicants for TANF are required to disclose their children's biological father(s). They can be required to attend marriage classes. The Personal Responsibility Act and the replacement of Aid to Families with Dependent Children by TANF (both under the Clinton administration) and the TANF reauthorization under the Bush administration, state that decreasing dependency on the government should be replaced with dependency on the labor market and marriage; i.e., privatized parenting.

In this political climate, when even holding back a conservative slide and maintaining the status quo is exhausting, a feminist recasting of the relationship between parents and children is beyond most of us. Thank goodness for artists. One of the best examples I have seen of separating adult romantic relationships from the raising of children is in Marge Piercy's (1976) *Women on the Edge of Time.* This work of science fiction allows us a glimpse of what is possible beyond what exists. In Piercy's imagined future, reproduction takes place in facilities outside of women's bodies. (One of the characters explains that women themselves decided that in order to achieve full equality they had to give up this one last gender-based differentiation.) When a person decides she or he is ready to parent, she or he requests to have a child born. Children have three adults who make a commitment to parent them. These parent/child relationships are distinct from, although they do not necessarily preclude, romantic relationships among the three adults.

Shared responsibility for children is not without difficulties. With it comes shared control. I have sometimes been critical of friends who want their partners to take more responsibility for the kids, but only if the men do it exactly as the mothers would. I admit to smiling inwardly when I hear couples squabbling over whether a child is hungry or in need of a nap, feeling relieved that I've never had that discussion. I am also keenly aware that even though I struggle to share decision-making and often solicit the opinions of friends, the ultimate decisions about my son's day-to-day life are mine and to some extent my son's. That is both the good news and the bad news. If support for, and legal recognition of, expanded networks of parenting come to fruition, I will have to loosen my death grip. I like to think I would rise to the occasion.

IT'S A TOUGH JOB, BUT SOMEONE'S GOT TO DO IT

Whether the path to liberation lies in assimilation or visibility is an enduring political question. In her overview of the politics in the dialogues surrounding three national marches on Washington (1979, 1987, and 1993) for gay, lesbian, and transgendered liberation, Nadine Smith (2002: 440) states:

> But as political and cultural gains lead sexual minorities out of the closet, increasing numbers lack the knowledge of, or the allegiance to, the liberationist roots of the movement. There is conflict between those who believe the movement is about visibility as a political act that challenges compulsory heterosexuality and those who tend more toward assimilation and believe equality will come from asserting we are more like heterosexuals than we are different.

Parenthood offers to lesbians and gays, for better or for worse, a connection to mainstream America that we might otherwise not have. For lesbians, it can be a way of declaring that we really are still women even if we sleep with women. Being a *single* lesbian parent gives me the option of passing as heterosexual (i.e., choosing invisibility) in settings such as my child's school. There are divorced parents and single women who have adopted children; I could easily blend in with either of these groups. I do not choose to pass for political, personal, and practical reasons: it is hard to imagine being closeted anywhere; I do not want my son to think it is something I am ashamed of; and he would probably blurt out something to out us anyway.

My son is also repeatedly faced with the choice of whether to come out about his family in response to his friends' questions. He is entering second grade, and his friends are asking more pointed questions. I am learning to help him navigate the choices. Most 7-year-olds I know are not wild about the idea of standing up and saying, "Hey – look at me, I'm different." To protect him (every parent's illusion, I imagine), I find myself being more conservative about the colors and styles of the clothes I buy for him than I suspect I would be as a straight feminist. My challenge is to help him simultaneously fit in and be bold, and to work with other parents and the school's staff so that he does not have to shoulder the responsibility alone. It is the elementary school version of the dilemma Smith describes.

While visibility is a step toward a liberationist strategy, it is not a replacement for one. In the political climate of the US Patriot Act that gives the US government unprecedented powers to investigate anyone suspected of less-than-flag-waving patriotism, it is difficult to imagine organizing to change the way we think about the parent/child relationship. Nevertheless, I think it is crucial to continue a dialogue about what we would really want. Otherwise, the political spectrum in the US runs from the right wing to an increasingly conservative Democratic Party, and I am reduced to confusing sending my son to school wearing subversive T-shirts with political action.

ACKNOWLEDGMENTS

I thank two anonymous referees for insightful comments that demonstrated the review process at its best.

NOTE

[1] With the recent ruling by the Massachusetts Supreme Court that says barring lesbians and gay men from marrying violates the state constitution, the battle cry to "save the family" is likely to get much louder.

REFERENCES

Lehr, Valerie. 1999. *Queer Family Values: Debunking the Myth of the Nuclear Family.* Philadelphia, PA: Temple University Press.

Ludtke, Melissa. 1999. *On Our Own: Unmarried Motherhood in America.* Berkeley, CA: University of California Press.

Martin, April. 1993. *The Lesbian and Gay Parenting Handbook: Creating and Raising Our Families.* Scranton, PA: Perennial.

Mattes, Jane. 1997. *Single Mothers by Choice: A Guidebook for Single Women Who Are Considering or Have Chosen Motherhood.* New York: Times Books.

Mink, Gwendolyn. 2002. "Violating Women: Rights Abuses in the Welfare Police State." Randy Albelda and Ann Withorn (eds.) *Lost Ground: Welfare Reform, Poverty, and Beyond.* Cambridge, MA: South End Press.

Nickles, Don. 1996. "The Defense of Marriage Act, Senate Bill 1999." Available http://nickles.senate.gov/legislative/releases/domafs.cfm (September 10, 1996).

Piercy, Marge. 1976. *Woman on the Edge of Time.* New York: Fawcett Press.

Saffron, Lisa. 1994. *Challenging Conceptions: Planning a Family by Self-Insemination*. London: Cassell.

Savage, Dan. 2000. *The Kid: What Happened After My Boyfriend and I Decided to Go Get Pregnant: An Adoption Story*. New York: Plume Press.

Smith, Nadine. 2002. "Three Marches, Many Lessons," in John D'Emilio, William B. Turner, and Urvashi Vaid (eds.) *Creating Change: Sexuality, Public Policy and Civil Rights*. New York: St. Martin's Press.

Young, Iris. 1996. *Justice and the Politics of Difference*, Princeton, NJ: Princeton University Press.

DIALOGUE
LONE MOTHERS: WHAT IS TO BE DONE?

Contributors: Susan Himmelweit, Barbara Bergmann, Kate Green, Randy Albelda and the Women's Committee of One Hundred, and Charlotte Koren

I. INTRODUCTION

Susan Himmelweit

For the Dialogue section of this special issue, the guest editors sought ideas about policies to help lone mothers. Although we gave the invited authors a free hand in what they wrote about, all of them chose to focus on the material deprivation many lone mothers face. The poverty of lone mothers is fundamentally rooted in a lack of time, often exacerbated by the low earning capacity of women in an unequal labor market. The problem is structural, not incidental, since lone parents who have no outside help must use their time for two competing purposes: to earn an income sufficient to support their families and to care for their children and themselves. Despite the many social changes that have affected parents' lives, the gap between the amount of time a lone parent has for these purposes and that available to a couple remains unchanged. Lone parents face an inevitable dilemma in allocating their time, and, as a result, societies face a similar dilemma in developing policies for lone mothers.

Although our authors live and work in three different developed economies (the US, the UK, and Norway), to some extent they write in a shared policy climate. Policy in most developed countries has moved toward an expectation that lone parents should provide at least some of their income through their own paid employment. In some countries, this expectation has always existed; others are moving in this direction in response to increasing numbers of lone parents, a normalization of the idea that mothers belong in employment, and an ideological shift against welfare "dependence." However, questions are now also being raised as to whether policy should enable mothers to care for their very young children themselves. Again, these policies have a variety of motivations, including ideas about child development, an increasing emphasis on individual choice, and cost considerations.

Even countries that are adopting labor-market activation policies vary in the extent to which they use coercion to pursue them. In the US, for example, mothers who do not take employment lose welfare payments. Other countries pursue similar ends by adopting policies designed to enable mothers to enter and stay attached to the labor market. The traditional Scandinavian solution, for example, is to provide high-quality, affordable childcare and sufficient paid parental leave to enable parents to have a reasonable work–life balance. There is also often a difference between rhetoric and reality with respect to enabling policies, for example, in whether childcare provision is affordable and adequate to meet demand, and whether the measures for balancing work and life are, in practice, available to all working parents.

Countries also vary in how much responsibility the state assumes for the welfare of children and how much is assumed to be a private matter for parents. These factors affect the provision of services for children and parents and the level of benefits paid to parents, both to those in paid work and those who do not take employment. Countries differ as well in whether their policies treat lone mothers differently from other (poor) parents, and in the extent to which lone mothers are stigmatized.

Although policies in most developed countries are now gender-neutral and apply to lone fathers as well as lone mothers, they do not operate in a world of gender equality. Most lone parents are women, and policies must be considered in the context of the specific features of a gender-divided labor market. Again these vary between countries, but there are some common themes:

(i) women's wages are low, often insufficient to support a family, especially when the mother seeks a working pattern compatible with having sufficient time with her children;

(ii)   many such jobs entail unfulfilling work, for which many mothers may feel it is not worth leaving their children;

(iii) reduced time spent in the labor market can have severe repercussions on current pay (for example, the low pay rates for part-time work) and even worse long-term effects on careers, and, in many countries, on access to vital pension and other employment benefits (even to healthcare in the US).

Against this background, a number of questions about policy arise. The first is about the role of social versus individual choice and responsibility. To what extent should the choice lone mothers make to work or to care for their children full-time be an individual or a societal one? Should society have an opinion on whether it is better for lone mothers to support themselves and their children through the labor market or to look after their children themselves?

If this is seen as an issue for society, should the state then be able to *enforce* its views on mothers – for example, by refusing them benefits if they do not look for jobs? Or should the state play an *enabling* role, by taking responsibility for making its chosen solution possible for all lone mothers? In that case, what happens to lone mothers who want to, or feel that they should, do things differently? What sort of help should they get?

Also, to what extent should such enforcing or enabling policies apply only to lone mothers or to all parents with similar needs? On the one hand, to be equally enabled, lone mothers may require special measures to compensate for the lack of a partner's income, time, and support. On the other hand, policies specific to lone parents may embody punitive measures that reflect a wish to impose social values (for example, that marriage is best) rather than a simple desire to relieve temporal and financial pressures.

The question remains: should all lone mothers be able to decide for themselves what they will do? What would that mean in practice, should all different courses of action be equally well remunerated? Should state support be income-tested or depend on other factors, such as the age of the youngest child? And at the level of the economy as a whole, should the amount of state support to enable choice be unlimited?

To what extent should the state protect mothers from the consequences of their own decisions? For example, if mothers choose to stay at home and look after their children, should they accept that they will pay a price for that choice later in reduced labor market prospects and a loss of the benefits attached to employment? Or should the state enact policies to reduce that price by, for example, ensuring that part-time workers are not discriminated against and that benefit entitlements are retained during career breaks? In sum, should policies prevent mothers from making "mistakes" about the consequences of their caring decisions, or should

239

policies try to ensure that the choices mothers want to make do not turn out to be mistakes in the long run?

Finally, what about the interests of children? How should they feature in these matters? Can we assume children's interests are encompassed in those of their mothers? Should the state assume that if it considers that mothers are better off in employment then that is the best solution for their children too? Or does government policy have a separate responsibility to look after the welfare of children?

Each of the following essays focuses on some but not all of these issues. In doing so, they lie to some extent along a spectrum. In the first piece, Barbara Bergmann, one of the founders of feminist economics and a former president of IAFFE, is most concerned with enabling lone mothers to take employment, though her solutions involve policies that go far beyond lone mothers, seeking instead to enable all women to enter the labor force. Kate Green, Director of One Parent Families, the leading charity representing lone parents in the UK, writes in a different policy context, one in which compulsion is not (yet) on the agenda. She supports enabling lone mothers to take employment, but also wants state policies to continue to respect the wishes of those who do not want to do so. Our third essay, an Immodest Proposal, was written by a group of US feminist scholars and activists (including Randy Albelda, one of the co-editors of this special issue) concerned to value and support caregiving. Their proposal would enable more mothers to receive support, whether they choose to be in or out of the labor market. Finally, Charlotte Koren, writing from a Norwegian perspective, goes one step further and suggests that we should develop policies that allow people to value their children more and spend more time with them in the few years when they are small.

II. WHAT POLICIES TOWARD LONE MOTHERS SHOULD WE AIM FOR?

Barbara R. Bergmann

The second half of the twentieth century witnessed a rapid and continuous rise in the proportion of children in developed countries living with lone mothers. The trend seems still upward; in any case a sizable reversal appears unlikely. Deprivation is the lot of large numbers of these mothers and children and is a grave blemish on the general prosperity of their societies. As time passes it may become clear (at least to more people than understand it now) that considerably more generous help from government to lone mothers would be desirable. In advance of that time, it would be useful to discuss how best to structure that help. If a program can be offered, discussed, agreed on, and advocated, it may speed the day when a more enlightened policy will be possible.

In considering the characteristics of such a program, there are three headings under which discussion is needed. First, what standard of living should such a program try to provide for these families? Second, should lone mothers receive enough support that they can, if they wish, give full-time care to their children? Finally, what sort of help should be given? That is, should lone mothers receive largely cash (from government grants and/or higher wages engineered by government policy) or, alternatively, should their support consist in large part in government-financed or government-provided services? The discussion presented here is based on US magnitudes, but the same issues arise in most developed countries.

What standard of life might be provided?

On average, the living standards of single mothers and their children are far below those of other families with children. The median income of single job-holding mothers in the United States was less than half of the median income of married couples in which only the husband was employed. These families do not need to buy childcare. Single-mother families average about one-third of the median income of two-earner couples.

The difficult situation of American lone mothers who hold jobs is illustrated in Table 1. A mother working forty hours a week year-round and earning the minimum wage has a disposable income that is close to the US official poverty line. That poverty line was set in the 1960s at three times the cost of a minimal food budget, and its value in constant dollars has since been kept fixed. A review of the methodology of setting poverty lines by a panel of experts assembled by the National Academy of Sciences (Constance F. Citro and Robert T. Michael 1995) concluded that at present a family should not be considered out of poverty unless it had an income after taxes that approximated the official poverty line plus the means to obtain healthcare, childcare, and other work-related items.

As the table shows, an American mother with two preschool children who earns the minimum wage and who must pay for healthcare and childcare is thousands of dollars short of being able to live at a minimally decent level. Even the mother who earns a sum equal to the median income for job-holding single mothers is still thousands short if she has to pay for those services. This means that a considerable number of such mothers are in a situation of serious deprivation.

Conservatives might advocate providing no help at all to such mothers, so as to promote self-sufficiency, buttress traditional rules of sexual conduct, keep the burden on taxpayers low, and discourage entry to lone

241

motherhood. However, reported reductions in the poverty rate, especially for children, are everywhere considered grounds for satisfaction. This suggests the public would sanction support that brings lone mothers who work at jobs at least to a poverty-line lifestyle.

This aim could be accomplished by providing lone mothers access to healthcare and childcare, either by increasing their incomes so they could pay for these services, or by simply providing the services. A considerably higher goal is possible: to provide sufficient help to get lone mothers and their children into the mainstream. A possible definition of "mainstream" would be a lifestyle not far below that of the median one-earner couple. The most important features of such a lifestyle would presumably include somewhat better food and clothing, an apartment in a safe neighborhood, and the possibility of higher education for the children.

Should full-time mothering be supported?

In the United States, stay-at-home single mothers were previously entitled to receive "welfare" payments as long as they had children under 18. Since 1996, the right to receive these payments has been greatly restricted. If it

Table 1 Financial situation of a US single mother of two preschool children, 2002

	Earning the minimum wage	Earning the median income of single jobholding mothers
(1) Wages	$10,712	$21,645
(2) Disposable income (after taxes and government benefits)	15,736	20,314
(3) Required expenditure for poverty-line living expenses exclusive of healthcare and childcare	14,494	14,494
(4) Amount left over that could be used to pay for health insurance and childcare [line (2) minus line (3)]	1,242	5,820
(5) Cost of licensed center care for both children	13,100	13,100
(6) Cost of health insurance for mother and children	4,000	4,000

Sources: (1) Unpublished tabulations of the US Census Bureau. (2) After subtraction of Social Security tax and federal and DC state income taxes, and addition of food stamps and Earned Income Tax Credit. (3) US Official poverty line, US Census Bureau, *Poverty in the United States: 2002.* (5) Children's Defense Fund, updated for price increases. (6) Website of Blue Cross/Blue Shield, a major health insurance provider in the US.

were to become politically feasible, should welfare payments to lone mothers who want to stay home with their children be re-established as an entitlement? The payments currently in force are low enough to keep the families receiving them beneath the poverty line, and they continue to decline in real value. If, in designing future policy, we were to advocate a right of support for stay-at-home lone mothers, the current level of welfare payments would be too low a standard to set if such families are to be at or above the poverty line. The stipends would have to be two or three times as large as welfare payments now are.

Further, if stipends (which would be viewed as wages for childcare) were given to stay-at-home mothers it would be politically difficult to confine them to lone mothers. Married or cohabiting mothers would have to receive stipends as well. The stipends for couples might be adjusted to take account of the family's wage income and greater time resources, but they would nevertheless be sizable in many cases.

Offering large stipends to lone and coupled mothers (or to parents of either sex) who stayed home with their children would probably increase the number of women who spent considerable time out of the labor force with the birth of each child. Today, 60 percent of mothers with children under 1 year old are in the US labor force. Employers can with some confidence depend on women workers' continuity on the job, treat them as fit for responsible jobs, and therefore consider them promotable. Prolonged absences on the part of many or most women would threaten to reverse the gains that women have made in the last half-century. Those gains – in educational opportunity, in the freedom to practice occupations and professions previously reserved for men, in the independence and status that come with working for pay, in the opportunities for a more interesting life experience than might be available to a long-term housewife – could be lost as employers ceased to assume that most of their women employees had a continuous attachment to the labor force.

One can see the effects of such a policy in Sweden, where the stipend is given in the form of paid parental leave, which can be taken for a year after a birth and extended for a longer period at a lower stipend. Although fathers are given incentives to share the leave, they take only a small percentage of the leave time. This system is thought to have contributed to the high degree of sex segregation of occupations in Sweden (L. Haas and P. Hwang 1999).

There is thus a tension between supporting mothers who wish to stay at home with their children and promoting gender equality, which arguably depends on men and women having similar life courses and activities (Barbara R. Bergmann 1998). Where one comes down in this matter depends on the value one puts on gender equality, what value one puts on validating and preserving women's specialization in caring roles, one's beliefs about the quality of familial care versus nonfamilial care, and what social arrangements one believes constitute gender equality.

My own view is that stipends for taking care of one's own children, including those in the form of lengthy paid parental leave, would cause a grave and unacceptable loss of gender equality. A compromise position that would preserve gender equality would be to provide two or three months of paid leave on the birth or adoption of a child to each of at most two adults residing in the household. Obviously, exceptions must be made for disabled adults, as well as for adults caring for disabled children.

The nature of the help: what mix of cash and services?

Government help to raise the standard of living of employed lone mothers could come in two forms – cash they could spend as they like and access to services. The cash could take the form of children's allowances, tax breaks, wage supplements, government-engineered rises in the wage rates employers paid, basic income grants, and lump-sum capital transfers. The services could be provided in government facilities or paid for in whole or in part by subsidies or vouchers to private providers that cover all or part of the cost.

In thinking about the appropriate mix of cash and services, the idea of "merit goods" is crucial (Robert Musgrave 1959). We label a good or service a "merit good" when we decide that, as a society, we should allow no one to do without it. We depend on government provision of such goods when we cannot rely on families buying it for themselves, either because they lack sufficient resources or because family priorities differ from public ones. It is important to emphasize that, as Table 1 shows, even a doubling of the minimum wage, or a hefty monthly child allowance, would not alone do the job of giving all families a set of "merit goods" that many people would endorse.

We already treat elementary and secondary education as a merit good. Healthcare is something that most people would agree also meets the definition of a merit good, something that we should not tolerate people going without. However, no government-engineered improvement in cash income through cash benefits or better wages could ensure that families would be covered. To achieve that, all families would have to be enrolled in a government-specified program of access to healthcare, with the government payment going to the provider.

I would argue that access to a decent standard of childcare, including after-school and summer care for school-aged children, should also be treated as a merit good. Childcare costs can run to $7,000 a year or more per child. Presenting parents with a check to cover the cost of such care, which they could spend as they wished, would not ensure that children received adequate care. Guaranteeing that would require government payments to the supplier or government provision of childcare itself, as well as government regulation of quality.

The above suggests that in ensuring lone parents at least a poverty-line lifestyle, the provision of healthcare and childcare services should take priority over further cash additions to their incomes. If we wish to allow a more mainstream style of life, we might give access to the services that constitute the major features of such a lifestyle: a dwelling unit in a safe neighborhood, and higher or vocational education, perhaps with a sliding scale of co-payments. Arguably, in a rich country these are also merit goods. Or, in addition to access to healthcare and childcare, a scheme of wage supplements might be developed, so that the wage income of those earning less than the median one-earner couple would be brought closer to the latter.

Services offered to lone mothers would gain in quality, equity, and popularity if they come from programs that make universal provision, rather than from programs serving single parents alone. So it would be best to provide all of the benefits above through programs available to the entire population, perhaps with co-payments on a sliding scale.

There are important services of a different type that government can provide that would greatly help lone mothers. One would be improved enforcement of child-support payments from absent fathers. Also useful would be a stepped-up campaign to reduce the sex discrimination that has kept women out of well-paying jobs, particularly those in the skilled blue-collar trades. Finally, lone mothers would benefit from a system of unemployment insurance that did not impose requirements – regarding length and continuity of tenure in previous jobs – that in practice exclude many lone mothers in the US.

Political feasibility of such a set of programs

All of the benefits proposed above already exist in some form in most countries, even in the United States. For instance, the US has public healthcare programs for the elderly, children, and low-income families. There is a federally funded program subsidizing childcare fees for low-income families and a subsidy program for housing. To aid with college costs, there are Pell grants and financial aid from the colleges themselves. The Earned Income Tax Credit (EITC) is a form of wage supplement.

However, these programs tend to be characterized by highly restrictive eligibility rules and to offer inadequate amounts of help. With the exception of the EITC they are also grossly underfunded, which means that the meager help they offer is denied even to many who are eligible. Nevertheless, the existence of these programs attests to an understanding by the public and politicians that they address serious problems that many families cannot overcome without help, and that government ought to be giving that help. The difficulty of transforming these existing programs into fully funded versions with improved benefits and appropriately broad coverage, which would bring the United States into line with the social democracies of Scandinavia and France, would be formidable. But we should not assume that it is impossible.

III. IS WORK WORTH IT FOR LONE PARENTS?

Kate Green

Social policy has long been concerned with the "problem" of lone parenthood. But in recent years, it is economic policy that has more strongly driven the political agenda for lone parents. The economic approach has extended across the political spectrum from the right-wing perspective that lone parents are a burden on the state, to the left's perception that social justice requires action to address the poverty and disadvantage that children growing up in lone-parent families face.

Increasingly, the two points of view have converged, resulting in efforts to move lone parents into paid work as a means of addressing the economic consequences of lone parenthood. And politicians are not alone in advocating for employment – most lone parents want to work when they feel that they can effectively combine their paid employment with caring for children (Louise Finlayson and Alan Marsh 1998). Thus, government policies seeking to bring more lone parents into the workplace have been pushing at an open door. In the UK, in the favorable economic climate of a period of exceptionally low unemployment, these policies have resulted in an increase in lone-parent employment from 44 percent in 1997 to nearly 54 percent by the spring of 2003 (One Parent Families 2003).[1]

Still, employment levels for lone mothers in Britain remain stubbornly below those of married mothers.[2] Moreover, married mothers are more likely than lone mothers to be in part-time work, despite the fact that most lone mothers would also prefer to work part-time (Carli Lessof, Jon Hales, Miranda Phillips, Kevin Pickering, Susan Purdon, and Melissa Miller 2001). Whether they cannot find jobs, cannot take the jobs that are available, or must work longer hours than they would like, many lone mothers find that employment is clearly not worth it or, in many cases, not possible.

When one examines policies designed to help lone parents into employment, three questions arise:

(1) Do the policies make employment worthwhile? That is, are lone parents sufficiently rewarded for being in paid work, and are there opportunities to progress once in those jobs?

(2)   Do the policies make employment possible? Are lone parents sufficiently supported so that they can balance paid work with caring for their children?

(3)   Do they work for lone parents for whom employment simply isn't possible or not appropriate; for example, those with disabled children?

Making employment worthwhile

Government policy is based on the assumption that lone parents moving into employment will improve their incomes, but for many lone parents paid employment may not be financially worthwhile. This is in large part due to the costs of childcare. While mothers with partners may be able to rely on them to share childcare responsibilities, making use of so-called shift-parenting arrangements, lone mothers often must look to other sources of childcare. In joint households, with the capacity of two earners, childcare can more easily be bought. For many lone mothers, childcare costs make employment unaffordable, especially part-time employment, for which the pay is often worse but childcare costs are proportionately higher. If the small financial gains from employment are eaten up in work-related expenses, such as travel, the necessary clothes, purchasing lunches, and meeting the social obligations of the workplace, lone parents are likely to conclude that employment simply is not worth it. Without additional income (such as in-work benefits and child maintenance), most lone parents would find it hard to escape poverty (Jane Millar and Tess Ridge 2001). Policies to increase earnings and strategies to help lone parents access better-quality, better-paid jobs with opportunities for progression are therefore key.

Paradoxically, policies to encourage lone parents into paid work must first focus on their out-of-work incomes. Lone parents who are struggling to make ends meet and hold their households together are less likely than those with a relatively stable income to be able to think about looking for employment. But this notion is counter-intuitive for many policy-makers, who focus on increasing levels of in-work financial support in the belief that increasing out-of-work financial support discourages parents from moving into employment.

The evidence suggests that they are wrong. In recent years, benefits for families out of work in the UK have increased significantly, yet labor market participation among these families has also increased.[3] Payment of child support maintenance (financial contributions from the absent parent) has also been identified as a key factor in building a stable income to enable lone parents to move into paid work.[4] Lone parents are highly risk-averse, and until they become confident about their economic stability while out of work, they will not consider a move into paid work. Increasing out-of-work

247

income also enables lone parents to manage the financial transition into paid employment (for example, meeting the costs of transportation, work clothes, etc.). It is important that the state sustain and increase its investment in out-of-work financial support as a prerequisite for moving more lone parents into employment. Policy-makers must recognize that rather than being a disincentive, good out-of-work support provides the best conditions for lone parents to move into work.

The move into employment must also bring benefits to the lone parent. Recognizing that most lone parents are women is key to understanding why so many are poor. Women are likely to earn significantly less than men, to be in low-paid work, and to be employed in the nonstandard or flexible economy. Policies need to recognize that whether lone parents will be better off in employment depends on the sort of jobs lone parents are able to get and the pay they receive. A cocktail of measures is needed to ensure that in-work incomes are maintained at a level that enables lone parents to make the transition to and stay in paid employment. These include imposing reasonable minimum pay rates, improving wages in the public sector (where many women work), and providing good in-work benefits.

Some of those policies are already in place in the UK. The introduction in 1999 of the National Minimum Wage has been important. So have various forms of financial help from the state, including the Working Tax Credit, a means-tested payment to workers in low-income households, which includes a childcare element to enable working lone parents to obtain help with childcare costs, benefit extensions (whereby out-of-work benefits continue for a limited period after formal entitlement has ceased), grants to cover living expenses until the first paycheck, and discretionary payments to help with the costs of moving into work. But still there are a few noticeable missing ingredients. One is a strategy to enable lone parents to gain, progress in, and remain in quality jobs with decent rates of pay.

We also need preventative measures so that women can gain secure places in the labor market before they become lone parents, and then be protected from falling out of work at the point at which they become lone parents. Policy-makers need to recognize that lone parenthood is a stage in the lifecycle that many women go through.

Robert Walker and Anthony Rafferty (2003), in particular, argue that some of the most pervasive factors that prevent lone parents from getting and keeping paid work have less to do with being a lone parent than with the generally disadvantaged position of women in the labor market. Again, we need universal policies that help women attain secure positions in the labor market before they ever become lone parents, with improved educational provision from an early age being key.

While improving women's education is clearly important as a long-term strategy, there is also a pressing need for greater investment in raising the skills and qualifications of those who are already lone parents. Many lone parents lack educational or vocational qualifications. Yet the work-first approach, which follows the principle that re-attachment to the labor market must be the immediate goal of all interventions, has proved inimical to lone parents' obtaining and progressing in well-paid jobs. This policy has dominated employment programs in both the UK and the US. It is based on early 1990s evaluations of US programs, which seemed to suggest that providing skills and training, the so-called human capital approach, was ineffective in promoting the employment prospects of lone parents. Yet more recent evidence from the US of successful programs of integrated education and training has shown that while the higher immediate employment rates and lower costs of the work-first approach provide immediate savings to the state, these savings are reduced over time. Over five years, the differences in positive outcomes for lone parents between the work-first approach and one focused on education and training narrowed so far as to be no longer statistically significant (Jane Hamilton 2002; Karl Ashworth, Andreas Cebulla, David Greenberg, and Robert Walker 2003). The most effective programs provided a mix of services (such as job search, life skills, work-focused basic education, and occupational training) to support employment (Martin Evans, Jill Eyre, Jane Millar, and Sophie Sarre 2003).

Investment in education and training before and during employment (and before and after lone parenthood) has an important role to play in improving lone parents' chances of getting work at all, and of obtaining well-paid jobs that enable them to lift themselves and their families out of poverty. The short-term fixes of minimum wage rates and in-work benefits will ultimately prove insufficient, and a strategic approach that enables lone parents to obtain better-paid jobs, and remain and progress in those jobs, must be the goal.

Making work possible

Beyond making work worthwhile, policies toward lone parents must also make work possible. The most striking factor linking high lone-parent employment and low child poverty rates is the availability of suitable, affordable childcare (Jonathan Bradshaw, Steven Kennedy, Marjella Kilkey, Sandra Hutton, Anne Corden, Tony Eardley, Hilary Holmes, and Joanna Neale 1996). When asked their reasons for not being in paid work, lone parents mention the lack of suitable childcare, and many believe employers will not employ them because of their childcare responsibilities (Lessof *et al.* 2001). Lone parents in paid work identified similar issues, suggesting that so-called barriers do not disappear on starting work, but instead become day-to-day "stressors" with which they must cope.

Increasing the quantity and quality of childcare is key to ensuring that lone parents enter and remain in employment. Governments have a choice of approaches. They could support and stimulate demand by providing parents with financial help towards the cost of childcare, thereby allowing the market to drive the increase in places. Or they could take a supply-side approach and directly support childcare provision.

Demand-led policies have not been especially successful in meeting the demand for childcare, particularly when the state will meet only a limited proportion of childcare costs (Daycare Trust 2003). So the UK government's emphasis is switching to increasing the supply. Despite the high cost of childcare provision, this strategy has potentially significant benefits, which go well beyond simply enabling more parents to take paid work. Aside from improving the educational outcomes and social well-being of children they serve, "children's centers" (which the UK government has pledged to introduce into the 20 percent most deprived areas by 2006, according to the government's own indices of deprivation) can be a hub for community regeneration and provide parent and family support. They can also support employment programs, facilitate links between training and education providers and the parents who use them, and act as "job shops." Increasing the supply of childcare will also, of course, increase the demand for a childcare workforce creating new job opportunities as well as the need for career progression in the health, education, and caring professions.

But parents need to be confident that high-quality, affordable childcare will be available *before* they start work. At the very least, children (and parents) will need a period to settle in to the new arrangements before a parent can confidently leave a child in childcare and go off to work. Taster sessions, during which parents can test childcare free of charge, and financial help with childcare costs for parents both in and out of work are an important but modest first step. They should be seen as just the beginning of a move toward a goal of universal, high-quality childcare as a social right, provided in all neighborhoods and affordable to all parents, essential to ensure gender equality and an equal start for every child. This goal would surely be a great vote winner as well.

Even with the best possible childcare available, all working parents should have the right to flexible employment that fits with their childcare responsibilities. Many lone parents prefer working part-time, during school terms and school hours; others may seek shifts that match when they can find available childcare. And all working parents need time off to cope with family emergencies and to be at home with their children when they feel they need to be. It is regrettable that the UK government has been so cowardly in this field. Employment rights for working parents remain limited, and the blame for slow progress in this area is frequently directed (quite unfairly) at perceived hostility from workers who are not parents. Remarkably, therefore, some of the drive for improvement in this area has come from employers, who recognize that family-friendly policies can help them to attract and retain good quality employees, and who argue the business case for providing them.

But relying on employers to blaze the trail will only take us so far. Not only must parents have a right to flexible working arrangements that enable them to balance work and family responsibilities, but they must also be economically able to take advantage of them. Unpaid parental leave is of little benefit to low-income parents who cannot afford to do without their pay; earnings-related paid parental leave is essential for this right to become meaningful.

Curiously, it is the recent extension of the right to parental leave to fathers that may have the most significant effect in improving rights for lone mothers. If fathers, apparently now clamoring for more time with their families, begin to assert their need for paid time off, then a political process that tends to pay more attention to the cries of men than those of women may yet bring about a step change in attitudes, to the benefit of all parents.

When employment does not work

Much remains to be done to bring about secure, stable, and long-term employment for lone parents. But before doing it we must ask one final question: is paid work *desirable (or even possible)* for lone parents? The answer to that is not clear-cut, and is best left to the lone parent to answer. Governments, opinion leaders, and policy-makers cannot and should not make that decision for individual families. Their responsibility is to ensure that all lone parents can maintain a decent standard of living and good opportunities for career progression regardless of the choices they make regarding work and parenting. This means recognizing the value of the parenting role and ensuring that policies to help lone parents work are not predicated on making caring less attractive (for example, by reducing out-of-work benefits), but on making work more attractive. It means, too, that more effort should be made to keep parents in touch with the workplace during periods they are out of work and fulfilling caring responsibilities. These efforts might include programs of education and training, support for volunteer activities, and a more holistic approach to return-to-work support.

IV. AN IMMODEST PROPOSAL

Randy Albelda and the Women's Committee of One Hundred

Introduction

Randy Albelda

The Women's Committee of One Hundred is a group of US feminist academics, professionals, and activists concerned with the relationship

251

between women, economic survival, and the work of caregiving. The Committee formed in the mid-1990s in response to proposed welfare reform in the United States. That legislation – the Personal Responsibility and Work Opportunity Reconciliation Act (PRWORA) of 1996 – abolished the six-decade-old Aid to Families with Dependent Children (AFDC) program and replaced it with a new program called Temporary Assistance for Needy Families (TANF). Some members of the Women's Committee prepared and circulated the statement below in 2000, in anticipation of the reauthorization of TANF scheduled for 2002.

The US Congress established the AFDC program as part of the Social Security Act of 1935, the same Act that created Old Age Survivors' Insurance (OASI, commonly referred to as Social Security) and Unemployment Insurance. It was (and, in its incarnation as TANF, still is) the only federal cash support program for poor, lone-parent families with no employment income. Many, including poor women and children and their advocates, disliked AFDC, as it provided only meager cash assistance to poor families with children (mostly lone mothers), scrutinized women's sexual and employment histories, and discouraged employment. Under AFDC, individual states had complete leeway in determining benefit levels and retained considerable flexibility in program design; still, federal guidelines provided some oversight and the program was an entitlement. Until the 1980s, only poor lone parents were eligible for AFDC. Since then, poor two-parent families have also been eligible, although the vast majority of families with adults receiving AFDC/TANF have been headed by lone mothers.

With TANF, individual states have even more flexibility and little oversight. The program is no longer an entitlement, and states may define "needy" as they wish. Under TANF, the federal government provides a block grant, from which individual states receive monies as long as they provide as little as 80 percent of the funds they had previously committed to welfare. This requirement can be reduced to 75 percent if states meet workforce participation goals.

TANF specifies that states must impose strict mandatory work requirements on adult recipients and sets a sixty-month lifetime limit on receiving TANF federal funds. Individual states may (and some do) have shorter time limits, stricter work requirements, and a host of other provisions. While states are not held accountable for providing for needy families, there is considerable oversight of families receiving assistance. By creating rules that impose sanctions – reductions of all or part of cash assistance – states have implemented policies that scrutinize poor women's lives and decisions even more than AFDC did. In some states, families can be sanctioned if parents fail to immunize their children, if children have too many unexcused school absences, if clients miss meetings with case workers or fail to report earnings and other income, if mothers fail to provide enough information about noncustodial fathers, if parents fail to find employment within specified periods of time (workfare), or if they have a child while receiving TANF (family cap). Research indicates that women of color receive differential treatment from their case workers (Susan Tinsley Gooden 1998) and that states with higher percentages of people of color on the welfare rolls have stricter policies (i.e., more rules that impose sanctions) (Joe Soss, Sanford F. Schram, Thomas P. Vartanian, and Erin O'Brien 2003).

As of May 2004, the US Congress and the President have not reauthorized TANF. However, changes promoted by the President and strongly supported by the US House of Representatives include increased work requirements (without a corresponding increase in childcare funds) and more funds for marriage promotion programs. The Women's Committee of One Hundred works with feminist and poor women's advocacy groups to fight these changes and promote the range of policies advocated in the Immodest Proposal. It will be a long struggle.

More on the Women's Committee of One Hundred and TANF Reauthorization is available at: http://www.welfare2002.org/ehome.html; information on TANF is available at: http://www.financeprojectinfo.org/WIN/summaries.asp; information on individual US state policies is available at: http://www.financeprojectinfo.org/WIN/state.asp.

An immodest proposal

The Women's Committee of One Hundred

Rewarding women's work to end poverty

In 2002 the Personal Responsibility and Work Opportunity Reconciliation Act (PRWORA) will expire, and Temporary Assistance to Needy Families (TANF), the policy it authorizes, will come up for abolition, renewal, or replacement.

In anticipation of the debate that will ensue, the Women's Committee of One Hundred/Project 2002 calls for a broadened perspective on women's poverty, including attention to the special economic vulnerability arising from the caregiving responsibilities that women often assume.

General principles

Women perform the bulk of caring work for children, elders, and dependent persons, both within their own homes and as paid employees. Our economic system undervalues caregiving work when it is performed in the labor market and penalizes caregivers when they work outside the labor

253

market caring for dependents. Although caregiving in families is indispensable to the welfare of families, communities, and the economy, research clearly shows that this work exposes women to poverty and other forms of economic inequality. Caregivers' poverty deepens as they encounter additional hardships and disadvantages. These include:

- low wages;
- discrimination based on gender, race, age, disability, and being the sole adult responsible for dependents;
- having a history of sexual abuse and/or encountering domestic abuse;
- lacking adequate education or skilled training.

When poor caregivers meet these hardships, they face destitution; when middle-class caregivers encounter them, they become vulnerable to poverty for the first time. This is why today poverty in this nation – and globally – assumes the face of a woman with children or other dependents.

If caregivers' poverty has a woman's face, that face also often belongs to a woman of color. Poverty in the United States is not color-blind. The debate preceding the 1996 welfare law made the color of poverty the fault of the poor. We insist that the color of poverty is the consequence of racism and related forms of discrimination. Accordingly, our proposal proceeds from the recognition that race affects the material basis for caregiving, privileging some women at the expense of others. We call for policies that address the shared vulnerabilities of women of all races, beginning with the particular vulnerabilities of the poorest caregivers, especially poor women of color.

Ending poverty, not ending welfare

As a crucial first step toward ending poverty as we know it, we call for social policies that recognize and reward the work of caring for dependents.

TANF, like its predecessor, AFDC, provides minimal assistance to those who are impoverished and have dependents in their care, but the arbitrary and punitive aspects of such policies prevent them from granting the type of recognition we have in mind.

We call for an end to:

- mandatory work outside the home as a condition of assistance;
- arbitrary time limits;
- child exclusion policies ("family cap").

To replace TANF, we propose a set of policies that will allow women to choose between performing caregiving themselves or purchasing high-quality services for those who depend upon them for care. Such policies should ensure that caregivers – whether they are caring for family members or nonfamily members – receive just compensation and provisions for respite, old age, health insurance, and other basic needs.

AFDC and TANF have given special, but inadequate, attention to poor families, especially those with a single adult responsible for dependent children. We, too, are especially concerned with this group of highly vulnerable caregivers, but propose that support should be extended more broadly for all caregiving work.

A caregiver's allowance

We call for the replacement of TANF with a guaranteed income for caregivers of minor children and other dependent family members requiring sustained care.

This program would work like survivor's insurance (OASI), in that it would provide cash payments for family caregiving that would be administered according to national standards and would be disbursed at the national level on a regular, automatic, and guaranteed basis. As with survivors' insurance (and social security) the caregivers' allowance would not authorize or condone government intrusion into the personal or family lives of recipients, including often racist intrusion into women's reproductive decisions. Those not now eligible for TANF would also receive a cash payment in recognition of their caregiving work, but the amount of compensation would be adjusted based on the total household income.

- The caregiver alone would decide how to spend the grant. For example, she/he could purchase surrogate caregiving services (child, elder, or other dependent care) and pursue paid employment, education, or training. Or, she/he could perform the carework herself/himself. Or she/he could devise a combination of carework and other pursuits.
- As with survivor's insurance, there would be no employment requirements and no oversight, and the allowance would be available to any primary caregiver, regardless of gender.
- Each caregiver would determine for herself/himself the balance of caregiving and other employment that is manageable and desirable.
- The value of a caregiver's allowance and the time spent doing caregiving work for dependents should be counted in an individual's work history for social security purposes.
- As an interim measure, the child tax credit should be expanded into a refundable Caregiver Tax Credit for all caregivers with dependents who need sustained care.[5]

To enable individuals to make meaningful decisions about care, we further advocate the creation of high-quality, universally available, caregiving services, including childcare for infants, toddlers, preschoolers, and school-age children, and elder care and noncustodial care for incapacitated dependents. All such programs should be federally funded and meet federally defined minimum standards that include adequate training, compensation, and benefits for workers as well as mechanisms for input from parents, guardians, and those responsible for the individuals under care.

Transforming wage-work

Ending women's poverty also requires transforming the labor market by valuing the work that women currently perform for wages, enforcing anti-discrimination law, and offering the opportunities and training for better-paying jobs.

Crucial for this transformation are an overall improvement in labor standards, including:

- A shortened standard work week. This should be available to both women and men so that both can meet their responsibilities for family caregiving.
- Effective protection of the right to unionize.
- A living wage achieved through an automatically indexed minimum wage. This should be a universal right. The minimum wage should be set high enough so that a single adult earns enough to bring a family of three above the poverty line.
- Application of the principle of comparable worth, or equal pay for work of equal value. This is necessary to undo the low wages in female-dominated occupations.
- Affirmative action law must continue to combat gender, race, age, and ability discrimination, and open up higher-paying positions.
- Universal access to higher education and skill-building training programs that lead to economic opportunity and enhance earning power. These should be developed to prepare women for existing and future occupations. Education and training should be free and students should be provided stipends, along with substitute caregiving services.
- A reformed unemployment insurance system. This should cover all workers, including the part-time, very low-waged, and intermittent. All jobs should provide paid family and medical leave. Legislation ensuring paid family leave should be phrased in such a way that it acknowledges caregiving responsibilities as a legitimate constraint on the types of demands an employer can make on an employee (for example, requiring overtime as a condition of employment).

Related programs

We envision additional social programs to enhance the quality of life of women and their families and to ensure that caregiving takes place in safety and with dignity.

- Broadly defined disability insurance/supports should protect those who cannot be employed, are not caregivers, or are not retired.
- Universal healthcare should be a right.
- Victims of domestic abuse require twenty-four-hour emergency assistance and temporary shelter and priority in subsidized housing.
- Child support responsibilities of noncustodial parents should be strongly enforced, but only at the request of custodial parents.
- The government should develop affordable housing in economically and racially integrated communities and provide adequate public transportation, including customized service to remote, especially rural, areas, and late-night service to accommodate night-shift workers.

We will not count it as a victory if the status of American women is improved at the expense of women from abroad, whose economic and social disadvantages are even greater, compelling them to relinquish their own

Authors of An Immodest Proposal	
Name	Affiliation
Mimi Abramovitz	Hunter College School of Social Work, CUNY
Randy Albelda	University of Massachusetts Boston
Eileen Boris	University of Virginia
Ruth Brandwein	SUNY at Stony Brook
Nancy Fraser	New School University
Cynthia Harrison	George Washington University
Eva Feder Kittay	SUNY at Stony Brook
Felicia Kornbluh	Duke University
Sonya Michel	University of Illinois-Urbana/Champaign
Gwendolyn Mink	University of California-Santa Cruz
Frances Fox Piven	Graduate Center, CUNY
Dorothy Roberts	Northwestern University School of Law
Rickie Solinger	historian, Boulder, Colorado
Jean Verber	welfare advocate/activist, Milwaukee, Wisconsin
Guida West	activist and author, Montclair, New Jersey
Ann Withorn	University of Massachusetts-Boston

Note: Since publication of this statement, several members have changed academic affiliations. Eileen Boris is at the University of California, Santa Barbara; Gwendolyn Mink is now at Smith College; Sonya Michel is now at University of Maryland, College Park.

caregiving responsibilities in order to find work – often in low-paying service occupations – here in the US. We therefore call for the recognition and promotion of policies that justly compensate the work of caregiving and improved labor standards for women across the globe.

V. WHO CARES?

Charlotte Koren

Children must be looked after, they need to be fed, dressed, and washed, and they need attention, consideration, and love. The material needs of children and their care draws heavily on economic resources: money and time. As more women have entered the labor force, and the opportunity cost of time has increased through rising wages, the full costs of childcare have become more visible. How to distribute these costs – between women and men, between the private and public sectors – has become increasingly problematic with the growing variety in family types, which includes a surge in the number of families headed by lone parents.

What is special about lone parents?

A married or cohabiting couple has access to a far larger economic output than the lone parent. Simply put, two parents have forty-eight hours a day at their disposal – for work, leisure, and childcare – while lone parents have only twenty-four. For the lone parent, both childcare and income earning must be pressed into a tighter schedule. One person alone must meet her child's need for both care and money.

According to the *Norwegian Time Use Survey* for 2000, childrearing is extremely time-consuming. Couples with small children together spend almost five hours more on household work and family care per day than those without children do (Odd Frank Vaage 2002). In addition to performing housework and carework, parents must also be present evenings and nights to keep an eye on the children. Even sleeping is being on duty. Unlike two parents, who can take turns looking after the children, the lone mother has no time off.

Lone mothers are also financially disadvantaged, compared with married and cohabiting parents. Not only do couples have twice the income-earning potential of single persons, but two-adult families also benefit from economies of scale in consumption: their household expenses per person are lower. Finally, a two-income household has greater financial robustness during times when one wage earner is ill, unemployed, or dealing with care responsibilities.

Social benefits for lone parents in Norway

Lone-mother families are a challenge for government policy in a society where the two-parent family is the norm for provision and care for children. Lone parents need greater public support than couples to compensate for having less time and earnings. The question is, what shape should this support take?

When the Norwegian welfare state was developed in the 1960s, it rested on the presumptions that families were stable, women were occupied with housework and carework, and men brought in the money. The housewife was not idle, but it was not her carework that stopped her from taking paid work. The predominant norm for mothers was to stay at home, and few mothers considered employment as an alternative. Thus, husband and wife covered one cost each: the father provided the money, the mother provided care. For the lone mother, the main problem was the absence of a breadwinner. In response, the state provided benefits that enabled lone mothers to stay at home temporarily while their children were small and needed care, or to allow the mother to receive education. Known as "transitional benefits" for lone parents, these stipends now amount to approximately $15,000 a year (Anne Skevik 2001 and in this issue).

Today, married and cohabiting mothers in Norway have high employment rates. Market work is also considered the norm for lone mothers. In accordance with the government's present "pro-work" policy the transitory benefit stops after three years; lone mothers are then supposed to support themselves (Anne Skevik in this issue). They must give up their care time in exchange for an income from work. This change of policy ignores the fact that lone mothers may still need support, since they must do the daily chores on their own as well as the income earning.

Government policy is now directed at helping all mothers take paid work. Highly subsidized daycare centers are provided for a majority of children – at least for children older than 3 years. When the number of daycare places is limited, lone parents have priority.

Financing the child's consumption is (in part) solved independently of the lone mother's need for income. Both parents are expected to pay for a child's expenses, whether they are living together or not. When parents are not living together, a child support payment is imposed on the noncustodial parent. The amount is decided by a complicated formula that stresses the responsibility of both parents to provide for their child: an estimated "cost of children's consumption" is divided between the parents in proportion to their incomes. This system is well-administered, and payments are collected from the majority of noncustodial fathers. When the father is unknown, evades paying, or has no income, the mother receives a minimum level of support from the state. If the father is dead, the child receives an orphan's pension from national insurance.

Are lone mothers a cost to society?

Some economists and policy-makers argue that lone mothers who stay at home receiving benefits are a burden for the welfare state. But this is not the case. Lone parents are willing to take care of their children at a far lower price than paid care workers. In Norway, the transitional benefit is lower than the production cost of daycare for a toddler and far less than the subsidy the government pays if a parent has two children in daycare.

When childcare is produced and sold in a market, the full costs of care become evident – even when the wages of workers in the childcare sector are disturbingly low. In Norwegian childcare centers there are 3.5 children per care worker (Statistics Norway 2003). Thus, the total production cost of providing care at a childcare center is approximately $20,000 per year, per child, for children up to 2 years old, and $10,000 for 3-to-5-year-olds (BFD 2003). These are the costs, not the actual price to consumers. Parents pay about one-third of these amounts with the rest covered by local and central governments.

The price of childcare produced in the home is seldom explicitly calculated. The figures above are an indicator of the economic value of childcare carried out in households, including in one-parent families. When lone mothers find that most of their wages must be used for childcare, transport to work, and other job-related expenses, this should indicate that there is also little real economic gain to society from lone mothers taking employment.

How should we think about family policy?

In economics literature, having children is often characterized primarily as an obstacle to parents' – especially mothers' – laborforce participation. Economists overlook the joy that parents receive from childrearing. For me, it was my job that felt like the obstacle, preventing me from being with my children. Generally, no one else cares as much for children as their parents do; just compare your own darlings to the neighbor's little brats! Society should take advantage of the strong force that parents' love for their own children represents. We get more adult involvement in children's lives, and at a lower price, when parents themselves attend to their children.

Also, when economists model or include the production of childcare in labor-supply models, it is typically the *parents'* utility that is maximized. The child's point of view is often forgotten or disregarded. But childcare is no ordinary commodity; it determines the life quality for the young, fragile, and vulnerable among us. Children's well-being is not determined by the parents' income level alone, but by consistent, loving care in a stable environment.

Childcare policy, for children of single, cohabiting, or married parents, should be designed so that parents' legitimate need for meaningful work does not overshadow the interests of children.

Conclusion

Allocating time between work and family is a challenge for all parents, mothers and fathers, married and unmarried. Parents' preferences for careers and childcare vary, and I see no reason why the government should prefer one, and only one, model for childcare. Nor do I see any reason for a policy that excludes lone mothers from choosing as freely as married mothers do.

Most lone mothers thrive at their jobs, socialize with colleagues, and enjoy making money. Their productive work contributes to our economic output, as does their childcare work, and they should be encouraged to continue working outside the home. But working mothers who live alone with children still need some income transfers to compensate for being on their own. A general benefit for lone parents – in the form of a child benefit or tax credit – is necessary. This cost for society must be seen as the price for all citizens to have the freedom to live in a family setting that is beneficial for them.

Part-time employment provides an attractive solution for lone mothers. Working part-time enables them to meet their dual obligations – of being care provider and breadwinner – by doing some of both. But currently, the tax and benefit systems are not designed to support part-time working. Taxes and tapered benefits need to be carefully designed not to create poverty traps for mothers that work less than full hours. Those few years when children are most vulnerable cover only a small part of a mother's working life. Labor-market policies should be improved to welcome mothers back into their careers after their most intensive childcare years are over.

This said, mothers who prefer to stay at home full-time for the first years of their children's lives should be enabled to do so. Providing a decent transitional benefit does not cost much more than subsidizing high-quality daycare. A rich society should not allow children to live in poverty. But for children themselves it may be just as important to live calmly with a content mother who has time for her child. A rich society can afford that too.

ACKNOWLEDGMENT

Kate Green would like to thank Kate Bell for her assistance in the preparation of this article.

NOTES

1 Figures commissioned by One Parent Families (2003). Estimates fewer than 10,000 are likely to be unreliable and estimates above this level are subject to a relatively standard error of about 20 percent and an approximate 95 percent confidence interval of $\pm$ 4,000. Crown copyright 2003.
2 In 2001, 51.4 percent of lone mothers compared with 71 percent of married mothers were in paid work (One Parent Families 2003).
3 The Institute for Fiscal Studies estimates that spending on children will have increased by 37 percent between 1997 and 2003 (Mike Brewer, Tom Clark, and Matthew Wakefield 2002).
4 Twenty-five percent of lone parents in receipt of child maintenance in 1999 had moved into work by 2000, compared with 12 percent of those with no child maintenance (Steve McKay 2002).
5 Editors' note: For clarification, the US childcare tax credit allows families with earnings to deduct up to US$4,800 (for two or more dependents) per year from federal taxable income. Legislation has been introduced to make that credit refundable so that families who have no income tax liabilities, but are eligible for the deduction, would receive a cash refund.

REFERENCES

Ashworth, Karl, Andreas Cebulla, David Greenberg, and Robert Walker. 2003. "Meta-evaluation: Discovering what Works Best in Welfare Provision." Paper to the Future Governance Seminars IFS Vienna and CEU Budapest, December 9–11, 2003. On-line. Available http://www.futuregovernance.ac.uk.

Bergmann, Barbara R. 1998. "The Only Ticket to Equality: Total Androgyny, Male Style." *Journal of Contemporary Legal Issues* 9: 75–86.

BFD. 2003. *Analyse av kostnader i barnehagene – resultater av en utvalgsundersøkelse [The Costs of Childcare Centers – Results from a Survey]*. Barne – og familiedepartementet (The Ministry of Children and Family Affairs) February 2003.

Bradshaw, Jonathan, Steven Kennedy, Marjella Kilkey, Sandra Hutton, Anne Corden, Tony Eardley, Hilary Holmes, and Joanna Neale. 1996. *The Employment of Lone Parents: A Comparison of Policy in 20 Countries.* York, UK: Social Policy Research Unit.

Brewer, Mike, Tom Clark, and Matthew Wakefield. 2002. "Five Years of Social Security Reforms in the UK." Working Paper No. WP02/12. On-line. Available http:// www.ifs.org.uk/taxben/workingpapers.shtml (July 2002).

Citro, Constance F. and Robert T. Michael (eds.). 1995. *Measuring Poverty: A New Approach.* Washington, DC: National Academy Press.

Daycare Trust and One Parent Families. 2003. *Informal Childcare, Bridging the Childcare Gap for Families,* London: Daycare Trust.

Department for Work and Pensions. 2003. *Households Below Average Income: 1994/95– 2001/02.* Leeds, UK: Corporate Document Services. On-line. Available http:// www.dwp.gov.uk/asd/hbai/hbai2002/contents.asp.

Evans, Martin, Jill Eyre, Jane Millar, and Sophie Sarre. 2003. *New Deal for Lone Parents; Second Synthesis Report of the National Evaluation.* Sheffield, UK: Department for Work and Pensions.

Finlayson, Louise and Alan Marsh. 1998. *Lone Parents on the Margins of Work.* Department for Work and Pensions Research Report No. 80. Norwich, UK: The Stationery Office.

Gooden, Susan Tinsley. 1998. "All Things Not Being Equal: Differences in Caseworker Support toward Black and White Welfare Clients." *Harvard Journal of African American Public Policy* 4: 23–33.

Haas, L. and P. Hwang. 1999. "Parental Leave in Sweden," in Peter Moss and Fred F. Deven (eds.) *Parental Leave: Progress or Pitfall? Research and Policy Issues in Europe,* pp. 45–68. Brussels: CBGS Publications.

Hamilton, Jane. 2002. *Moving People from Welfare to Work: Lessons from the National Evaluation of Welfare to Work Strategies.* New York: Management Decision and Research Center.

Lessof, Carli, Jon Hales, Miranda Phillips, Kevin Pickering, Susan Purdon, and Melissa Miller. 2001. *New Deal for Lone Parents Evaluation: A Quantitative Survey of Lone Parents on Income Support.* ESR 101. Sheffield, UK: Department for Work and Pensions. On-line. Available http://www.dwp.gov.uk/jad/2001/esr101rep.pdf.

McKay, Steve. 2002. *Low/Moderate-Income Families in Britain: Working Families Tax Credit and Childcare in 2000.* Department for Work and Pensions Research Report No. 161. Leeds, UK: Corporate Document Services.

Millar, Jane and Tess Ridge. 2001. *Families, Poverty, Work and Care.* Department for Work and Pensions Research Report No. 153. Leeds: Corporate Document Services.

Musgrave, Robert A. 1959. *The Theory of Public Finance.* New York: McGraw-Hill.

One Parent Families. 2003. *Employment and One Parent Families: The Facts.* London: One Parent Families.

Skevik, Anne. 2001. "Lone Parents and Employment in Norway," in J. Millar and K. Rowlingson (eds.) *Lone Parents, Employment and Social Policy.* Bristol, UK: Policy Press.

Soss, Joe, Sanford F. Schram, Thomas P. Vartanian, and Erin O'Brien. 2003. "The Hard Line and the Color Line: Race, Welfare, and the Roots of Get-Tough Reform," in Sanford F. Schram, Joe Soss, and Richard C. Fording (eds.) *Race and the Politics of Welfare Reform,* pp. 225–53. Ann Arbor, MI: University of Michigan Press.

Statistics Norway. 2003. *Barnehager 2000 [Kindergartens 2000]*, NOS 684. Oslo: Statistics Norway.

Vaage, Odd Frank. 2002. *Til alle døgnets tider. Tidsbruk 1971 – 2000* [*At All Times. Time Use 1971– 2000*], Statistical Analyses No. 52. Oslo: Statistics Norway.

Walker, Robert and Anthony Rafferty. 2003. in Djuna Thurley (ed.) *Working to Target: Can Policies Deliver Paid Work for Seven in Ten Lone Parents?* London: One Parent Families.

Women's Committee of One Hundred. 2002. "An Immodest Proposal." On-line. Available http://www.welfare2002.org/ehome.html

NOTES ON CONTRIBUTORS

Randy Albelda is Professor of Economics at the University of Massachusetts in Boston. She is the author of *Economics and Feminism: Disturbances in the Field*, co-editor of *Lost Ground: Welfare Reform, Poverty and Beyond*, and co-author of the books *The War on the Poor: A Defense Manual* and *Glass Ceilings and Bottomless Pits: Women's Work, Women's Poverty*. She is an Associate Editor of *Feminist Economics* and a former vice-president of IAFFE. Her research and teaching focus is on poverty, women's economic status, welfare reform, income inequality, and policies for low-income families.

Barbara R. Bergmann is co-author with Suzanne W. Helburn of *America's Child Care Problem: The Way Out*, and the author of *The Economic Emergence of Women, In Defense of Affirmative Action, Saving Our Children from Poverty: What the United States Can Learn from France*, and *Is Social Security Broke? A Cartoon Guide to the Issues*.

Karen Christopher is Assistant Professor with a joint appointment in Women's Studies and Sociology at the University of Louisville. Her research interests include the feminization of poverty; gender and the welfare state; and gender and race in labor markets. She has published several book chapters and journal articles on these topics, most recently in *Social Politics, Journal of Poverty*, and a co-authored article in *Sociological Perspectives*. She is beginning a qualitative study of post-secondary education among TANF recipients in Kentucky.

Irene Dingeldey is Assistant Professor at the Center for Social Policy Research at Bremen University. She earned a Ph.D. in Social Sciences from the University of Bielefeld in 1996. She has published on industrial relations in Great Britain, family tax systems, marginal part-time employment, and labor market policies in Germany and Europe. Her present research interests are new forms of governance, particularly the coordination of labor market and family policy as new challenges of welfare-state reform. She has published articles in *Politische Vierteljahresschrift* (1996), *Journal of Social Policy* (2001), *Aus Politik und Zeitgeschichte* (1998 and 2001), and *Österreichische Zeitschrift für Politikwissenschaft* (2003).

Lisa Giddings is Assistant Professor of Economics at the University of Wisconsin at La Crosse. She obtained her PhD in August of 2000 from American University in Washington DC. Her research interests include women and ethnic minorities in labor markets of transitioning economies as well as in the area of pedagogy and economics. She has published articles in *Feminist Economics*, the *Eastern Economic Journal*, the *Economics of Transitions*, and the *Journal of Manpower*.

Kate Green was Director of One Parent Families, the leading UK charity campaigning for the one in four families in Britain headed by a single parent. The charity works to tackle the poverty, disadvantage, and isolation so many lone parents face. Kate is a member of the Council of the Institute for Fiscal Studies and of the National Employment Panel, which advises Ministers on labor-market programs and employment initiatives.

Susan Himmelweit is Professor of Economics at the Open University. She co-chairs the UK Women's Budget Group through which she advises the UK government on the gender implications of social and economic policy. She is an Associate Editor of *Feminist Economics*, a joint guest editor of this special issue and *Children and Family Policy*, published in 2000. Her research is on gender issues in economics, particularly those located at the boundaries between employment and family care. She recently completed a study of the interaction between identities and behavior in mothers' decision-making with respect to childcare and paid employment.

Jane Humphries is Reader in Economic History at Oxford University and Fellow of All Souls College. Women's work and family lives both in the past and in the present has long been one of her principal interests. She is currently writing a book on child labor during the British Industrial Revolution.

Shireen Kanji is currently writing her PhD thesis on child poverty in lone-mother households in Russia. Her main research interest is the relation-ships between family policy, child poverty, and socially constructed definitions of household types. She is also interested in the methodological issues that arise when combining quantitative and qualitative methods of social inquiry.

Randi Kjeldstad is Senior Research Fellow and Deputy Director of Research at Statistics Norway, Division for Social and Demographic Research. She has written several books and articles on work and income from a gender perspective.

Charlotte Koren is Senior Research Fellow at Norwegian Social Research (NOVA) in Oslo. Her research experience ranges from the development of micro-simulation models, applied analysis of income distribution, studies of taxation and social security for women, and discussions of the value of unpaid work, to the evaluation of laws for cohabitants. She is presently a board member of IAFFE. In addition, she is on the editorial board of *Feminist Economics* and was an Associate Editor from 1997 to 2002.

June Lapidus is Associate Professor of Economics and Mansfield Professor of Social Justice at Roosevelt University in Chicago. She has published on women, work, and welfare in *Feminist Economics, Review of Radical Political Economics, Work and Occupations,* and the *International Review of Applied Economics.* She received her PhD in 1990 from the University of Massachusetts, Amherst. She is also a staff economist with the Center for Popular Economics.

Judith Record McKinney is Associate Professor of Economics and Director of the Russian Area Studies Program at Hobart and William Smith Colleges in Geneva, New York. Her current research focuses on the effects of the transition on women and children in Russia and on Russian demographic issues.

Margaret K. Nelson is Hepburn Professor of Sociology and Women's and Gender Studies at Middlebury College. Her most recent book is *Working Hard and Making Do: Survival in Small Town America* (University of California Press, 1999) co-authored with Joan Smith. She is currently writing a book on single mothers in Vermont.

Marit Rønsen is an economist and Research Fellow at Statistics Norway, Division for Social and Demographic Research. Her main research interest is in the field of fertility and female labor supply, including the effects of public policies. Her writings are published in national and international books and journals.

Kanchana N. Ruwanpura is an Assistant Professor at the Department of Economics, Hobart and William Smith Colleges, U.S.A, where she typically teaches courses in labour market issues, political economy, and feminist issues in development. Prior to her appointment at the colleges, she was a Humboldt Research Fellow attached to the Department of Economics and Post-Colonial Studies Program at the Ludwig Maximilians University (Munich) and before that a Research Officer at the International Labour Office, Geneva, Switzerland. A native of Sri Lanka, she completed her Ph.D. (2001) at Newnham College, University of Cambridge, where she

267

explored her research interests in gender and development, ethnicity, labour market issues, and feminist methodology through her dissertation.

Anne Skevik is a senior research fellow at NOVA – Norwegian Social Research – in Oslo, Norway. She holds a doctoral degree in sociology from the University of Oslo. Her main research interests are provision for children after family break-ups, changing policies toward lone parents, and comparative family policy. Recent publications include the doctoral thesis 'Family Ideology and Social Policy: Policies towards Lone Parents in Norway and the UK' (NOVA, Oslo, 2001), and 'Children of the Welfare State: Individuals with Entitlements, or Hidden in the Family?' *Journal of Social Policy* 32(3): 423–40.

Susan Ulbricht is a doctoral candidate in Sociology at the University of Leipzig. She organized the Congress of Sociology in 2000 in Leipzig. Her thesis topic is 'Income Mixes – Structural Changes of the Sources of Income in Germany.''

INDEX